FALSE DOCUMENTS

GLOBAL LATIN/O AMERICAS
Frederick Luis Aldama and Lourdes Torres, Series Editors

FALSE DOCUMENTS

INTER-AMERICAN CULTURAL HISTORY, LITERATURE, AND THE LOST DECADE (1975–1992)

Frans Weiser

THE OHIO STATE UNIVERSITY PRESS
COLUMBUS

Copyright © 2020 by The Ohio State University.
All rights reserved.

Library of Congress Cataloging-in-Publication Data
Names: Weiser, Frans, author.
Title: False documents : inter-American cultural history, literature, and the lost decade (1975–1992) / Frans Weiser.
Description: Columbus : The Ohio State University Press, 2020. | Series: Global Latin/o Americas | Includes bibliographical references and index. | Summary: "Examines the work of writers and journalists from Hispanic America, Brazil, and the US from the 1970s to 1990s who appropriated history as a tool for repositioning democracies in a hemispheric context in order to expose how governments controlled and misrepresented events"—Provided by publisher.
Identifiers: LCCN 2019041117 | ISBN 9780814214367 (cloth) | ISBN 9780814277737 (ebook)
Subjects: LCSH: Latin American fiction—20th century—History and criticism. | American fiction—20th century—History and criticism. | Literature and history—Latin America—History—20th century. | Literature and history—United States—History—20th century. | Comparative literature—Latin American and American. | Comparative literature—American and Latin American. | Latin America—Historiography. | United States—Historiography.
Classification: LCC PQ7082.N7 W42 2020 | DDC 809/.897—dc23
LC record available at https://lccn.loc.gov/2019041117

Cover design by Laurence J. Nozik
Text design by Juliet Williams
Type set in Adobe Minion Pro

CONTENTS

List of Illustrations		vii
Acknowledgments		ix
INTRODUCTION	The Ends of History and "American" Studies	1
CHAPTER 1	Interdependent Methods: Postwar Cultural History, Historical Literature, and False Documents	27
CHAPTER 2	History's Return: Literary Revisionism in North America, Hispanic America, and Brazil during the Lost Decade	47
CHAPTER 3	The Ends of Argentine Democracy: The False Memoir(s) and Cultural Hybridity behind Tomás Eloy Martínez's *The Perón Novel*	73
CHAPTER 4	The "Dialectics" of Feminist Caribbean History: Laura Antillano, José Martí, and the Venezuelan Lost Decade	97
CHAPTER 5	History at the Periphery: Postdictatorial Literature and the Abandoned Generation of Ana Maria Machado's *Tropical Sun of Liberty*	125

CHAPTER 6	Allegorizing Brazilian History: Silviano Santiago's *In Liberty*, Invisible Texts, and Ideological Patrols	149
CHAPTER 7	The Many Deaths of Che Guevara: Jay Cantor's Anxiety of Origins and the Limits of Transnationalism	173
CHAPTER 8	Renewing History? John Updike's Critique of Cultural Studies and the Two Americas in *Memories of the Ford Administration*	195
POSTSCRIPT	Fake News and the New Lost Decade	217
Works Cited		221
Index		235

ILLUSTRATIONS

FIGURE 1 Juan Perón on the front cover of the *Panorama* 1970 special edition — 75

FIGURE 2 The cover of COPRE's 1987 special issue of *Estado & Reforma* — 99

FIGURE 3 "Cli-ché," part of D*Face's 2007 collection "Eyecons" — 183

FIGURE 4 *Time* Magazine's 1974 cover on President Ford and the economic crisis — 198

ACKNOWLEDGMENTS

IT HAS BEEN almost a decade since the seeds of this project first took root, and I have many people to thank for not getting lost along the way. Earl Fitz is not only the trailblazer of Inter-American studies, but he is also a generous mentor to young scholars who work in and across comparative fields. Luiz Valente, who took a chance on including an unknown graduate student on his MLA panel many years ago, offered responses to early chapter drafts, but even more importantly, has offered friendship over the years. While participating in the Futures of American Studies Institute, John Carlos Rowe kindly offered to correspond and provide suggestions, while Winfried Fluck furnished honest feedback regarding the project's intended American Studies audiences. Luciano Tosta likewise offered helpful encouragement during moments of self-doubt. In addition to Kristen Elias Rowley's editorial interest, I would like to thank the press readers who offered insightful commentary and suggestions for improving the clarity of the entire manuscript's historical and disciplinary discussions.

At the University of Georgia, Richard Gordon made himself available to provide advice at many junctures, and his support offered through the Latin American and Caribbean Studies Institute has helped inform my academic trajectory in numerous professional contexts. The Willson Center for the Humanities is a vital resource; its assistance via a Research Fellowship gave me crucial time to finish key theoretical chapters of the project, while the Sarah

Moss Fellowship first put me in conversation with Inter-American programs at European institutions in Austria and Germany. Additionally, Peter O'Neill, from Comparative Literature, and John Inscoe, from History, have patiently mentored me in both official and unofficial capacities.

I have interrupted this project on multiple occasions to pursue new lines of inquiry, only to discover how important these detours would be for formulating my scholarly and philosophical foundations. It was during a postdoctoral fellowship at the University of Pittsburgh that I was first truly introduced to the purchase of Latin American cultural studies, and where my interest in historiography began to assume Brazilian dimensions. Access to the collections and archives at Indiana University's Lilly Library, through its Everett Helm Fellowship, and the Organization of American States' Columbus Memorial Library was beneficial in the final stages of revising the book. At the University of Massachusetts Amherst, I also owe a debt of gratitude to Daphne Patai, whose acerbic criticism has no doubt shaped my research and methodology more than any other mentor. Additionally, David Lenson and Luis Marentes reminded me that, in the midst of bureaucracy, academia could still be pleasurable and rewarding, while Bill Moebius provided many forms of institutional support.

Speaking of institutional assistance, I am indebted to the work of both librarians and administrators. This includes the collaboration of Laura Shedenhelm on Latin American funding proposals and the industriousness of Cindy Flomm at the University of Georgia's Interlibrary Loan Department, as well as the advocacy of Jill Talmadge and Martha Babendrier in Comparative Literature. Martin Kagel, Jean Martin-Williams, Robert Moser, and Ben Ehlers have also encouraged me with academic opportunities that have led to domestic and international partnerships.

Finally, I owe the most to those outside the academy: to Hermine and Stephen Weiser for their patience and acceptance over so many years, to Jim Weiser for his angry letters to the editor, to Emile Wessels for the dreams of books and music, to Cecília Rodrigues for companionship across the travails of academia and the world, and to Marcel for the valuable reminder(s) of what the most important project in life is.

INTRODUCTION

The Ends of History and "American" Studies

TASKED BY new US President Richard Nixon with surveying the failure of the Alliance for Progress to stimulate economic development in Latin America, Nelson Rockefeller and his team conducted interviews with government officials across twenty participating countries, yet also witnessed frustrated citizens' public demonstrations at various stops. The resulting document, *The Rockefeller Report on the Americas* (1969), predicts multiple challenges during the 1970s to Washington's long-standing hemispheric paternalism, including increased authoritarianism, general unrest with the changes wrought by accelerated modernization, and growing nationalist sentiment fueled by the desire to be free of US hegemony. While he advises against further attempts to improve infrastructure through developmental democracy, Rockefeller also directs criticism inward, claiming US media representatives' ignorance of their southern neighbors as a continued obstacle to cooperation. To combat this, he exhorts the president to promote the circulation of "journalists, teachers, intellectuals, writers, musicians, artists, and other representatives of the United States to other American republics" (*Report* 139). In this regard, Rockefeller reprises a balancing act that dated back to World War II, when as head of the Office of Inter-American Affairs he championed cultural diplomacy as an instrument of advancing US democratic ideals and shoring up regional partnerships, at the same time acting as an economic advisor to governments attempting to limit the negative impacts of wartime inflation across the hemisphere.[1]

If Rockefeller's formula for winning Latin American hearts and minds was not unique, neither was it unilateral. In her history of Hispanic American cultural responses to the Cold War, Jean Franco details how the CIA covertly subsidized multiple journals that internationally circulated regional authors' work, in theory to support an anticommunist agenda (*Decline and Fall* 30–35). Yet, as Deborah Cohn has also shown, the Center for Inter-American Relations began promoting Latin American cultural production within the United States in 1963 via public affairs initiatives and literary subsidies—frequently touting representatives whose progressive viewpoints were at odds with official national policy.[2] Nonetheless, while Rockefeller's predictions regarding nationalist, authoritarian trends proved well founded, his emphasis upon balancing economic and intercultural investment made little impact. In the early 1970s, the fear of communism's spread to Latin America had diminished, and the region appeared to provide less national security risk, leading the Alliance for Progress to be dissolved. Although after Nixon's resignation, Rockefeller became Gerald Ford's vice president (1974–1977), his tenure was beset by party infighting and a focus on repairing fractured domestic policies. Only in 1984 with the conservative Kissinger Commission would the US formally turn its attention southward again, even if this was largely to justify financial and military aid to right-wing Contra groups in Central America charged with human rights abuses. Despite processes of redemocratization in thirteen Latin American countries during that same period, scholarship focusing upon economic hardship reinscribed the "two" Americas concept based on insular national models, downplaying the humanitarian crises rocking the region. Wedged between the remnants of Pan-American idealism in the 1960s and the hemispheric turn of the 1990s, then, the penultimate decade of the Cold War represents an anomaly in US–Latin American relations.

Yet these same events provoked a radically different response in cultural producers across the New World than Rockefeller might have imagined, as journalists and authors became newly free to contest nationalist narratives of progress, unity, and inclusion by situating them in the long history of Inter-American relations. Simultaneous to this popular development, the consolidation of cultural historiography as a field during the 1970s advanced new

---

1. Cramer and Prutsch provide an accessible history of Rockefeller's role in the Office of Inter-American Affairs. See Rockefeller's "Discurso del Excmo." for his reproving address to the Inter-American Financial and Economic Advisory Committee.

2. For a history of the CIAR, see Cohn (145–92), whose study of US outreach programs and nationalism during the Cold War is an important resource.

methodologies for recuperating marginalized groups previously ignored by the official record.³ While in the United States predominantly white writers had embraced ironic ahistoricism throughout the 1960s, the fall of Vietnam in 1975 marked a return to "serious" history (Rowe, *New American* 25), as it allowed for minority counternarratives to the 1976 bicentennial celebrations of US social inclusion. The publicized "historical turn" in academia followed shortly thereafter, as the social sciences and humanities began to both historicize their own disciplines and incorporate historical methodology in the 1980s.⁴

Despite receiving less attention, the concurrent critical return of history had even greater implications for Latin America, albeit for distinct political causes, as noted by both Uruguayan and Brazilian cultural critics.⁵ After years of dictatorial censorship during which journalists and artists either had been prevented from criticizing the national past or had given their energies to documenting contemporary humanitarian crimes by the state, the decline of regimes provided writers a new liberty to examine colonial and modern history. The purpose was equally to diagnose the origin of current social inequalities and to disturb the discourses of nationalism that military regimes had utilized to legitimize their dictatorships.

Under the postwar charter of the Organization of American States, the Inter-American moniker became increasingly associated with commissions on human rights, banks, courts, and treaties—organizations that largely supported a model of democracy emerging from within the United States. Thus it is important from the outset to establish that in its academic formation, Inter-American studies predates the creation of Cold War area studies programs, comprising an international array of scholars working precisely to destabilize US hemispheric sovereignty by decentralizing the manufacture of knowledge and analyzing the contradictory roles of cultural activism and economic development within transnational diplomacy. *False Documents: Inter-American Cultural History, Literature, and the Lost Decade (1975–1992)* explores the sudden "return" of popular history that swept across the Americas during the final two decades of the Cold War as Latin American nations emerged from dictatorships and US multiculturalists responded to conservative bicentennial

---

3. See Levine's discussion of pushback against US cultural history (*Unpredictable Past* 3–31).

4. McDonald's cross-disciplinary account examines the three forms this transformation took: critique of postwar opposition to history, examining history as a conceptual process, and reexamination of the discipline itself.

5. In Chapter 2, I discuss the first two scholars to highlight this historical return, Ángel Rama and Silviano Santiago, the latter of whom wrote "Prosa Literária Atual no Brasil" in 1979, though it was first collected in *Nas malhas da letra* (1989).

backlash. It does so through the examination of the work of journalists, writers, and academics from Hispanic America, Brazil, and the United States who turned to fiction during the 1980s to reconsider national discord through the prism of cultural history. In order to publicly expose the misrepresentation of recent events by their respective governments, however, these writers neither took recourse to testimonial deposition or fashionable satire, but rather developed a shared approach to history that I will shortly define as "false documentation." By assessing the cultural nature of this Inter-American intersection, this project not only draws attention to productive overlaps between neighbors that emerged in response to the so-called "lost decade," but it also revises predominantly economic accounts of the period that either portray the hemisphere in national isolation or reinscribe the reductive "two Americas" model.

As the first book to contextualize the parallel Cold War evolutions of cultural historiography and literary criticism in three primary sociolinguistic regions of the Americas, *False Documents* provides alternative models to two key challenges that continue to trouble the humanities. The first is the methodological impasse between local and global area studies. While the political projects of Latin American and American studies are frequently framed as mutually exclusive, I seek to contribute to both fields by demonstrating productive points of confluence. Building upon the work of Latin American scholars who repurposed traveling postmodern theory, including Silviano Santiago and Néstor García Canclini, as well as activating the type of postnational American studies encouraged by Juan Poblete, John Carlos Rowe, and Caroline Levander, I posit the Inter-American paradigm as an understudied intermediary that synthesizes each domain's cultural specificity, in part because it avoids the trappings of institutional area studies. Thus while underlining the unique social and political realities to which each author responds, this book also demonstrates that the regional revisionist turn was characterized by similar strategies and mutually constitutive ends.

Second, I provide a reparative reading of the antagonism between history and literature. The dominant tendency within literary criticism has associated representation in this period with emerging postmodern currents, reductively characterizing historiography as supporting hegemonic interests. In order to intercede in the debate, I propose the alternative model of "false documents," which recognizes the mutually constructive relationship between the two disciplines. Jewish American author E. L. Doctorow first adopted the term in 1975 to describe his experimental historical works *The Book of Daniel* (1971) and *Ragtime* (1975) in contrast to "true" political documents such as "the Gulf of Tonkin Resolution or the Watergate tapes" (Gussow 5). Curiously, these novels provoked conflicting responses as a form of postmodern skepticism—

a description Doctorow rejected—or self-aware documentary fiction. In fact, reviewers' and historians' hyperbolic pronouncements prompted Doctorow to chastise academic audiences in an essay titled "False Documents" (1977; Bevilacqua 130–32), where he expanded upon the concept to describe literary publications in which an author disingenuously claims to be the editor of a found text.

In other words, by suggesting they are merely disassociated literary executors of a discovered or existing document, writers lend seeming verisimilitude to their narrative depictions. Looking to foundational examples such as Miguel de Cervantes's *Don Quixote* (1605) and Daniel Defoe's *Robinson Crusoe* (1719), Doctorow claims that audiences are frequently aware of the context of publication, thus unlike hoaxes, this creative disavowal focuses attention on the rhetorical or documentary status of the text. In his terms, the most important public trials in our history "are those in which the judgment is called into question: Scopes, Sacco and Vanzetti, and the Rosenbergs. Facts are buried, exhumed, deposed, contradicted, recanted. There is a decision by the jury and, when the historical and prejudicial context of the decision is examined, a subsequent judgment by history" ("False Documents" 23). In essence, Doctorow creates a metaphor for placing historical attitudes themselves on trial by reconsidering the evidence and eyewitness accounts that inform the jurisdiction of facts, for the public ascribes greater authority to nonfiction discourses than those of fiction. As a human rights activist, Doctorow not only advocated for US multiculturalism but he also joined a group of North American writers in protesting Washington's institutionalized efforts to silence the circulation of left-leaning Latin American Boom authors by denying entry visas and permits (Cohn, *Latin American* 62). Unlike many contemporaries who sought to undermine historiography's cultural role, Doctorow recognizes inherent rhetorical difference between the production of history and fiction, a distinction that narratologists and historians would corroborate in the following decade.[6]

As will become apparent in the following chapters, the term "false documents" may have North American origins, yet other theorists catalogued remarkably similar tendencies across the hemisphere during the same period, from Brazilian critic Antonio Candido to Cuban Roberto González Echevarría, whose concept of "archival fictions" has been enormously influential in Latin American studies. Synthesizing these distinct conceptions of literary history that provide alternative models to postmodern periodization, I refocus Doctorow's definition to instead consider texts that appropriate the conventions of primary documentation, forms of journalism, and archival research

---

6. See LaCapra as well as Cohn ("Signposts of Fictionality").

with the express purpose of exposing the processes leading to the construction of dominant national narratives. I argue that in contrast to postmodern parodic distortions of the agreed-upon record, these dissociative works interrogate—rather than dismiss—what historians term the "documentary model," the definitive practice of ascribing special authority to primary written documents that undergirds the field. After discovering that entire minority groups were written out of postwar consensus history, Doctorow acknowledges the need for redressing marginalized groups' exclusion. Yet rather than pretend to supplant historiography, he adopts a complementary stance, admitting that "history as written by historians is insufficient. And the historians are the first to express skepticism over this 'objectivity' in the discipline," yet it "turns out that history, as insufficient and poorly accommodated as it may be, is one of the few things we have in common [in America]" (Levine, "Independent Witness" 42).

This declaration of commonality has repercussions beyond self-determination. In revising the official narrative of Latin American loss and North American prosperity at the end of the Cold War, my purpose is to establish how this postnational model continues to have relevance for area studies today, for establishing the symbiotic relationship between literature and history is also relevant for examining broader academic issues. As growing numbers of scholars perceive humanities funding and status to be under attack, the antagonistic framing of internal humanistic disciplines detrimentally limits the types of collaborative opportunities that reinforce the importance of culture for ethical decision-making. By drawing on a combination of internationally recognized writers as well as those celebrated primarily within their own national traditions (thus largely unexplored in the rest of the hemisphere), the goal of my comparative scope is also to bring awareness of these intersecting traditions to a larger audience. Inter- and Latin American comparisons have predominantly focused upon two languages by either highlighting US/Hispanic American comparison or Hispanic American/Brazilian production, though as Earl Fitz has repeatedly lamented, all too often Brazil has played a token role, if it is acknowledged at all.[7] The triangular approach of this book is designed to resist unintentionally reproducing such cultural binaries. And while comparative analyses are typically organized around the reading of two or more texts in unison, my approach to chapters will instead examine individual case studies both in order to rigorously locate the cultural specificities of each tradition and to avoid reinforcing categories of difference.

---

7. See, for example, Fitz ("Spanish American") in *Comparative Cultural Studies and Latin America*.

As a means of highlighting the consolidation of Inter-American studies before the rise of hemispheric and border studies during the 1990s, this book therefore seeks to contribute not only to revisionist scholarship on Latin American and US history, literature, and cultural studies but also to our ability to come to terms with a period of hemispheric relations that witnessed deepening democratic divisions.

Drawing on correspondence with multiple authors and scholars, I analyze six case studies between 1975 and 1992 in which writers whose countries were affected by the lost decade demonstrate overlapping strategies of Inter-American historical revisionism: from Hispanic America, Argentine Tomás Eloy Martínez's *The Perón Novel* (1985) and Venezuelan Laura Antillano's *Alone but Committed* (1990); from Brazil, Ana Maria Machado's *Tropical Sun of Liberty* (1988) and Silviano Santiago's *In Liberty* (1981); and from the United States, Jay Cantor's *The Death of Che Guevara* (1981) and John Updike's *Memories of the Ford Administration* (1992). Several of these authors initially worked as either journalists or academics before turning to fiction to reexamine national issues, yet whether writing about feminism in the Hispanic Caribbean or failed transnational revolution, all develop similar strategies of presenting their work as official historical documents while directly commenting upon the uses to which history has been purposed. Furthermore, I approach each case study through a range of Inter-American theories that appear contemporary to the lost decade, both to draw attention to key pioneers in an undertheorized field and to expand the footprint of Inter-American studies' relevance for eroding the political boundaries of area studies. In the process of examining how founding figures or documents were used under dictatorships to marshal national solidarity in some cases, while in others to question free market consensus, these authors evoke a reconsideration of the relationship between nationalism and democracy within the contemporary Cold War context under which they produce their texts.

THE LOST DECADE AND THE END OF HISTORY

While the authors I examine revisit the 1970s from the vantage of the 1980s, the dates defining the scope of this study are as symbolic as they are functional. The year 1975 both marks when Doctorow first used the term "false document" and corresponds with the critical recognition of Augusto Roa Bastos's *I, the Supreme* (1974), credited with initiating new historical fiction in Latin America, although it is also a paradigmatic example of the false document. The endpoint of 1992 coincides with both the demise of the Cold War and the quincentennial of Christopher Columbus's arrival to the New World, the latter of which occasioned numerous literary interrogations of Europe's colonial legacy. At the same time, these dates overlap with two economic theories used to describe opposing trajectories of the Americas in relation to democracy and neoliberalism—the Latin American lost decade (1982–1991) and the US-celebrated end of history (1975–1992)—which merit unpacking because they reinforce the "two Americas" approach I mentioned previously through sociological rather than cultural analysis.

The important convergence of Inter-American and cultural history during the 1980s can perhaps best be illustrated through the inability of structural economic theories to account for the everyday reality of local social experience. The most common application of the term "lost decade," for example, describes the paralyzing effects of the financial debt crisis across Latin America. Rampant inflation and unprecedented loss of international investment were consequences of the global recession upon international debt that had accumulated to support nationalist modernization projects. While Mexico had begun devaluing its currency in response to the oil crisis after 1975, its default on foreign debt payment in 1982 initiated a chain reaction across the region that soon involved Argentina, Brazil, Venezuela, and Peru.[8] After the unsuccessful implementation of Inter-Monetary Fund guidelines, US-educated policy makers across the region adopted neoliberal measures to halt inflation, though this would come at great cost to social programs, and by then the decade had already had disastrous consequences for millions of the middle class who fell below the poverty line (Green 85–86). The effects were not limited to the region, for great losses in trade affected the United States as it entered into its own recession in 1981.

Largely overlooked, however, is the concurrent cultural application of the description "lost decade" within the hemisphere that expands the term's temporal and financial referents. Thus, scholars have used this rubric to characterize Central America's bloody civil wars and the state-sanctioned genocide that led hundreds of thousands to flee the region during the 1980s.[9] And in Brazil under military dictatorship (1964–1985), the decade preceding the 1979 Amnesty Law that permitted an "absent generation" of political exiles to return was equally known as a "cultural void," a consequence of the regime's institutionalization of torture and strict censorship upon forms of public expression (Sussekind 59). And the term has not only been applied to Latin America. During the 1970s, the United States also experienced a "lost decade"

---

8. See both Green's chapter 3 and Almandoz on differing Latin American financial crisis responses.

9. See Tedesco and Barton's introduction (1, 9).

(Hurup 10), its national identity crisis a concatenation of economic and social factors stemming from the 1973 Arab oil embargo as well as existential uncertainty fueled by growing anti–Vietnam War sentiment.

On an Inter-American level, however, the economic crisis surprisingly stimulated unprecedented regional cooperation, a collaborative form of postnationalism contrasting that of neoliberal globalization. Divided during a century of Pan-Latin American activism, country leaders suddenly succeeded in banding together against US domination of the Inter-American System, coordinating responses to foreign debt and actively negotiating peace in Argentina's Falklands War as well as the civil conflicts that plagued Central America.[10] It is this comparative, paradoxical, and inclusive Inter-American analogue to the economic lost decade that informs the scope of this book.

If the lost decade invites Latin American response to US economists, Hemispheric American scholars tend toward exposing the type of US exceptionalism found in narratives such as Francis Fukuyama's "The End of History?" (1989).[11] By now largely discredited, the essay was written in the months before the Berlin Wall was dismantled, and it recounts in triumphant terms the global ascendancy of Western liberal democracy at the expense of fascism and communism, a feat brokered under the stewardship of the United States. While the developing world might remain "mired in history" and therefore continue as a site of armed nationalist or religious conflict, the Department of State analyst sees the proof of free market viability in both the "ineluctable spread of consumerist Western culture" (3) and the inevitable homogenization of modernizing nations. From Jean-François Lyotard's end of historical "metanarratives" to Fredric Jameson's superficial nostalgia, as well as Jean Baudrillard's "vanishing" history, the currency of contemporary accounts of posthistory paved the way for Fukuyama's initial association with postmodern nihilism. Yet far from destabilizing universal narratives, the conservative repackages US political hegemony in philosophical terms.

Fukuyama's article ignited a firestorm of controversy,[12] both because of its appropriation of Marxist reference points and its problematic understanding of history, prompting the one-time policy advisor to Ronald Reagan to clarify in *The End of History and the Last Man* (1992) that his title's end-limit does not portend the destruction of the discipline or deny the material events that

---

10. Mallmann both provides a succinct history of Inter-American relations and examines the region's newfound diplomatic cooperation during the 1980s.

11. Rowe has labeled Fukuyama a cultural apologist ("Culture, US Imperialism" 288).

12. For a list of historians' many harsh responses, consider Jenkins and Munslow's discussion of "Endisms," Perry Anderson's concluding chapter of *A Zone of Engagement*, and Windschuttle.

make up the historical record. Rather, it describes the abolition of ideological and national competition under global democracy, repurposing Hegel's original use of the phrase "end-of-history" as a form of universal progress. As proof of the intersection of political and economic paradigms, the North American points to 1975 as the starting point for an unprecedented collapse of dictatorships across the globe—both military-authoritarian and leftist communist-totalitarian regimes—that would extend through the next decade.

While Fukuyama is most concerned with the collapse of communism in the Soviet Union, his thesis seemed by many accounts equally applicable to the Western hemisphere (Brands 252), even if it glossed over the CIA's role in establishing the nondemocratic Latin American regimes that would fall during the 1980s. As Noam Chomsky has pointed out, despite the rhetoric of preserving democracy, the United States inaugurated the post–Cold War era by invading one-time ally Panama (144–45), yet due to a systemic lack of media coverage, knowledge of Central America's plight was largely limited to efforts of engaged writers and activist groups.[13] Given the tendency of Cold War models to privilege East–West dynamics, it is not entirely surprising that Latin America is virtually absent from Fukuyama's expanded thesis, where he reductively attributes the economic stagnation that precipitated the 1980s debt crisis to the "fundamental" aspects of its people's social structure (*Last Man* 103–4).

I dedicate time to characterizing the economic motivations behind Fukuyama's discriminatory end of history and the negative implications of the lost decade for three reasons. First, they provide examples of the types of competing narratives toward which Latin American and American studies have alternately gravitated. Second, by contextualizing the political and economic claims of each text, it becomes apparent that their focus upon systems and collectivities fails to account for individual agency, the ethnological specificities that alter social norms, and the increasing inclusion of women and minorities into political life—all key critiques that cultural historians directed at social historians' economic focus during the 1970s and 1980s. Finally, several of the authors whose work I explore have responded vehemently to the postmodern end-of-history in essays that help place into relief both the objective of their comparative writing and the role of history as a philosophical concept in their critiques.

Indeed, cultural historians have observed how Fukuyama glosses over the past, for the type of development diplomacy he attributes to the end of the twentieth century has been practiced by Washington for more than a cen-

---

13. See also De la Campa's discussion of postmodernism and revolution (32–33).

tury within Central and South America.[14] More damningly, others claim that what Fukuyama unwittingly describes is the end of white male dominance of the historical record (Poster 64), and Latin American historians have gone one step further to intimate that the "loudly proclaimed End of History is the beginning of histories in the plural: not the forced paralysis of the future of the world in accordance with the interests of a hegemonic power, but the right to alternatives" (Britto-García 526). In line with these pluralities, comparatist George Yúdice promoted local responses to postmodern identities as a method for rethinking capitalism and reimagining democracy—a task notably as important for North America as it was for Brazil and Hispanic America ("Puede hablarse" 109). Significantly, then, despite the distinct political realities of the "two" Americas, the historical turn can only be comprehended within a hemispheric constellation, for cultural historians' radical approach to revisionism manifested through remarkably similar strategies across the region. Moreover, this postnational critique of history therefore unfolded concurrently with a discrete postnational desire to reconfigure "bounded" American identities.

This book is thus not a survey of historical literature in the final quarter of the twentieth century but rather seeks to examine the *ends,* or designs, of hemispheric American history by tracing the confluence of the above revisionist trends, for both new Inter-American and new historical literary studies were formulated as correctives to their fields. Each shift sought to disturb fixed structures of knowledge and identify the dominant forms of exceptionalism these structures benefited. My project consists of reframing scholarly relationships whose division has been intensified by the antagonism undergirding postmodernism—specifically that between the domains of literature and historiography as well as Latin American and American studies—in order to establish the basis for understanding the humanities in a mutually constructive framework.

While the end of the Cold War has been separately fashioned in American and Latin American studies as a turning point that led to distinct views on global positionality,[15] the phenomenon has not been explored comparatively. From the 1980s onward, iconoclastic historical literature has been theorized under a variety of rubrics and associated with divergent concepts in

---

14. Citing the 2002 National Security Strategy's findings regarding the "single sustainable model for national success: freedom, democracy, and free enterprise," Grandin notes that long-standing US imperialism in the Americas has since informed post-9/11 foreign policy in the Middle East (195, 166).

15. Cohen examines transnational US historical fiction written between the end of the Cold War and 9/11, while Hoyos takes the end of the Cold War as the starting point of the global Latin American novel.

the Americas, though this theorization has, much like accounts of the end of history and the lost decade, almost exclusively ignored neighboring linguistic and literary traditions. From apocryphal history (McHale) to historiographic metafiction (Hutcheon *Poetics*) and postmodern history (Parrish), North American models have extended a global politics of poststructuralism, while Latin American considerations such as new historical fiction (Aínsa; Menton; Valente, "Viva o povo"), archival fictions (González Echevarría *Myth*), and intra-history (Rivas 1997) have interrogated the perceived ethical nihilism of Anglo-American experimentation. I will explore the synergy of these approaches in chapter 2, for the contextualization of such responses involves documenting how a particular historical moment was processed in localized yet nonetheless compatible ways.

As will therefore become clear, my purpose is not to legitimize a postmodern agenda, nor will I pursue more commonly repeated assertions regarding the supposed crisis of representation or the inherent fictionality of historical practice, for this imperative of rupture often did not translate to cultural production in the southern sector of the hemisphere. In fact, the viability of postmodern historicism is a particularly vexed issue in Latin America, where its implementation in cultural studies was initially met with great resistance and where it has had little association with the end of ideology (Rodríguez, "Postmodern Theory" 607), instead serving as an incentive for revisiting the past in order to recuperate history suppressed during authoritarian regimes. As John Beverley makes clear in perhaps the most widely cited collection on the subject, whereas the goal of democratization in Euro-American paradigms emerged within aesthetic categories, it was initiated from within the social sciences in Latin America, leading to a blurring of disciplinary boundaries (6).[16] Because several writers evaluated here seek to negate postmodernism's perceived apoliticism, I will take up this question in the case studies that follow by exploring region-specific scholarship, for cultural history and cultural studies are not synonymous ventures.

AGENCY AND IMPERIALISM IN AMERICAN, LATIN AMERICAN, AND INTER-AMERICAN STUDIES

I will probe the exceptionalism underlying the history-literature divide in the following two chapters, yet it remains to first address disciplinary distinctions

---

16. See also Rodríguez's "Postmodern Theory" for an overview of the primary debates in both Hispanic and Lusophone America.

relating to how analyses of inequality in the New World are organized. My intent is to read the paradigms of Hemispheric American and Latin American studies in productive dialogue, for the critical capital of American studies has meant that its emergent hemispheric turn in the 1990s has in many ways overshadowed the existing valence of established, yet less institutionally visible, practices like Inter-American studies. Despite significant overlap in their exploration of transnational networks, however, the different fields of study are not necessarily compatible, even if at times scholarship has used the terms interchangeably.[17]

This is particularly notable with regard to questions of methodology and the specter of the nation-state, which has meant vastly different things to intellectuals across the region. If, for example, US multiculturalism has focused on "issues of citizen empowerment" in a post–civil rights context, the history of neocolonial exploitation in Latin America yields a more urgent agenda to "take over (or take back) nation-states and wrest more economic control from 'outsiders'" (Shukla and Tinsman 10). Whereas American studies scholars decry the constructed borders and imagined geographies of the United States as forms of hegemony, Latin Americanists have in turn seen state-formation as a safeguard against US military and cultural expansion (Bauer, "Hemispheric Studies" 235). At the same time, American studies has effectively extended the methodological paradigms it first developed with regard to domestic multiculturalism, including postcolonial and race theory, to draw attention to the asymmetrical relationship between ethnic minorities and US border regions. Yet because its ostensible goal is to cast off the legacy of US imperialism, the United States essentially remains the theoretical locus for such maneuvers, prompting the rejoinder from Inter-American scholars that the lack of cultural and linguistic referents beyond North America is not meaningfully postnational (McClennen, "Imperial Studies" 402).

The potential for miscommunication between like-minded scholars expressing regional solidarity is evidenced by the polarizing response to Janice Radway's 1998 Presidential Address at the American Studies Association, titled "What's In a Name?" In it, Radway revisits the politics behind the Cold War formation of the association in the 1950s, and in an attempt to formalize the transnational turn earlier in the decade, she suggests several potential rebrandings of the field, one of which is the "Inter-American Studies Association" (20–21). Americanists applauded Radway's gesture toward inclusion and her advocacy for the training of US scholars to be bilingual, and the essay has

---

17. Bauer provides the most comprehensive account of Inter-American and Hemispheric American institutional distinctions in his "Early American Literature" and "Hemispheric Studies."

been reproduced in Donald Pease's *The Futures of American Studies* (2002) as an example of posthegemonic studies. By contrast, Inter-Americanists have understood the gesture as paradoxically widening the territorial realm of US Americanists and perpetuating intellectual imperialism, for Radway speaks as if the field of Inter-American studies did not already exist, an oversight unimaginable for Latin American scholars who must appraise their field through US cultural activity.[18]

Indeed, while the beginning of the 1990s marked a key shift for all three disciplines, it was perhaps most notable in Latin American studies. The field is one of several Cold War area studies initiatives, yet the exodus of Latin American intellectuals to the United States in the 1980s helped reshape its politics and demographics, serving as a catalyst for the consolidation of regional cultural studies. Thus during the 1992 quincentennial of Columbus's arrival, Enrico Santí drew upon Edward Said's *Orientalism* (1978) when he suggested the corollary "Latinamericanism" to gauge the impact of imagining and constructing a regional other as a form of "scientific colonialism" (89–90). Román de la Campa further considered the term in *Latin Americanism* (1999) to examine the roles that postmodernity and poststructuralism had played in the field's appropriation by the US academy, ranging from the inclusion of forgotten groups—through the subaltern and female *testimonio*—to forgotten regions—through recognition of Hispanic and Francophone Caribbean contributions.

At the same time, a second development had an equally important effect on the field's transnational ambitions. In her foundational manifesto *Borderlands/La Frontera* (1987), feminist activist Gloria Anzaldúa not only blends personal and critical genres, but also mixes English and Spanish to epitomize how the geopolitical and social borders that divided the identities of minority subjects also served as sites of cultural hybridity. Her interdisciplinary work helped pave the way for academic activism through the subsequent emergence of border and queer studies in the early to mid-1990s, which became central tenets of cultural studies agendas. By being able to problematize area and ethnic/multicultural models, Juan Poblete would suggest that Latinx studies not only bridged Latin American issues, but it was also a central component of "critical Americanism" in the face of globalization (xxv–vi), attested to by the productivity of Anglophone-American scholars' subsequent exploration of border inequality. As extensions of Latinamericanism's increased attention to the Caribbean and deconstruction of the canon, border and queer

---

18. Bauer's "Hemispheric Studies" provides a measured reaction, yet McClennen adamantly criticizes Radway, suggesting that such disciplinary border disputes reinforce the monopoly of power imbalance in US-centered area studies ("Imperial American" 402).

studies helped drastically expand the social and geographical inclusivity of approaches to the region. Nonetheless, the focus upon Hispanic and indigenous patterns of culture meant that the most populous country and the largest regional economy after the lost decade—Brazil—was still largely absent from consideration.

Recognizing the similar erasure of Canada from hemispheric comparative models (Sadowski-Smith and Fox), the decentralized, synthetic approach of Inter-Americanism shares more in common with Latin Americanism than US studies, yet its own roots lie in historiography and outside institutionalized area studies. Despite a surge of scholarship disparaging US President Theodore Roosevelt's 1904 corollary to the Monroe Doctrine—and receptive to the First International Conference of American States in 1889—formal Inter-American practice is generally traced to Herbert Bolton's 1932 Presidential Address for the American History Association, "The Epic of Greater America." By the 1970s, the cultural turn led the field to expand exponentially from political history to include literary analysis.[19] Earl Fitz, who has stratified expressions of "Americanism" into six distinct periods dating back to European conquest,[20] founded the first Inter-American Literature Program in 1978, and by 1980 his ambition was that the practice would become a central component of comparative literature programs nationwide ("Old World Roots" 10). Fitz's prognostication did not ultimately materialize, though comparative literature began to confront its problematic Eurocentric foundations and comparatists led a bevy of Inter-American criticism during the following decade.[21]

Coinciding with the end of the Cold War, Cuban Gustavo Firmat's *Do the Americas Have a Common Literature?* (1990) institutionalized this critical tendency with the declared purpose of establishing dialogue between Americanists and Latin Americanists (2–3), and I specifically draw on the related work of several emerging contributors to his volume to inform my own analyses. In addition to José David Saldívar, the collection notably showcased the work of Lois Parkinson Zamora, the founding figure in comparative historical studies of the Americas, whose two "companion" works—*Writing the Apocalypse* (1989) and *The Usable Past* (1997)—demonstrate how preoccupations with the beginning and the end of history, respectively, have pervaded twentieth-century US and Hispanic American writing. Significantly, the rhetorical question posed by Firmat's title is not designed to be answered but rather pay homage to the field's origins in historical studies; in *Do the Americas Have a Common History?*

---

19. Holden and Zolov divide Inter-American history into five periods in their introduction.
20. Both Fitz's *Inter-American Literary History* and *Rediscovering the New World* provide examples of his linguistic and ethnic comparative literary scope.
21. See Aldridge, Valdés, and Chevigny and Laguardia.

(1964), influential Latin Americanist Lewis Hanke tasked Cold War historians from the United States, Canada, and Latin America with deconstructing the resurgence of Good Neighbor "Boltonism" during the Cold War.

Yet less than two decades after Firmat's conciliatory gesture, Sandhya Shukla and Helen Tinsman displayed their apprehension with the trend of transnationalism in more acerbic terms, asserting that throughout the

> important new work in US American studies there is a glaring absence of the appearance and thick description of other places in the world, not just as specters of victimized objects but as actors, producers, and sources within transnational circuitry. Recent books on empire may do the important work of explaining in detail the role of the United States in the world, but they do so, often, without the cultural or linguistic fluency of those acted-upon sites that would help us understand the depth of impact and the possibilities for resistance. (11–12)

While this formulation sets the critique of imperialism at odds with the agency of non-US cultural traditions, it does not entirely do justice to the evolving field. In the decade that followed Radway's intervention, a group of scholars from across the globe partnered to create the independent International Association of American Studies, while the transnational trend was tempered by European Americanist concerns that it unintentionally helped facilitate the spread of neoliberalism.[22] Thus, Caroline Levander and Robert Levine's collection *Hemispheric American Studies* (2008) recalls Firmat's earlier Inter-American sentiment, as the editors contend the recent tendency to conceive the United States solely in terms of imperialism essentializes the complexity of contingent national encounters. Aiming to create the cultural history of a "polycentric American hemisphere with no dominant center" (7), Levander and Levine seek to revitalize conversations between the regions by juxtaposing distinct "national and extra-national histories and cultural formations . . . to contextualize what can sometimes appear to be the artificially hardened borders and boundaries of the US nation, or for that matter, any nation of the American hemisphere" (2–3). During this same period, comparative hemispheric contributions such as Zita Nunes's *Cannibal Democracy* (2008), Gretchen Murphy's *Hemispheric Imaginings* (2005), and Anna Brickhouse's *Transamerican Literary Relations and the Nineteenth-Century Public Sphere* (2004) explored issues as diverse as national and racial identity as well

---

22. Fluck is skeptical of Levander's optimism regarding the "rejuvenating" promise of transnationalism, as he suggests that the actual application of the theory frequently downplays its own role in the processes of globalization that it critiques (375).

as the Monroe Doctrine's role in shaping the US empire. And most recently, the intersecting approaches of Inter-Americanist Claire Fox's *Making Art Panamerican* (2013) and Americanist Stephen Park's *The Pan American Imagination* (2014) have demonstrated productive regional and historical overlaps between the two fields.

Yet Shukla and Tinsman's critique of imperialism is ultimately a response to an earlier evolution of American studies, namely the hemispheric turn in the 1990s. Historian Robert Berkhofer noticed in 1989 that Americanists' preoccupation with myth and identity had been usurped by questions relating to the exercise of power, in which culture was no longer a unifying force but rather a multicultural marker of division ("A New Context" 280).[23] Initiated by Pease and Amy Kaplan's groundbreaking collection *Cultures of United States Imperialism* (1993), the study of empire emerged as the most transformative paradigm within US American studies. Making explicit the transnational and historical implications of such a charge, Pease couches the volume as a response to both the end of the Cold War and the problematic 1992 quincentennial celebration of Columbus' arrival to the New World. The future of American studies, he argues, will be determined by two conflicting post–civil rights developments: multiculturalism and "new historicism," the latter of which subverts the US nationalist metanarrative by exposing the "bankruptcy" of its foreign diplomatic policy (25). Yet despite the overlap in terms, the new historicism Pease labels is not related to the 1980s literary movement, but rather is roughly equivalent to 1970s social history in its focus on class rather than the plurality of identities central to cultural history.

By contrast, the Inter-American conceptualization of the past resists locating the United States at the core of a neocolonial system whose prevailing concern is the control of power, using traditions outside the dominant center—the beginning of "histories" in the plural—to revise its isolationism. If for Pease new historicism and multiculturalism act as opposing US paradigms, historian Gilbert Joseph notes a similar Latin American tension between interventionist models and dependency theories. While he acknowledges the formative influence of Washington upon the region, Joseph worries that exclusive focuses on imperialism risk becoming one-dimensional by presuming a lack of local agency, for "the master narrative of 'dependency,' like that of 'imperialism,' has presupposed a bipolar relationship that subsumed difference (regional, class, racial/ethnic, gender, generational) into the service of a greater machinery" (12). Thus for Joseph, it is the postmodern approach to historical agency in

---

23. For histories of the field's various phases, consult Wise's "Paradigm Dramas," as well as Pease's update in his introduction to *The Futures of American Studies*.

collaborative, cultural history that can most likely account for local production while interrogating national categories previously assumed to be fixed.

Americanist Paul Giles has worried that used indiscriminately, hemispheric considerations merely replace nationalist essentialism with geographical essentialism (649), yet broad comparison does not inherently lead to parallelism. As a key Americanist and postmodern historian, Berkhofer contends that unlike the "textualism" of traditional scholars, the "contextualist" approaches favored by cultural studies are skeptical of comparative synthesis because they presume the uniqueness of local events (*Great Story* 42–43). Yet in the process, such categorical assumptions of difference may also inadvertently reinscribe national models by disqualifying extranational analysis. Rather than erase disciplinary borders, then, the following case studies expand the range of comparative Inter-American scholarship by articulating a framework for surveying historical and democratic representation as part of a network of mutually constitutive developments.

CHAPTER OUTLINES AND CRITERIA

False Documents is divided into two sections. The first two chapters perform an overview of the parallel disciplinary evolutions of historiographic and literary historical criticism in the second half of the twentieth century. The six chapters constituting the second section are comprised of two paired case studies of false documents from each region embodying the geographical and cultural hybridity of Inter-American comparison during the lost decade. I begin with paradigmatic examples from Argentina and Venezuela, and then consider two specimens from Brazil, before extending the analysis to two North American narratives. Each author disentangles the recent national past by representing traumatic events from his or her own lost decade, in some cases incorporating a previous historical era to dialectically draw attention to systemic inequalities reproduced in the author's contemporary setting.

As will become apparent, considerable overlap emerges between the distinct strategies of apocryphal primary documents, lost archival texts, and supposed professional scholarship, though not all of the writers here share the same understanding of postnationalism. Each regional pairing therefore features one example of an explicitly transnational comparative framework and one author who in contrast critiques undemocratic methods of the nation-state by incorporating extranational political markers. At the same time, while several writers considered here have not crossed into circulation in neighboring parts of the hemisphere, their inclusion is not merely a token gesture.

Each text has been claimed as a form of postmodernism or historiographic metafiction, yet I will propose how rereading them instead as false documents establishes a prototype for revising the construction of democracy within the nation-state, whether as a means of self-determination or a critique of neoliberalism. To reinforce this dynamic, I read each of the six representations of the lost decade against an Inter-American theory contemporary to the study's scope, which demonstrates the applicability of regional resolutions to a wide variety of disciplines and contexts.

Including Deborah Cohn's *History and Memory in the Two Souths* (1999), a number of important Inter-American scholars/works have emerged since roughly the turn of the twenty-first century, particularly in the fields of Colonial American studies, border studies, and transnational race and ethnicity studies. These include, among others, Ralph Bauer, Claire Fox, Robert Newcomb, Zita Nunes, Antonio Barrenechea, Lesley Feracho, Kirsten Silva Gruesz, and Claudia Milian. Nonetheless, because my intent is to examine the particular milieu of the final quarter of the twentieth century prior to the surge in border studies, I have privileged Inter-American analyses of history from the beginning of the 1990s corresponding to the rise of the field, particularly by participants in Firmat's collection such as José Davíd Saldívar and Lois Parkinson Zamora, with nods to Doris Sommer and Enrico Santí. In other cases, analyzing the work of Silviano Santiago and Néstor García Canclini, or historians David Harlan and Robert Berkhofer, I demonstrate how theories first proposed within specific geographic traditions contain unexplored postnational dimensions.

In the preceding pages, I have elaborated some of the methodological differences between Inter-American, Latin American, and Hemispheric American studies, which the individual case studies will further elucidate. Before examining these distinct hemispheric engagements, however, the first two chapters must first deconstruct the other axis of this study, the antagonistic relationship between postwar literary scholars and historians. Chapter 1 traces the social and cultural turns in revisionist historiography in relation to cognate concepts in postnational literary studies of the past. The purpose of highlighting methodological shifts that led to this postwar American convergence is to establish the basis for false documentation to transcend disciplinary divisiveness by the chapter's end. Before turning my attention to historiography, I evaluate as an endpoint historiographic metafiction, the Canadian postmodern model that has had the most currency in Anglophone literary historical studies, yet which has been taken to task for essentializing Latin American traditions in the process. After briefly examining the origins of the history-literature debate by contextualizing the traditional historical novel and the resulting documentary model of historiography, I trace the rise of social history and then the transition to cultural history that took place across the hemisphere through the work of Gilberto Freyre, Hayden White, Natalie Zemon Davis, and Fernando Retamar, demonstrating that the literary-based critique of "traditional" history had been anticipated by cultural historians themselves. While Latin American historians were instead influenced by the French *Annales* school as well as economic dependency theory, social and cultural history nonetheless began to gain traction at exactly the same moments. Having established a pattern of mutual influence, the chapter culminates by analyzing the principal methodology of historiography: the documentary model, which privileges primary documents and official archives over oral and unofficial sources. It is precisely because of the continued dominance of these conventions that false documents provide a model for literary revision to apply historians' own distinct revisionist methodologies.

Chapter 2 considers the historical turn in the humanities within the United States (1970–1989), Hispanic America (1974–1992), and Brazil (1976–1992). Tracing the arc of revisionism within the three traditions reveals that each has been defined by two opposing tendencies, postmodern parody that distorts the official record and self-reflexive false documents that appear to reproduce the conventions of history, although the latter has received significantly less attention. Thus, the first section investigates the procession of postmodern revision in North America, moving from apocalyptic comedy that emerged in the 1960s through Brian McHale's apocryphal history (as a precursor to historiographic metafiction). After identifying a corpus of iconoclastic postmodern historical fiction from this period, I propose reconsidering this canon through the undertheorized documentary tendency developed by Doctorow as well as the New Journalists.

The subsequent exploration of Hispanic America's return of history, where the task was distinct from US multicultural agendas, follows a similar pattern. Because political history had been tightly censored under authoritarian regimes, discourses of national unity became a prime target for intellectuals seeking to provide agency to citizens. Many intellectuals rejected North American deconstruction, although they reached surprisingly commensurate conclusions in their independent theorization of the "new historical novel" during the 1980s. Yet as González Echevarría's "archival fictions" demonstrates, an equally important countertendency saw authors present their works as nonfictional discourse. Finally, a similar dynamic played out in Brazil, with Luiz Valente and Tânia Pellegrini's examination of how the gradual loosening of the dictatorship facilitated the use of history as a means of diagnosing the nation's current democratic and social ailments. Significantly, the tension between allegory and documentary fiction that developed during the military dictatorship provides the clearest case for examining several of Brazil's canonical "new" texts as false documents.

Part 2 is organized around regional typologies of false documentation—though these categories are not meant to be either exclusive or definitive. Thus chapter 3 features the first of two Hispanic American analyses through *La novela de Perón* (1985, *The Perón Novel*), which journalist Tomás Eloy Martínez largely wrote from exile in Venezuela during Argentina's Dirty War (1976–1983). In 1970, as exiled President Juan Perón sought to return to power with a new regional populist message, Martínez interviewed him and published his "canonical memoirs," despite discovering numerous inconsistencies. After unsuccessfully attempting to discredit the memoirs as propaganda through journalism and biography, however, Martínez turned to experimental fiction, combining apocryphal fragments of the original interview with fictionalized interviews he conducted with Perón's ex-associates, a mixture of journalism taken by some national historians as fact. Rejecting the label of postmodernism, Martínez increasingly provided academic reflections of the novel as cultural history, thus I explore Martínez's hybrid writing alongside Argentine anthropologist Néstor García Canclini's *Hybrid Cultures* (1990) to provide a contemporary cultural framework for distinguishing modern and postmodern historical approaches. Finished on the eve of the military dictatorship's public trials, the novel views Perón's return in 1973 as the catalyst for the end of democracy, yet as García Canclini's approach to hybridity helps demonstrate, Argentina's response to the lost decade developed as part of a larger network of transnational relations.

Chapter 4 expands the typology of Hispanic American postnationalism by analyzing Venezuelan author Laura Antillano's *Solitaria solidaria* (1990, *Alone but Committed*). Written as the country's democracy unraveled during the financial crisis, the work simulates a female historian's research and "reproduces" a nineteenth-century woman's diaries discovered in the university archives, revealing surprisingly parallel, epochal gender politics. As a literature professor, journalist, and a screenplay writer, Antillano had firsthand experience of the culture industry during the 1970s and 1980s, when a generation of women began to enter the workforce. Yet the influential role in the diaries of Cuban author and activist José Martí, who arrived in Venezuela in 1881 to launch a political magazine, also highlights Antillano's postnational politics. I thus read the work as a feminist revision of "Nuestra América," Martí's famous call for pan-Hispanic American solidarity. While numerous Latin and American scholars have resignified this canonical work, in *The Dialectics of Our America* (1991) José David Saldívar notably draws on Doctorow's "false documents" to complicate the prevailing tendencies to consider the periphery a mere recipient of global cultural flows. Synthesizing Saldívar's dialectical approach to the Americas, I demonstrate how Antillano distinguishes between the patriarchal official record and marginalized feminist microhistories, revealing a shared identity across history that feminist scholars have demonstrated extends beyond Venezuelan national politics to encompass Hispanic Caribbean regional identities.

Chapter 5 turns its attention to Brazil's absent generation, the political exiles during the military dictatorship's most repressive period. After the 1979 Amnesty Law, as exiles returned to tell their side of the nation's recent history, the popular success of testimonial and parajournalistic literature—its focus upon middle-class dissidence markedly different from its Hispanic American counterpart—paradoxically limited outlets for aesthetic intellectual experiments. Although Ana Machado's *Tropical sol da liberdade* (*Tropical Sun of Liberty*, 1988) in fact critiques the limits of such genres, her novel has been reductively categorized as a form of truth literature. After detailing the different responses to the dictatorship that dominated the Brazilian marketplace, I argue that Machado's book is in fact a paradigmatic example of "postdictatorial" literature, a concept coined by Idelber Avelar in *The Untimely Present* (1999). In this Inter-American analysis of the Southern Cone's redemocratization, Avelar maintains that the military regime's model of consumerism erased meaningful historical referents, encumbering attempts to grieve and bring guilty parties to justice. Drawing partially on her own experience, Machado follows a returned female journalist during the democratic transition as she seeks to create a literary document of her generation, though she loses the ability to write after being mysteriously afflicted with dyslexia. Locating herself on what she terms the "periphery of history," the protagonist is haunted by not having participated in the national recuperation of this lost period, despite numerous interviews she conducts with exiles from across South America. Exposing the psychological consequences of censorship, Machado reveals that the recovery of collective memory must begin with local and regional partnerships or run the risk of becoming trapped by the very discourses of nationalism returning writers sought to criticize.

Operating at the heart of chapter 6, Brazilian Silviano Santiago's *Em Liberdade* (1980, *In Liberty*), which claims to be a fictional edition of the postincarceration diaries of communist writer Graciliano Ramos, initially confused multiple critics who believed the text was a legitimate discovery. While Santiago performed archival research in order to mimic Ramos's confessional writing style, the fictional diary's critique of intellectuals' complicity during the 1930s civilian dictatorship is in fact a thinly veiled attack upon the left's infighting and so-called "ideological patrols" under the contemporary military dictatorship. Indeed, the fictional diary not only subtly references the secret police's 1975 murder of a journalist, but it also adversely reflects the emerging trend in exiles' confessional literature. While Santiago initially viewed *In Liberty* as a negation of Brazilian modernism, I instead read it as the paradigmatic expression of his most famous essay on Inter-American intellectual resistance, "The Space In-Between" (1971). Detailing a means of subverting European cultural models by creating a false imitation or an invisible text, Santiago not only anticipates Hispanic American debates on postmodern peripheral hybridity, but he also creates the very blueprint that *In Liberty* utilizes to reassess the limits of discourses of realism during periods of censorship.

The first of two chapters by North American writers inspects the commodification of Che Guevara as an Inter-American revolutionary, which owes much to the fetishization of his posthumous diaries as primary documents of guerilla warfare. While Argentine and Brazilian writers have since also claimed to reproduce Guevara's apocryphal diaries, Jewish American Jay Cantor's *The Death of Che Guevara* (1983) remains the only novel to utilize Guevara's own words to trace the history of anti-US sentiment across the Americas. Playing on the Bolivian government's claim that a Cuban version of Guevara's confiscated diaries was fake, Cantor juxtaposes a mixture of legitimate documents and invented entries from the failed campaign, his title taken from the famous 1967 magazine article that broke the news of the revolutionary's death. Lois Parkinson Zamora argues in *The Usable Past* (1997) that hemispheric authors are bound by an "anxiety of origins" unique to the Americas, and I draw on her examination of newspaper and novelistic discourse to demonstrate how Guevara's false diaries reveal a new strategy for reclaiming historical figures within a transnational context. Although Cantor views Guevara as an embodiment of the failed modernist project, he has been a vocal critic of postmodernism and Fukuyama's end-of-history claims. While the titular death refers to the appropriation of Guevara by competing political agendas, Cantor overtly ties the political repercussions of Guevara's demise to the 1975 US withdrawal from Vietnam through multiple historical timelines of anti-imperial movements across Latin America and Asia.

In the final chapter, I read David Harlan's *The Degradation of American History* (1997) against the work of John Updike, whose interest in Latin American literature culminated in his unsuccessful experiment *Brazil* (1994). While Harlan claims postmodern and New Left scholarship corroded historiography's ability to distill universal lessons, he argues the trends had exhausted themselves by 1992, permitting the renewal of history's ethical imperative. The stark realism of Updike's "Rabbit" tetralogy documented a postwar history of the United States, yet the author's less-studied *Memories of the Ford Administration* (1992) instead complicates the possibility of celebrating the national past. Despite the nostalgic discourse of the bicentennial during Ford's term, economic challenges had progressively led to the existence of "two Americas" separated by class and geography. Ostensibly framed as a historian's submission about Gerald Ford's presidency to an academic journal, the narrative actually reproduces a common strategy in American cultural history, detailing the historian's challenges to complete a biography during the 1970s, in this case about President James Buchanan and the imminent Civil War. The inclusion of large segments of the historian's monograph that cave under the weight of relativism is an explicit critique of American studies, from which the narrator opportunistically borrows his postmodern theory only to unwittingly exposes its limits. At the same time, Updike draws parallels between the dissolution of the Union and Ford's attempts to reconnect a divided country in the wake of the Vietnam War. Yet if Updike's historian exemplifies what Harlan describes as the crisis in historiography, the novelist also provides a roadmap to the ethical renewal of the discipline that rejects consensus nationalism.

Establishing a representative assemblage of texts always involves difficult choices and exclusions, especially because Inter-American studies' eschewal of an organizing geographical center necessarily results in partial encounters rather than total histories. Analyzing Spanish-language works from the Southern Cone and the Spanish Caribbean, I seek to not only demonstrate a breadth of geographical and gender concerns but also to draw attention to works that incorporate a discussion of cultural history most directly into their narratives. While I examine the three most linguistically and politically prominent traditions in the hemisphere, this is not to negate the importance of the false document within those spaces outside the study's purview. Cuban authors and theorists are central to the rise of new historical conceptions, though Puerto Rican Ana Lydia Vega's *False Chronicles from the South* (1991) exemplifies elements of the false document relevant to a different historical era, and it has not been possible to include Anglophone and Francophone Caribbean authors. Additionally, while Central America's civil wars have received postmodern treatment, several of its false documents—from Nicaraguan Sergio Ramírez's *Divine Punishment* (1988) or Costa Rican Tatiana Lobo's *Between God and the Devil* (1993)—similarly deal with historical events outside the frame of this study's reference. Fortunately, Ana Patricia Rodríguez's *Dividing the Isthmus* (2009) has grappled with a transnational corpus of testimonial and fictional works that deal with Cold War history and immigration across the region.

The question of canonicity also looms large. Brazilian literature has historically been written by and for the educated minority, a disconnect further exacerbated by rapid modernization and the sudden accessibility of visual culture during the 1960s. As Leila Lehnen has shown in *Citizenship and Crisis in Contemporary Brazilian Literature* (2013), the market has become more multicultural and inclusive of the social and geographic periphery since the turn of the century, yet the two institutionalized authors included here clearly continue to have much greater international circulation and currency. Both Santiago and Machado have been awarded the prestigious Jabuti Prize, although during the 1980s, their countercultural voices first emerged outside the field of literature, and Santiago's controversial *Stella Manhattan* (1985) would prove to be a formative work for Latin American queer studies and the nation's underrepresented tradition of homosexual literature.

The issues of multicultural representation and sexual identities are more contentious in American and Latinx studies, for while Jewish American Cantor has embraced continental civil rights and ethnic activism in his work, John Updike may seem to represent a more conservative canon. Updike won the Pulitzer Prize twice during the period under examination, yet along with Doctorow and John Barth, his prominence allowed him to be an important figure in the reception of Hispanic American and Brazilian literature during the 1980s. Even more importantly, his specific discussion of historiography-as-process is particularly relevant to the then-contemporary debates on cultural history and nationalism central to this book. Because I will argue that the indiscriminate application of the term "historiographic metafiction" has robbed the concept of much of its original iconoclasm, my own attention to temporal specificity has obliged me to exclude important works from marginal and canonical producers alike. Thus, while outside the scope of this study, US–Cuban relations under President Kennedy have received false documentary treatment in works as varied as Don DeLillo's *Libra* (1988), Oliver Stone's controversial film *JKF* (1991), and neo-noir texts by James Ellroy such as *American Tabloid* (1995).

Once again, this does not mean that false documentation has been limited to specific gender and ethnic spheres, but rather that practitioners were adopting distinct epochal focuses. While Japanese-Canadian Joy Kogawa's *Obasan* (1981) and Dominican-American Julia Alvarez's *In the Time of the Butterflies* (1994) both incorporate female diaries as informal archival texts, for example, their primary goal is not to meditate on transnational historiography and media presentation. Toni Morrison's *Beloved* (1987) is famously based on a discovered newspaper article, yet the novel ultimately partakes of magical realist strategies. And while Leslie Marmon Silko's *Almanac of the*

Dead (1992) both contains supposed fragments of its eponymous historical indigenous text and connects North and Central America, its focus is not upon passing off invented documents as institutional discourse. The book has occasioned numerous responses within the context of border studies, and its history has received Inter-American treatment in Antonio Barrenechea's *America Unbound* (2016). Finally, Danny Santiago's supposedly semi-autobiographic *Famous All over Town* (1983) was received as a milestone contribution to Latinx literature until it was revealed that Santiago was in fact the pseudonym of a white Hollywood screenwriter, yet this type of dissimulation is more aligned with literary hoaxes than it is false documentation.

Taken together, the chosen texts provide insight into the expanding, transnational uses of history. In each instance, the recent past, whether a lost decade or a lost heritage previously restricted for its citizens, provides a heightened understanding of the stakes of public democratic debates in the present. Additionally, the abstract critique of historical practice becomes rooted in specific texts and attitudes that provide a means for analyzing the motivations and machinations behind the popularization of particular narrative trends. Perhaps most importantly, the broadening scope of historical sources and methodologies further bolsters the availability of history as a complementary model that establishes continuity between underrepresented critical junctures and similar issues in the twenty-first century, as the current resurgence of nationalism and political history attest.

CHAPTER 1

Interdependent Methods

Postwar Cultural History, Historical Literature, and False Documents

THE MODERN historical novel serves a political function. It has done so since its inception in early nineteenth-century Europe and its export a decade later to fledgling nations across the Americas. And while it became linked to postindependence projects via what Doris Sommer in 1991 famously termed Latin American "foundational fictions," the characteristics have been noted across the hemisphere.[1] Paradoxically, through their shared desire to cast off the influence of European models by inventing local and indigenous mythologies, early practitioners in fact established a common Inter-American strategy of dissociative writing (Buchenau 199). The specific nature of both the historical novel's form and its political ends, however, was radically reconfigured in the final decades of the twentieth century, when experimentation in the genre took on the implications of counterhistory. Long associated with articulating nationhood and facilitating, in Benedict Anderson's words, "imagined communities" in the New World, the classic historical novel had by the 1980s become affiliated with an implicitly conservative political outlook, and postmodern forms of cultural production were consolidated as trends to challenge the idea of both nation and history as coherent narratives of progress.

---

1. Samuels (*Reading*) traces the adaptation of Scott's nationalist mythology in Fennimore Cooper's 1820s novels. Unzueta and Ribeiro, respectively, each discuss Scott's equivalent adoption in Hispanic America and Brazil.

Because these new variations spanned an extensive variety of forms and strategies, complicating specific categorization, scholars generally define them in contradistinction to "traditional" or modernist history/fiction, the implicit assumption being that realist discourses represent dominant state and social interests. But the epithet "traditional" does not clarify exactly what this means in a twentieth-century context. Instead, the term can act as a false benchmark, a discursive strategy for essentializing the diverse practices of historiography under a single rubric and insinuating complicity with hegemonic power. My goal here is to reconsider the politics of exceptionalism underlying the rupture between history and literature, which has given rise to postmodern misunderstandings of historiography as a static category. For how and to what ends the new historical novel's politicization has been cast often reveals just as much if not more about the enterprise of scholars than the agenda of a particular assembly of writers.

Although I argue that postmodern literary revisionism overlooks its indebtedness to postwar evolutions of social and cultural historical methods in both Anglophone and Latin America, this chapter will not address each field in chronological order. In order to break down the critical slippage behind both "traditional" history and "traditional" historical literature that is central to postmodern criticism, it will be necessary first to establish the context and importance of historiographic metafiction, the most prominent literary theory from the period. Not only do the shifting social and cultural axes of postwar historical schools of thought complicate any single demarcation of traditional, but they also anticipate and reinforce the displacements in hemispheric literary theory that I will explore in chapter 2. Exposing the misguided rhetoric of disruption allows me to more fully flesh out false documents in this chapter's conclusion as an exploitation of the documentary model, the defining trait of history that has notably continued to dominate the field despite poststructural challenges. Rather than provide anything resembling an exhaustive account, my goal is to trace in broad strokes the major junctures in theory and practice, along with their attendant critiques, which document constructive interdisciplinary dialogue.

HISTORIOGRAPHIC METAFICTION AND THE POSTMODERN PARADIGM

Numerous scholars have suggested rubrics for postmodernism dating back to the 1970s, yet the importance of Linda Hutcheon's companion volumes *A Poetics of Postmodernism* (1988) and *The Politics of Postmodernism* (1989) for comprehending the purchase of historicity within these paradigms cannot be overstated. It is here that the Canadian scholar first defined "historiographic metafiction," the term she chooses to describe the intersection of history, fiction, and theory (*Poetics* 5). If today Fredric Jameson's assertion that video represents the most distinguished new medium of postmodernism seems old-fashioned (*Cultural Logic* 76), how much more so must the historical novel be, yet Hutcheon argues that this reformulated genre is the paradigmatic expression of cultural postmodernism. Of course, as Hutcheon readily admits, self-reflexivity is not new, and she traces it back to the same source that Doctorow does the false document: Cervantes's *Don Quixote*. What distinguishes contemporary applications of metafiction is the obsessive frequency with which ironic self-awareness has been employed in the latter half of the twentieth century (*Poetics* x–xi). Historiographic metafiction has been enormously influential in the fields of postmodern and cultural studies. Although three decades have passed since its coinage, the model still serves as the primary interpretive theory for contemporary historical fiction, despite being, by several accounts, outdated (Robinson xiii).

Its lasting currency is due less to immunity from criticism than the particular ways in which Hutcheon explicitly sets her theory in opposition to Jameson's influential dismissal of postmodern historicity as superficial "pop" nostalgia in "The Cultural Logic of Late Capitalism" (1984). First, the Canadian maintains that far from being ahistorical, postmodernism is defined by its ironic interrogation of the past that in fact foregrounds historicity as a problem. Second, Hutcheon takes issue with Jameson's description of postmodern aesthetic as empty imitation or pastiche, contending that historiographic metafiction engages in substantive parody of discursive conventions and accepted forms of knowledge. Third, rather than offer a cultural-economic contextualization of the dominance of capital, she gives expression to a decidedly literary approach to the problematic of postmodernism by offering a text-based account of the phenomenon. Finally, as opposed to understanding the postmodern subject as a passive consumer, she envisages the writer as an active agent capable of producing change. As evidenced by the immediate proliferation of studies recasting reflexivity as political critique, parody and intertextuality offered a blueprint for a generation of scholars struggling to find constructive value in a hermeneutic often criticized for its ethical relativism.[2] Nonetheless, it is telling that Jameson would view the "innovative" historical politics of leftist writer Doctorow—whose work I will return to at the

---

2. The number of Anglophone and Latin American monographs is too vast to exhaustively catalogue, though I will analyze specific examples in each target region in chapter 2. For examples testifying to Hutcheon's continued currency, see Gauthier and Weldt-Basson.

end of the chapter—as providing the antidote to Hutcheon and postmodern nostalgia (*Cultural Logic* 21).

One of historiographic metafiction's principal defenses against the pitfalls of relativism has been its application as a corrective to a historical record that has represented the interests of dominant groups, for self-reflexive texts are credited with dismantling "hegemonic discourse" by incorporating voices traditionally suppressed by the producers of narrative history. This occurs both by undermining the authority of history's claim to objective truth and by actively distorting the agreed-upon record to champion alternative counterhistories. If history is aligned with the institutions of power, literature is by contrast both a vehicle for previously excluded groups and a means of improving the vigilance of information sources through fiction's unique set of strategies. In addition to parody and intertextuality, these include the use of fragmentation, multiple perspectives, provisionality, anachronism, self-consciousness, and doubleness or paradox. According to the argument, because fiction is not limited by historiography's codification to be objective and factual, it is better equipped to educate the public about the past, because it is also less likely to be written in the service of political institutions. These politicized claims have created a central base around which to rally underrepresented writers and taboo themes as authors began to explore the politics of representation in the 1980s, no doubt bolstered by emerging feminist and postcolonial reconsiderations of underrepresented American minorities. Thus after experimental writers like Ishmael Reed and Toni Morrison underscored the importance of black history for reconstituting African American cultural identity starting in the 1970s—even if other authors to explore racial dynamics were less parodic—Latina writers signaled a new wave of women's histories starting in the 1980s.[3]

The application of Hutcheon's model over a global canon of works has led to a quandary, however. If all experimental fiction intersecting with history is subsumed under the blanket of historiographic metafiction, the term loses its descriptive power. Despite editorial involvement in collaborative projects such as *Literary Cultures of Latin America: A Comparative History* (2004), Hutcheon has been taken to task for "misappropriating" the region because she applies a "first-world" methodology to a corpus of peripheral transnational literatures, in which Latin American production figures prominently. One of the consequences of her decidedly literary basis is the exclusion of social and political conditions out of which postmodernism emerged in either North or Latin America. This results in a universalizing impulse that compromises her

---

3. See Nunes on African American female writers, Spaulding on the "neo-slave narrative," and Byerman on black postmodern writers' nonparodic approach to combat falsified history (10).

claim to contest totalizing metanarratives and also fails to account for uneven social development in the two sectors of the hemisphere (Colás 3–4). This is by no means to say that hemispheric models of literary production during the 1960s were incompatible, according to Santiago Colás, for the tension between the documentary impulse of New Journalism and "apocalyptic" parody in the United States found its correlation in Latin America through the rise of testimonial truth literature and certain "Boom" authors' magical realism (3).

More problematically still, the trend toward epistemological skepticism also facilitated a general opposition to history as an establishment. Aggrieved that the rise of scientific methodology in the nineteenth century permitted an epistemological divorce between the fields, literary critics have taken umbrage with the greater value accorded to truth discourses of history. While for the majority of its existence, historical fiction has been evaluated regarding how accurately it has reflected the accepted historical record, postmodernism's inherent critique of scientific discourse also served as a pretense for attacking the authority of historians' truth claims. Whereas postmodern historical fiction was originally defined as a break with realist fiction, Hutcheon extends this critique to the entire discipline of historiography by conflating literary realism and nonfiction: "Historians are readers of fragmentary documents and, like readers of fiction, they fill in the gaps and create ordering structures, which may be further disrupted by new textual inconsistencies that will force the formation of new totalizing patterns" (*Politics* 83). In this account, historians do not seek to record the past so much as "master" it and conceal their own agendas. Even though no guilty historians are ever named, craftily equating a critique of modernist conventions with one of academic disciplines doubly empowers literature to do the work of cultural studies and expands the authority of literary scholars in an attempt to validate their own field's political relevance.

Unfortunately, these claims are based on a gross mischaracterization of the field of history, whose landscape was also reshaped by poststructural theoretical challenges during the same era. Concurrent to Hutcheon's manifestoes, Peter Novick's *That Noble Dream* (1988) remains one of the richest accounts of American historiography and is emblematic of historians' own attempts to grapple with the questions of objectivity and subjectivity over the course of a century. Such chronicles suggest that historiography is neither immune to self-evaluation nor the static discipline supposed by the reductive indictment of "traditional."

In fact, as the following overview of interrelated developments reveals, the conditions for postmodern historical fiction's rise were first created by specific shifts toward feminist and cultural practices within history departments; exemplifying their interdependence, the linguistic turn in historiography then occasioned a historical turn in literary criticism. Although literary critics legitimately identify social history's antinarrative stance, in seeking to erase this problematic divide by deconstructing a strawman version of historiography, they have succeeded in further divorcing the two forms of accessing the past. While Hutcheon's model had productive implications for the academic environment in which it was formulated, the conditions necessitating such disciplinary skepticism have changed significantly in the last thirty years. How telling, then, that a postmodern hermeneutics exalted for unmasking metanarratives has itself become an institutionalized, totalizing theory.

THE TRADITIONAL HISTORICAL NOVEL AND THE DOCUMENTARY MODEL

If postmodern historical fiction is defined in conscious opposition to the classical historical novel, this earlier genre's definition is credited to Marxist Georg Lukács's *The Historical Novel* (1937), the first text to pursue a relation between economic and social development relating to artistic production of the past. Originally published in Russian, the touchstone study remains the most sustained engagement with the form of the historical novel, as the author distinguishes its particular attributes from the shortcomings of theater and the historical epic traditions while tracing the shift to historical consciousness contemporary to Scotsman Sir Walter Scott's *Waverley* (1814).

Writing on the eve of World War II, the Marxist critic is, like Scott himself, concerned less with the factuality of events than the way in which such narratives can be used to generate collective social identity. Nonetheless, Lukács's ambitious study of the rise and fall of European traditions does not advocate for nationalism, but instead represents his unrealized hope of finding a response to the rise of continental fascism (13). According to the Hungarian critic, prior to the nineteenth century, while authors had certainly evoked history, it had been used as merely a form of background costumery, with no attempt to historicize the specific qualities of their age. Just as postmodern history responded to diverse traumatic experiences related to war, domestic repressions, and the advent of the atomic bomb, the foundation of historical consciousness necessary for such an endeavor was also provided by a series of social and political ruptures. In conjunction with the rise of conscripted armies against Napoleon, the appearance of capitalism "for the first time made history a *mass experience,* and moreover on a European scale" (23, emphasis in original). Thus, Lukács contends that the social realist novel emerged to satisfy the attendant need to engender national identification because of transnational tensions.

Yet rather than highlighting what Hegel characterized as the "world-historical individual" (i.e., the recognized "great men" of history) central to epic literature, Lukács asserts that classical historical fiction is peopled with minor historical characters or completely fictional individuals so that "society is the principal subject of the novel . . . with the different social institutions or customs which mediate the relations between individuals in social life" (139). In contending that it is not the events that matter, but rather the poetic awakening of a people through an imagined past, Lukács desires that both the novel's characters and the reading audience perceive "the gulf which separates the 'top' from the 'bottom' of society" (209). In other words, Lukács's example reveals that the representation of disenfranchised actors was already a preoccupation in modernist scholarship well before it was claimed in the name of postmodernism. What had changed was the viability of realism in an era where language played a newly formative role.

Ironically, however, the birth of historical fiction is partially related to the nineteenth-century emergence of the documentary model in historical studies. Emblematic of disciplinary miscommunication, writers in both camps sought to truthfully represent the essence of the past, though what they perceived that essence to be provoked radically discordant responses. Scott claimed in 1823 that his work performed a didactic function by making readers "anxious to learn what the facts really were, and how far the novelist has justly represented them."[4] Yet during the 1820s, historian Leopold van Ranke also aspired in his oft-translated maxim to represent the past "as it actually happened," albeit to contrasting ends. When comparing Scott's fiction to a historian's objectivity, Ranke was disturbed by what he perceived as inaccuracies, distortion, and romantic fictionalization, in part inspiring his own desire to stamp out inexactitude by removing all hint of imagination and sticking with "facts" (Evans 16; Weinstein 264). Consequently, his implementation of empirical methodology revolutionized the field of historiography, establishing it as a distinct discipline from literature, while professionalizing and legitimating its practice as a pursuit of objective, scientific truths. Unlike Scott, who peopled his fiction with unremarkable individuals to draw greater attention to the particular period, Ranke judged the lives of men of action. In his estimation, the purpose of modern historians was to "root out forgeries and falsifications from the record. [Historians] had to test documents on the basis of their

---

4. See Scott's fictitious prefatory letter in *Peveril of the Peak* (xxviii) where he appears as a character defending his public legacy.

internal consistency and their consistency with other documents originating at the same period. They had to stick to 'primary sources,' eyewitness reports . . . which could be shown to have originated at the time under investigation" (Evans 16–17). This positivist model operated under the implicit assumption that archival research would uncover facts hidden within yet-to-be discovered documents. As I will demonstrate later in this chapter, despite a variety of challenges to the practice of "traditional" history, the documentary model has survived as the central organizing methodology, placing false documents in a privileged position to exploit this dynamic through the critical reproduction of historical conventions.

THE POSTWAR SOCIAL TURN

Given the climate in the North American literary critical establishment during the 1930s, Lukács's historical materialism may well not have found sympathy had it been available in English. New Criticism's jettison of material historical contextualization eventually prompted the first generation of American studies graduates to advocate for greater affinity with both the social sciences and "cultural" studies after World War II (Reising 15–16; Smith 6–7). This tendency was radicalized within two decades, as the emergence in North America of new technologies and the civil rights movement led the New Left to embrace Marxist class-based techniques. Hence, in 1962, twenty-five years after the initial publication of *The Historical Novel*, an English-language translation coincided with a series of Anglo-American methodological innovations known as (new) social history, which more closely resonated with the Hungarian critic's claims about the importance of everyday individual experience.

Famously described in 1966 by E. P. Thompson as "history from below" in an essay of the same name, the "bottom-up" approach to social history examined working-class cultures, rather than the more visible "great men," as social agents who engaged in forms of resistance. Thompson's *The Making of the English Working Class* (1963) revolutionized the teaching of history for decades after its publication, and in similar terms to Lukács's argument regarding historical consciousness, Thompson avers that the nineteenth-century working class emerged when it became conscious of itself as a social group. Claiming that history too often remembers the successful at the expense of the "losers," Thompson sought, in his words, to "rescue" the working people, whose agency in the making of history has been obscured (*Working Class* 12). By foregrounding inequality in the past, initiating the study of social class as an emancipatory project, and introducing the disenfranchised to the historical record—attributes that would be claimed by historiographic metafiction over two decades later—Thompson not only complicated claims that the field served dominant interests alone, but he also provided an alternative basis of solidarity to that of national consensus. While a resurgence of national pride led postwar US scholars to initially promote consensus unity, the civil rights movement and the accompanying rise of the New Left created a potent cocktail that firmly established social history as a dominant force on North American soil (Harrison 110–12).

Across Latin America, by contrast, the 1960s corresponded to the first generation of professional full-time historians, a role that had typically been played since the independence period by privileged middle-class writers and politicians who saw history as a means to enhance national causes. Despite the more direct influence on Latin American historiography by the concept of "longue durée," the French *Annales* School's focus on the institutional structures that define history and resist change over time, social history arrived at the same moment as it did to the north. Yet unlike the New Left's rally around African American inequality, the southern counterpart to "history from below" examined the marginalization of peasants, indigenous groups, and the subaltern dating back to the colonial period.[5]

The transformational power of Latin American social history can be traced to multiple factors. On the one hand, French structuralists such as Fernand Braudel and Claude Lévi-Strauss arrived as some of the earliest visiting scholars to Brazil and established a longstanding intellectual exchange with Latin American universities (Rojas 26–32). Even more important, however, was the opportunity presented by quantitative methods and data collection to counteract stereotypes of chronic underdevelopment posited by US economists. Fukuyama's interventionist model, for example, ultimately recalls the Cold War modernization theory that economic historian Walt Rostow developed in *The Stages of Economic Growth* (1960).[6] In the 1960s, social scientists from Argentina and Brazil formulated dependency theory to demonstrate that the systemic inequalities of trade through which dominant centers controlled the terms of manufacturing occurred to the detriment of producers at the periphery. This reactionary attitude transferred to both literature and historiography after the 1959 Cuban Revolution, for as US historians began visiting Latin American archives in droves, their rebranding of local events through the lens of capitalism and liberal democracy smacked of intellectual imperialism that

---

5. Archila reflects on the first generation of Latin American social historians, while Grover distinguishes between nonprofessional and university historians in the twentieth century.

6. See Pérez-Brignoli and Ruiz for more on the experiment of Latin American quantitative social history.

facilitated agendas of expansion (Grover 359). Dependency theory required a focus on asymmetric economic, political, and social relationships between Latin America and more advanced countries, thus the question of nationalism was similarly placed under scrutiny, while statistics provided a means of presenting indisputable "facts" that narrative methods could not match. Paradoxically, deconstructive readings of existing documents that went against the grain, as well as a turn toward oral and women's histories, in many rural areas stemmed not from the cultural turn but rather precisely from a lack of access to education. Although many aspects of the structural approach overlooked individual agency, dependency theory not only revolutionized Latin American critical response, but also heavily influenced North American scholarship in the following decades.

THE LINGUISTIC AND CULTURAL TURNS OF THE 1970s

Despite the important shift that social history initiated in undermining the nation as the primary unit of study, it soon became the object of critique in the United States, whereas in Latin America the border between social and cultural traditions was more fluid. On the one hand, structural concerns with economics and social mobility meant that practitioners turned away from narrative history and sought greater identification with scientific models of quantitative analysis. Yet a new faction diverged to argue that the discipline still understood history as a totalizing force, largely applying universal concepts such as working-class formation, capitalism, and modernization to a nationalist framework (Welskopp 217, 206). On the other hand, emerging feminist and ethnic history alleged a neglect of gender differentiation in Thompson's conception of laborers, along with his generic treatment of race. In fact, Thompson lost sight of the individual in the midst of making collectivities the unit of analysis, leaving little room to discuss agency in a way that microhistories would soon enable (215).

Influenced by Clifford Geertz's *The Interpretation of Cultures* (1973), scholars increasingly shifted their interdisciplinary focus from sociology to anthropology to account for ethnographic shifts through everyday experience, and the cultural turn was born. Distinctively, historians understand postmodernism to describe a historical era and poststructuralism as the deconstructive practices within this period that interrogated representation over reality (Green and Troup 297; Passmore 119; Thompson, *Postmodernism* 14–15). Thus if social history's return to scientifism became emblematic of structuralism, poststructural debates acted as correctives to the "'four sins' of modernist (social) theory": reductionism, functionalism, essentialism, and universalism, transhistorical assumptions that were contradicted by postmodernism's preference for local knowledges (qtd. in Joyce 212).

Another challenge came from Hayden White, whose deconstruction of Thompson's narrative strategies signaled a new shift in which historical meaning was reconceived as a product of language rather than a particular theoretical approximation (*Tropics* 15–17). Along with Michel Foucault, White's examination of the ontological primacy of language anticipated a general paradigm shift that came to be known as the linguistic turn, particularly in North America where scholars more openly embraced questions of postmodernism and multiculturalism (Joyce 221). From his first published article, "The Burden of History" (1966), White has self-consciously attempted to account for the historian's complicated location between the humanities and hard sciences, and his deconstruction of Thompson is indicative of his most famous publications *Metahistory* (1973) and *Tropics of Discourse* (1978). White's narrative deep structure, from which the trope of emplotment has received the most attention, resonates with Geertz's "thick description," for the historian contends that literature and history employ similar processes of fictionalization by using language as means of representing reality. More radically, he posits that historians' need for causation presumes a beginning and an end to a series of related events, in effect prefiguring their field of study (*Metahistory* 30). Because chapter 8 explores emplotment in detail, I will not belabor the point here. Suffice it to say, the reader recognizes the particular plot structures and in turn understands how to interpret the arc of a historical narrative along with its attendant protagonists and villains, which can be as important as the actual content (*Tropics* 83). Perhaps unsurprisingly, after the 1970s White has exerted considerably more influence over the literary establishment than upon the discipline of history.[7]

Another key figure in the politicization of the linguistic turn, Foucault left many unsure how to categorize his work with regard to the field of history (Flynn 28). By examining the ways in which power is exercised to normalize attitudes toward control of the body and mind, many of his books seek to recover the histories of marginalized groups, including *Madness and Civilization* (1961), *Birth of the Clinic* (1963), *Discipline and Punish* (1975), and the multivolume *The History of Sexuality* (1976–1984). While the terminology he employed to suggest modes of history—archaeologies, genealogies, problematizations—changed over the course of his career, the centrality of power

---

7. Since White's narrative turn after *Metahistory*, less than fifteen percent of his scholarly citations have come from historians, the majority found in literary criticism (Vann 148).

relations remained constant (Flynn 29). As opposed to the Marxist binary between dominant and oppressed, however, Foucault's concept of "discourse" understands power as diffuse, whether being exercised on the level of social and state institutions or through the means of organizing knowledge. In an oft-cited quotation, Foucault blurs the boundaries between history and the ideal of truth, claiming, "It seems to me that the possibility exists for fiction to function in truth. One 'fictions' history on the basis of a political reality that makes it true, one 'fictions' a politics not yet in existence on the basis of a historical truth" (193). By arguing that forms of knowledge are fundamentally situated within their historical epochs, he demonstrates that many phenomena considered natural developments are actually constructed through ideological forms beyond the awareness of individual producers.

The language, in particular the categories, that we utilize to group events and people in the past inherently reflects contemporary discourses, and it follows that Foucault does not support the linear Enlightenment model of historical progress. To the contrary, he celebrates rupture and discontinuity, averring that individually chronological epistemes are not intellectually commensurable, and therefore historical change is neither progressive nor rational. Rather than explain the relationship between events and time periods, he favors treating them as diagnoses of the present in order to imagine alternate futures (Flynn 44), not only providing a basis for the postmodern challenge to metanarratives but also identifying presentism, one of the central strategies utilized by new historical authors.

FROM CULTURAL HISTORY TO NEW HISTORICISM IN THE 1980s

In contrast to structural analyses, the trademark of new cultural history was microhistory—first tested in Mexico and Italy[8]—a narrowly defined investigation of an individual or a single event that could in theory reconstruct the worldview of greater society. US historian Natalie Zemon Davis is perhaps the most famous practitioner in North America, in part because she adopted the approach to a feminist framework. She had already demonstrated the transition between schools with her first book, *Society and Culture in Early Modern France* (1975), but it was her second that caused a storm of controversy. In *The Return of Martin Guerre* (1983), Davis explored the sixteenth-century case of imposture for

---

8. Examples include Carlo Ginzburg's *The Worm and the Cheese* (1976) and Luis González's *Pueblo en vilo* (1968).

which she had written the screenplay for a film of the same name that actually premiered one year earlier. Yet rather than content herself with the incomplete existing documentation, she openly fills in the gaps in the record through her own interpretation of contemporary society as an example of "thick description." Defying the accepted account wherein a woman had been duped by an impersonator claiming to be her husband returning from a decade of war, Davis contends that the wife recognized the deception from the beginning but accepted the arrangement because of the social benefits provided by having a husband-figure. Some critics labeled this self-conscious revelation of the historian's intervention as postmodern (Evans 245–46), though for many cultural proponents, it demonstrated the possibilities that studies of everyday life had for uncovering the unique experiences of women and the postcolonial subaltern, about whom little to no official records had been kept.

Thus although US compilations like Lynn Hunt's *The New Cultural History* (1989) and *Annales* representative Roger Chartier's *Cultural History* (1988) emerged at the same time as Hutcheon's postmodern guides, these exponents were classifying tendencies that had been discernible for more than a decade. In fact, cultural history had already heralded the postmodern approach to the relationship between literature and documents by erasing three binary oppositions central to social methods: the divisions between high and popular culture, production and reception, and reality and fiction (Chartier 37–45). This allowed literature to be considered as part of the historical method, although its performative dimension meant that it "should not be treated as simple documents or realistic reflections of a historical reality," for all texts are invested with the "obsessions of their producers" (43).

In Latin America the cultural turn was perceived differently, for the divide between fiction and history had not been as widely enforced, and social history in multiple cases took popular culture into account, especially in the case of rural and agricultural focuses. Perhaps the most famous example of this is Brazilian sociologist and anthropologist Gilberto Freyre, whose infamous *The Masters and the Slaves* (1933) initiated a historical trilogy that finished with *Order and Progress* (1957). Variously revising Brazil's democracy through the lens of race and urban studies, Freyre's translation introduced the concept of cultural history to audiences around the globe (Burke, "Gilberto Freyre" 335–37). In 1959, Colombian German Posada Mejía repurposed the title of José Martí's famous essay "Nuestra América" as a cultural history of the colonial period, although by contemporary standards his focus on chroniclers and historians constitutes an intellectual approach. While female historians began to enter the field, the 1970s corresponded to the tightening of dictatorial control in several countries, leading to a decrease in leftist-leaning publications. Influenced by dependency theory, humanities scholars began to approach culture with the intent of determining specifically Latin American qualities through a rejection of foreign historical imposition. Cuban critic Roberto Fernández Retamar's *Calibán: Notes toward a Discussion of Culture in Our America* (1971, published in English in 1989 with a foreword by Fredric Jameson) responds to the implication that "our entire culture is taken as an apprenticeship, a rough draft or a copy of European bourgeois culture" (7). Exploring the ways Shakespeare's Caliban has been employed by Latin American and Caribbean intellectuals during the nineteenth and twentieth century to metaphorically describe the New World, Retamar both revises the region's literary history and turns the logic of colonialism on its head.

If the primacy of social history was challenged during the 1970s via the anthropological and linguistic turns, however, the 1980s saw the pendulum swing back as history infiltrated literary practices. Whereas cultural history foregrounds the agency of local knowledge in shaping social relations, its literary counterpart was new historicism, which explores texts as historically specific objects (Green and Troup 304). Stephen Greenblatt's *Renaissance Self-Fashioning* (1980) is one of the texts that initiated new historicism, yet the term was first associated with the field later in 1982, and Greenblatt ultimately preferred the description "cultural poetics" ("Poetics") to better represent the everyday reality of American culture. Known in Great Britain as cultural materialism, the field laid claim to Davis's feminist microhistories, though it has had far more purchase in literature departments.[9] The influence of Foucault is particularly visible in the disavowal of standard periodization practices and the focus upon the circulation of literary texts as sites of power. While, similar to cultural history, it expands the range of artifacts that can be analyzed as historical sources, it does so by refusing to recognize any difference between formal and creative texts, thus fiction and documents are read alongside one another as signs of hidden cultural expression. Literature therefore reveals itself to be an agent in constructing and circulating accepted discourses of control, embodied by a "need to develop terms to describe the ways in which material—here official documents, private papers, newspaper clippings, and so forth—is transferred from one discursive sphere to another and becomes aesthetic property" (Greenblatt, "Poetics" 11). In effect echoing the thick description central to microhistories, scholars often focus on ignored or minor texts as symptomatic of an entire historical moment. Eschewing traditional objectivity, the anecdote is frequently personal, and in focusing upon

---

9. Brannigan is helpful for identifying regional differences of these culturally oriented practices.

chance, points to the provisionality of the scholar's own position in relation to his or her subject.

Although new historicists are notoriously resistant to labels that suggest participation in a uniform program of criticism, H. Aram Veeser's two anthologies, *The New Historicism* (1989) and *The New Historicism Reader* (1994), have approximated an underlying methodology regarding the circulation of texts. In addition to situating each expressive act in a network of material practices and capitalist relations, Veeser notably articulates the same paradox at the heart of Hutcheon's postmodern history, namely that "every act of unmasking, critique, and opposition uses the tools it condemns and risks falling prey to the practice it exposes" (*The New Historicism* xi). Literature is not seen as an antidote to formal documents, but is instead explored as another space where the exercise of power is made visible. In new historicist terms, it is not history that is revealed to be fiction but rather identity as a stable category, as the latter is constantly being negotiated and performed in relation to prevailing historical conditions. Whereas Thompson associates the birth of the working class with historical consciousness, then, Greenblatt first traced the origin of the concept of the individual to the birth of capitalist society. By treating literary texts as cultural signifiers of equal importance to formal documents, new historicism anticipates some of the key strategies historiographic metafiction would popularize later in the decade. Yet given its disempowering view of literature, which is never afforded the chance to act as an "oppositional cultural agent in history" (qtd. in Brannigan 65), it is small wonder that Hutcheon's politically active model served as a watershed for the field.

NEW HISTORY, THE DOCUMENTARY MODEL, AND FALSE DOCUMENTS

Each of the disciplinary shifts touched upon so far has illustrated the tension between literature/language and facts/documents. While poststructuralism did infiltrate history departments later than other humanities fields, many of its general considerations are now taken for granted in the discipline. Without falling into the trap of nihilism, for example, healthy skepticism regarding assumptions behind objectivity, the reliability of sources, and the unseen politics behind how archives are created and preserved can be powerful conceptual tools, while feminist and ethnic inroads toward a more inclusive record have been significant. One of the early identifiers of the new historical novel in Latin America, Fernando Aínsa, declares that the exclusive status of documents ultimately underwent a process of democratization, having expanded from written texts alone to include unofficial cultural production, such as icons, images, advertisements, and even public graffiti (*Reescribir* 60–61). Did this signal the end of Ranke's documentary model, however?

By the early 1990s, the distinct social, cultural, and feminist tendencies had coalesced under the general rubric of "new history," a recognized alternative to the "traditional" paradigm. Familiar with both Anglophone and Brazilian traditions, historian Peter Burke assessed the field in 1992 by juxtaposing an oppositional set of old and new practices. These axioms not only integrate the social, cultural, and metahistorical challenges detailed earlier in this chapter, but they also demonstrate a striking degree of overlap between traditional and new historical fiction across the Americas:

1. Traditional history is concerned with politics; new practice takes all aspects of human production as its sources.
2. Traditional history appeared as a narrative of events; new history analyzes the different structures that lead to events.
3. Traditional history's focus on "great men" glorified the role of social elites; popular culture has infused new history with a "view from below."
4. Traditional writing is based on recognized documents that privileged official sources and perspectives; new approaches turn to less formally recognized oral and photographic sources.
5. History habitually explored individual motivations of recognized individuals; new historians highlight the power of collective trends in shaping events.
6. The Rankean focus on documents presents history as objective; cultural relativism predominates through the recognition that conditioned points of view affect how the past is explored. (*New Perspectives* 3–6)

All these assertions will by now sound familiar, except the final one, where the old/new binary breaks down. With its more inclusive focus upon nonarchival sources, from oral testimony to popular cultural, the practice of historiography has certainly adapted to considering a greater array of formal and informal (con)texts as sources. Yet what has not changed is that new history must on some level continue to privilege the use of primary documents as sources. Indeed, this remains the defining element of historiography in its quest to accurately and responsibly provide insight into events without first-person access, one of the reasons postmodernism has not been able to destabilize the field the same way it has other fields.[10] Even if it is suggested that historians perform poetic acts in constructing narratives, in contrast to imaginative literature, historiography is constrained by its obligation to acknowledge accepted sources within the public domain and work within the agreed-upon record. Within the context of public revision of attitudes toward the past, it is for this reason that fiction that purposefully distorts the record is interpreted differently from literary texts that offer documentary access into the past.

Yet the specific understanding of revision must be put in perspective. While literary scholars have tended to understand revision in terms of its function as a subject or theoretical focus, another important question within history has been the revision of the practice itself. Throughout the 1980s, Dominick LaCapra responded to what he believed was a resurgence of the documentary model, which he defined as "an explicit or implicit hierarchy among sources whereby a preferential position is accorded to seemingly direct informational documents such as bureaucratic reports, wills, registers, diaries, [and] eye-witness accounts" (18). LaCapra believes that the fetishization of the archive led to the marginalization of all texts not deemed primary or referential. Although social history generated a new awareness of class inequality that helped unseat the essentialist nationalism of consensus history, its quantitative displacement of narrative ironically further ingrained previous empirical approaches to the field as a form of scientific discourse.

Thus LaCapra worries that discourse analysis diverts attention away from the textual dimensions of documents, which process and transform the reality they purport to represent while eliding complex questions regarding the ambiguity of interpretation, for if "the novel is read at all in history, it is typically because it may be employed as a source telling us something factual about the past. Its value is in its referential functions . . . its representation of social life, its characters, its themes, and so forth" (125). The resulting affirmation of social realism is damaging because it disavows the ability of imagination in reconstructing the past, but also because literature is rendered redundant when its value is limited to communicating what is already present in documentary sources. In fact, in terms similar to the false document, LaCapra notes that the novel's strength has historically lain in its experimentation, which consisted of cannibalizing other genres and testing the barriers of classification (122).

---

10. See Berkhofer's *Fashioning History* for extensive exploration of contemporary historical practice's reformulation of the traditional documentary model.

LaCapra's examination of the inherent rhetorical dimensions of texts is intended as a critique of historiographical tendencies, but it also ends up highlighting important differences in terms of how truth-value is unequivocally accorded to nonfiction and fiction discourses. For better or for worse, cultural texts presented within the vein of realism have provoked the greatest response from historians, for while literature that foregrounds distortion and parody of the past record may provide an alternative to the discourse of objectivity, by departing from these norms, irony does not suggest a means of revising the practice of history from the inside-out or the bottom-up in the way texts that self-consciously appropriate conventions do.

In the context of LaCapra's rhetorical concerns about documents, Doctorow's "False Documents" provides a means for exploring the rhetorical function of history more aligned with the methodology of the field, for Doctorow argues that "language is seen as a property of facts themselves. . . . This is the bias of scientific method and empiricism by which the world reveals itself and gives itself over to our control insofar as we recognize the primacy of fact-reality" (17). He therefore creates a political distinction between two kinds of power in language, that of the regime and that of freedom. Bearing similarity to LaCapra's documentary model, the power of the regime is effectively a consensus realism employed by politicians, journalists, and scientists, and is encountered in the form of market studies, contracts, polls, presses releases, and headlines. In contrast to this characterization of nonfiction, the creative liberty afforded by literary discourse, that which cannot be verified, exemplifies the power of freedom, which is formidable precisely because it does not have the obligation to fact that "dulls" nonfiction. While both discourses are constructs, the North American author privileges that of literature—not because it is inherently more truthful, but because it must be more transparent, belonging to the "only profession forced to admit that it lies" (26).

My interest lies less in legitimizing Doctorow's claims than in restaging the pseudo-factuality of false documents as a means of productively addressing the bias of the documentary model. One of the unfortunate legacies of historiographic metafiction's sweeping gaze is that any contemporary text evincing self-awareness is subsumed under the category of postmodernism, though like the documentary model, this does a disservice to the different affective functions of literature. While false documents are clearly not throwbacks to social realism, their reflexive awareness is guided by an attempt to work within conventions rather than explode them and thus revise the manner in which indexical textual authority is construed. Harboring multiple discourses, these apocryphal documents inhabit a middle ground between the extremes of strict mimeticism and the parody of "apocalyptic" fiction to be discussed in the next chapter.

The previous sketch represents a compressed summary of methodological shifts in historiography during the latter half of the twentieth century. Given the artificiality of periodization that such theories have spotlighted, there are of course dangers in attempting to demarcate specific points of historical transition as informing both literature and historical studies. Ultimately, significant overlap exists between many works of historical practice and philosophy, despite the former being claimed by political, social, cultural, or other philosophical schools. Rather than make cases for the viability of one particular procedure over another, I have instead presented a general picture of the types of innovations that emerged along with their critically identified blind spots, and my purpose has been three-fold. The first is to contextualize the emergence of postmodern attitudes toward historical fiction by demonstrating how the landscape of historiography was equally modified by poststructural debates. Thus, despite being a favorite point of assault, the interrogation of disciplinary and doctrinal boundaries is not the invention of literary studies. Accordingly, postmodern literary critics' claim to deconstruct or revise conventional history essentializes the field, for one of the paradoxes of historiographic metafiction is that it has not examined the history of the conditions for its own manufacture.[11]

This observation leads to a second point, namely that while the discourse of deconstruction is convenient because it solidifies a position with which few critics would take issue, it is also teleological, largely ignoring the fact that the complex intersection of discourses that became postmodernism were a product of the same shifts in historiography that it purports to subvert. The third goal, therefore, has been to lay the basis for the false document's application within interdisciplinary methodologies to which the following case studies respond. Chapter 2, then, will explore the various theories of new literary history across the Americas and demonstrate how these canons can be reinterpreted through the lens of critical documentary awareness before testing the theories through an Inter-American cohort of writers, journalists, and academics.

---

11. See Olster and Wesseling as important exceptions to this ahistorical trend.

CHAPTER 2

History's Return

Literary Revisionism in North America, Hispanic America, and Brazil during the Lost Decade

IN A 1991 keynote address to the Modern Language Association, Hispanist Mary Louise Pratt coined the term "contact zone" to describe the border sites and social spaces where cultures come into conflict (34). Although her purpose was to rethink the asymmetrical power of colonial American history, specifically how a "lost" indigenous chronicle revises the European canonical account of the conquest, the term was adapted to a number of American postcolonial contexts. Hemispheric Americanist John Carlos Rowe, for example, deploys the expression to imagine a more internationally comparative US multiculturalism that "focuses with special interest on just the points of historical, geographical, and linguistic 'contact' where two or more communities must negotiate their respective identities" (*Post-Nationalist* 25). And Inter-Americanist Luciano Tosta effectively updates the concept in his *Confluence Narratives* (2016), whose titular expression identifies postcolonial histories of American nations via their recurrent contact with Brazil. My purpose in the following pages, then, is to illustrate how approaches to history have evidenced a type of cross-disciplinary, postnational contact zone. If chapter 1 outlined half the story of the mutually informative relationship between historiography and literary studies, this chapter contrapuntally traces the flourishing of "new" historical literary camps in North America (1960–1989), Hispanic

America (1974–1992), and Brazil (1976–1992) as a means to characterize false documents' constructive critique of such paradigms.

In order to demonstrate the similar patterns informing both creative and scholarly sensibilities in the above regions, I will return to the same period in which we previously saw that social history fractured the field in both North and Latin America. Thereafter, I will follow the chronology in which these experimental attitudes first began to be accepted within the literary marketplace, although the establishment of a hemispheric lineage is not so clear cut. While one of the first US exponents of postmodernism, John Barth, critiqued the continued currency of nineteenth-century realism in "The Literature of Exhaustion" (1967), his self-conscious style was heavily influenced by Jorge Luis Borges, whose "Pierre Menard, Author of the Quixote" (1939) helped initiate the Argentine's period of playful false documents and revolutionized international literature over the next several decades. And Barth also admitted the influence of even earlier postmodern antecedents from Brazil, most famously Machado de Assis's satirical *The Posthumous Memoirs of Bras Cubas* (1881). Barth's contemporary, historian Barbara Tuchman, declared that the postwar decline of the novel, undercut by the market's turn to works of "reality" such as biography and sociology, meant that to "look for the reason why fictional truth has gone askew is [now] part of the historian's task" (52). Nonetheless, within a decade, poststructuralist scholars reversed the terms to instead celebrate history's ailments, although despite sharing goals of historical revisionism, it will become clear that the term "postnational" has different implications for each region of writers, for Latin American preoccupation with colonial exploitation has focused less upon deconstructing geopolitical borders than reconceiving sovereignty as a form of social participation.

In each of the following three regional literary histories tracing the rise of new historical fiction, I provide a basic canon of texts that have become associated with the genre, explore the origins and development of the critical response to the canon, and evaluate the importance of parodic subversion to each model. Finally, in each case I draw attention to the alternative false documentary response that emerged simultaneously in each network of theories, yet which has been downplayed and thus remains undertheorized in any kind of comparative sense. In addition to representing an authorial scheme, then, the false document is a strategy of reading and circulation, for several foundational parodic texts actually derive their effects from supposed referentiality to recognized sources, and reconsidering them with this new awareness reveals productive zones of contact and confluence.

THE NORTH AMERICAN ORIGINS OF HISTORICAL REVISIONISM (1960–1989)

The 1980s saw the adoption of historical methods in the humanities and social sciences across the United States, yet for literary authors, the shift began back in 1975. This is the moment that marked the "return to neglected history" led not by male postmodernists who had trivialized the past during the preceding decade, but by committed minority and women's voices (Rowe, *New American* 25). Thus, while the concept of a "historical turn" in the humanities is helpful for categorizing the marked escalation in poststructural analyses of the role of history, for all the rhetoric regarding critical ruptures with modernist paradigms, this new phase actually represented the gradual accretion of theoretical shifts. Lukács's fears that the genre's days were numbered notwithstanding, the US historical novel had gained prominence during formational national traumas such as the Civil War and the Great Depression, and it again became a dominant paradigm on the heels of World War II. As Ernest Leisy would argue, far from equating to escapist literature, as some claimed, the genre healed by offering a "usable past" from which models of democracy could profit, while also anticipating new techniques that the "modern skeptical temper" (19) used to demonstrate that "there is no such thing as objective history" (6–7).[1] Although the period of American modernism during the first half of the twentieth century is chiefly associated with the representation of individual experience rather than the collective associations of social realism, John dos Passos's *USA Trilogy* (1930–1936) and William Faulkner's *Absalom, Absalom!* (1936) had challenged the conventional conception of historicism. Alternately understood as self-aware documentary fiction or as radical modernism,[2] such novels reconceived the representation of biographical history and complicated the role of historians, yet because they were not initially classified as historical literature, this disruptive challenge to stable categories of representation would only be explored in the 1960s by likeminded authors (Wesseling 74).

Although subsequent scholars would point to Hayden White's "literariness" of history to bolster their own cross-disciplinary claims as nonhistorians, a number of literary scholars reached metahistorical conclusions independent of his influence. Thus, just as White first began writing in the

---

1. Leisy's appendix of historical novels written 1820–1950 is an excellent resource on the genre's evolution.

2. See chapter 3 of Foley's *Telling the Truth* for a historical analysis of the modernist documentary novel.

1960s about the historian's contradictory "burden," likeminded literary scholars reminded readers that before Ranke's nineteenth-century popularization of scientifism, both disciplines had shared the same philosophical epistemology.[3] David Levin, writing *In Defense of Historical Literature* (1967), maintained that history was inherently a literary art and that its pedagogical value was enhanced—not hampered—by its imaginative interventions (5–6). Yet in a 1968 roundtable between the historian C. Van Woodward and three historical novelists (Ralph Ellison, William Styron, and Robert Warren Penn), it is noteworthy that Van Woodward was the most adamant about affirming the kinship of "priggish" history with fiction in opposition to his historian colleagues' claim that it was a science (Ellison et al., "The Uses of History" 58–59). Indicative of the ability of false documents to elicit strong responses to historical veracity, the roundtable was dominated by African American critiques of Styron's controversial false document *The Confessions of Nat Turner* (1966), which purports to reflect the final days in prison of the eponymous leader of the 1831 slave uprising. Confusing the line between deposition and fantasy, the novel reproduces a portion of the only official documentation of Turner's rebellion, the same pamphlet from which the novel derives its name.

Ultimately, the 1970s proved to be a turning point in which literary critics first had the necessary distance from the previous decade to recognize a break between the realism of the 1950s and the experimental skepticism that characterized a growing body of 1960s publications. The preliminary nature of their findings did not lead to a definitive paradigm, though by reappearing in distinct studies, a corpus of postmodern historical fiction began to take shape: John Barthes's *Sotweed Factor* (1960), Thomas Pynchon's *V.* (1963) and *Gravity's Rainbow* (1973), Thomas Berger's *Little Big Man* (1964), Kurt Vonnegut's *Slaughterhouse Five* (1969), Ishmael Reed's *Mumbo Jumbo* (1972), E. L. Doctorow's *Ragtime* (1975), and Robert Coover's *The Public Burning* (1977). In the following decade, this male-dominated group would be increasingly augmented by women and authors of color. Even at this early stage, however, it was clear that US literary shifts could not be viewed within a vacuum, but instead were directly influenced by Hispanic American Boom translations such as Carlos Fuentes's *The Death of Artemio Cruz* (1962) and *Terra Nostra* (1975) as well as Gabriel García Márquez's *One Hundred Years of Solitude* (1967; Foley, "Historical Consciousness" 101; Wesseling 2–3).[4]

---

3. Russel Nye suggests that history and fiction are equally defined by ethical imagination, though historians are limited by the problem of "pastness," while novelists have greater means to treat different temporalities (146, 154).

4. Cohn (*Literary Boom*) provides a multipronged history of how North and Latin American writers supported each other through informal and institutional programs to improve mutual regional understanding.

Avrom Fleishman's attempt at a universal theory of British historical fiction in the early 1970s, narrowly defined as heroic depiction of individuals and time periods that occurred prior to that of the author's lifetime, was maligned by North American critics as a conservative throwback. In order to avoid the essentialist trappings of Fleishman's classification, US evaluations tended toward a catalogue of stylistic novelties as well as the suggestion of multiple forms of historical representation that moved away from "true-to-life" portrayals. Many of the new innovations—self-consciousness, irony, skepticism, the blurring of the line between fact and fiction, fragmentation—would be encompassed under the umbrella of metafiction after 1970, though these analyses preceded the widespread implementation of the term.

Hence, at the end of the decade, Joseph Turner critiques Fleishman's continued assumption that history and fiction are stable categories of knowledge and proffers multiple kinds of historical novel—documented (biographical), disguised (fictional characters whose experiences parallel known figures), and invented (historical romance). Based on this typology, Turner councils that traditionally, "if fiction is to carry the weight of history, the novelist does well to distract any attention from himself or the artifice he has created, a gesture through his text to the past he seeks to recapture" (350), though the literary critic ultimately believes otherwise. Frequently overlooked is the fact that Turner also highlights the materialization of a new, fourth strategy in 1960s literature. What he terms the comic historical novel, in contrast to hiding the role of the novelist, begins to self-reflexively flaunt the inherent artifice of its own creation. Turner hastens to add that the descriptor "comic" has little to do with humorous treatment of the past, but rather the parody of generic conventions. Despite setting the stage for more radical theorizations in the 1980s, Turner's "metahistorical" conclusion that the best historical fiction reflexively concerns its own construction is evidence that Hayden White's literary influence had already begun to assert itself.

Though Turner downplayed the role of humor, many of his contemporaries took the notion of comedy literally when making the case for replenishment of exhausted conventions, proudly asserting that literature's creative impulse could no longer be treated as or limited to a form of social documentation. Harry Henderson's important survey of US production is one of the first to explore this shift toward postwar attitudes of deception. The two predominant structures of classical historical fiction during the nineteenth century, the progressive and the holistic frames, respectively measured history as a form of human progress or drew upon the relativism of historicist thought to represent past eras as quantifiable within themselves alone. Yet after World War II, these traditional axes were supplanted by two new structures that would permanently alter the vocabulary of literary scholars: liberal conscience and "apocalyptic" parody (270). The former category explores the ethical consequences of historical trauma, while the latter frame describes absurdist authors such as John Barth and Thomas Pynchon, who evoke an end to history through ironic critiques of progressive assumptions. Several contemporary critics expand upon the "apocalyptic" tendency to observe black humor's use as a counterintuitive means of rebelling against institutional authority while depicting uncomfortable forms of victimization (Dickstein 191; Olderman 19, 22). Satirical fiction could suddenly rewrite accepted history rather than be measured against it, whether Coover's surrealistic treatment of Nixon and contemporary American politics in *The Public Burning* or Doctorow's reimagining of the United States's entrance into the twentieth century in *Ragtime*. By contrast, Latin American examples of literature defying mimetic conventions would be labeled magical realism, and while those translated for Anglophone audiences starting in the 1970s were marketed heavily within the Hispanic American Boom, several US writers were mutually influenced by the technique in their own historical texts.[5]

These examples point to perhaps the greatest change in both criticism and production during the 1970s, namely an expanded consensus regarding what constituted historicity, though this was accomplished through competing agendas. In contradistinction to Fleishman's claims earlier in the decade, no longer was historical fiction obliged to take place in a distant past prior to the author's birth, but instead could expand its scope to reinterpret the relation between the recent past and current events. Although critics might not yet have employed the term "presentism" in Foucault's sense, their approaches clearly located the past's value explicitly in its use for explaining the state of contemporary events and issues.[6] Thus they share the understanding that historical literature can no longer be gauged solely as an adjunct to the past to be judged by its accuracy (i.e., adherence to accepted facts). In much the same way structuralist and poststructuralist formations theorized language's primacy, these fictions were revealed to not only reflect but also construct the reader's perception of historical reality. In this way, fiction writers could openly challenge the positivist basis of history as linear progress, in some cases even deconstructing it as a means of drawing attention to the inherent

---

5. See Zamora and Faris for a collection of hemispheric historical contributions through the prism of magical realism.

6. Joseph Heller's *Catch-22* (1961), for example, is in fact a satire of Cold War US politics (Dickstein 186), and Ralph Ellison and Ishmael Reed reveal parallels between historical events and the civil rights movement in order to force readers to think about the origins of institutionalized racism. At the opposite extreme, Mailer's realist *The Armies of the Night* represents history as synonymous with the "immediate now" (Weinstein 276).

contradictions involved in representing the past "as it actually was." History's new defining characteristic became its plasticity, its representation contingent upon the ideological framework underlying the individual or party seeking to disseminate its interpretation.

Its origins documented two decades earlier, iconoclastic historical representation finally gathered under a single banner in the 1980s when it was explicitly theorized as a postmodern phenomenon by Hutcheon. What made this shift possible was the need to recognize the stakes of experimentation and determine what such rupture with preceding literary models accomplished. The solution—revisionism, both literary and scientific—was radical, even if how exactly the process worked was not entirely clear. This revisionist imperative has been central to the political platform upon which the postmodern historical novel has been studied within North America. In fact, the combination of revisionist power with social history is perhaps the most important legacy of Hutcheon's criticism, and while her prominence suggests that historical consensus within literary studies reached a turning point as a consequence of postmodern intervention, not all scholars attempted to treat the phenomenon as a form of cultural studies or identity politics.

This revisionist distinction can be illustrated by briefly comparing moderate and radical formulations evident in Hutcheon's contemporaries. David Cowart, for example, makes the case for the provisionality of historical knowledge, which, "if it can be known at all, can be known best by historically informed artists" (30) rather than historians, yet he stops short of positing a rupture between postmodernist and modernist practices. Cowart prefers the term "Age of Anxiety" to that of postmodern periodization, and instead of highlighting the black humor of apocalyptic frames frequently evoked during the 1970s, he turns to the serious moral implications of narrating history after the advent of nuclear technologies when the threat of apocalypse had become the most serious of possibilities for the general population.[7] In presenting a postwar corpus, he too stresses the instability of narrative representation, but this volatility does not refer to epistemological categories so much as the question of human survival in the nuclear present. Despite revealing a recognizable postmodern corpus, Cowart highlights pluralism over parody, focusing on women's contributions and understanding the recent trend as a subset of modernism's preoccupation with perception.

In contrast to Cowart's proposed continuity, radical postmodernists such as Brian McHale theorized revisionism as a break with verisimilitude and

---

7. Cohen maintains that the 9/11 attacks initiated a return to the anxiety that had characterized earlier Cold War rhetoric (4–7).

the ideals of modernist progress. For McHale, postmodernism presents an entirely new form of cultural dominant, for whereas the system of modernism is governed by epistemological questions, the new dominant shifts to a set of ontological strategies for exploring modes of being (9–10). This explains why traditional forms of the historical novel had attempted to discreetly camouflage the seams between fiction and accepted history—the only spaces where authors were permitted to fill in the undocumented dark areas of the historical record—while "apocryphal history" proudly advertises the artificiality of such a transition by violating realist conventions. Thus, McHale is the first to imagine apocalyptic parody as constructive revision debunking/demystifying the official record:

> The two meanings of revisionism converge especially in the postmodernist strategy of apocryphal or alternative history. Apocryphal history contradicts the official history in one of two ways: either it *supplements* the historical record, claiming to restore what has been lost or suppressed; or it *displaces* official history altogether. . . . In both cases, the effect is to juxtapose the officially-accepted version of what happened and the way things were, with another, often radically dissimilar version of the world. (90, emphasis in original)

As we have previously seen, Hutcheon's historiographic metafiction built on the above revisionist imperatives to focus on whose—rather than what—story was being privileged, because representation is never a neutral act. Yet while the model proved powerful for US multicultural and ethnic analyses, Latin Americanists were wary of its undiscerning transnationalism. At the same time, while the critical tendency may have been to privilege novelty within forms of periodization, postmodern interventions accounted for a small percentage of texts being published, for the production of conventional or romantic historical fiction continued unabated.

Geocultural and genre objections, however, are not the only limitations of radical revisionism, as demonstrated by a discrete contemporary treatment of history that specifically problematized documents, the very building blocks of history. Under the banners of the nonfiction novel and New Journalism, subjective works of history designed to blur the line between artifice and knowable truth emerged through Truman Capote's *In Cold Blood* (1966), Tom Wolfe's *The Electric Kool-Aid Acid Test* (1968), and Norman Mailer's *The Armies of the Night* (1968) and *The Executioner's Song* (1980) (Foley, "Historical Consciousness" 101). And while this core group of men is most closely associated with national history, Joan Didion's *Salvador* (1983) and *Miami* (1987) demonstrated an Inter-American capacity by examining US political influence on topics ranging from Central American civil war to Cuban immigration.

Significantly, self-reflexive "documentary" novels took their reference from these theatrically subjective works rather than apocalyptic parody. If during the nineteenth century sociohistorical novels had formed a predominant current of documentary fiction claiming to represent real events, during the twentieth century this referential approach shifted to encompass fictional autobiographies and subtly "metahistorical" novels in which the "documentary effect derives from the assertion of the very indeterminacy of factual verification" (Foley, *Telling the Truth* 25). But this was no mere return to uncritical realism. Unlike the nonfiction novel, which provided plot and signification to specific historical events without makings claims to a broader historical interpretation, documentary fiction did not subordinate fact to fantastical discourse, nor did it "deify facts," in Doctorow's words. By considering the documentary strategies of Dos Passos's *USA Trilogy*, he characterized his own novels as a subversion of New Journalism, a "false document" that existed "halfway between fiction and history" (Gussow 5). And rather than suggest indebtedness to postmodernism, Doctorow acknowledges the political pamphlets and the mock realism of Daniel Defoe's *Robinson Crusoe* (1719) and *Moll Flanders* (1722), for the Englishman's "narrators assume the pose of real persons telling of real events, and much of the reader's pleasure in these narrative derives from this pronounced effect of historicity—even if at times it is, paradoxically enough, felt to be an illusion" (Foley, "Historical Consciousness" 97).

This designed unmasking of authority is a key element of such works' challenges to empirical factuality. Thus, far from aligning his stance with the narrative strategies of the nonfiction novel, Doctorow also distances himself from Capote's work by presenting facts expressly for the purpose of uncovering the mirage of authority. This pseudo-factual strategy not only has significance for "a whole host of writers of the contemporary period" (Foley, "Historical Consciousness" 98), but it also demonstrates that metahistorical reflexivity need not only take the form of parody in order to target truth claims. Doctorow and other disillusioned members of the Old Left essentially practice "subjective historicism," an ethical examination of both the Left's failures and the structures undergirding US history (Olster 137–51). Yet while this distinct form of self-aware literature appears across the Americas, its implications have been lost in the allure of iconoclasm promised by apocalyptic strategies to distort the agreed-upon record. Shifting the focus from irreverence to an actual examination of the conventions of documents and their application through the device of false documents reveals an important means of reconsidering (and revising) how the historical turn in literature was underscored by various, and at times, contradictory tendencies. Nor is this an isolated situation within North America, as examination of Hispanic America and Brazil bolsters the case for approaching the canon of new historical fiction as a conditioned cultural response to ways in which documents had been constructed and rhetorically put to work in the latter half of the twentieth century.

AGAINST POSTMODERNISM: THE NEW HISTORICAL NOVEL IN HISPANIC AMERICA, 1974–1992

In his 1969 attempt to define the unique possibilities of "new" Latin American fiction, Carlos Fuentes argues that contemporary revision consisted of inventing a literary language to reveal the events that historical discourse had long silenced (30). While Fuentes would go on to write several parodic examples of historical fiction during the 1970s and 1980s,[8] few authors immediately responded to his challenge, though there were legitimate obstacles. As Uruguayan cultural critic Ángel Rama suggested in 1981, history as a critical concept had only recently begun to "reenter" public discourse at the end of the 1970s, for the need to respond to political and social oppression under dictatorships required a social realist focus on the present, as evidenced by the rise of testimonials and the nonfiction novel (18). By the end of the decade, however, Rama reveals that authors began abandoning romanticized reconstructions of the past to create new "interpretive diagrams of history" that circumnavigated the historian as middleman (20). Predicting what would soon be more formally termed Latin America's "new historical novel," Rama identifies its two foundational works in Augusto Roa Bastos's *I, the Supreme* (1974) and Carlos Fuentes's *Terra Nostra* (1975). Similar to the United States, the shifts established by artists in the latter 1970s were quickly followed by burgeoning academic attention, testified to by two collaborative conferences featuring both North and Latin America scholars that culminated in published collections. Yale University organized a 1979 homage to the father of the field, Cuban writer Alejo Carpentier, and the influence of White's metahistory upon Latin American scholarship was on full display at a symposium at Tulane University soon thereafter.[9]

---

8. Examples include Fuentes's *The Death of Artemio Cruz* (1962), *Terra Nostra* (1975), *The Old Gringo* (1985), and *Christopher Unborn* (1987).

9. The former conference resulted in Roberto González-Echevarría's *Historia y ficción en la narrativa hispanoamericana* (1984) and the latter Daniel Balderston's *The Historical Novel in Latin America* (1986).

At the same time that Hutcheon politicized writing about the past in North America through the schemes of parody and intertextuality, then, a new type of historical preoccupation within Latin American letters also acquired significance, and while debate exists with regard to whether the catalogue of this profoundly new attitude was first quantifiable in the late 1960s or 1970s, there is consensus that by the 1980s it had become a dominant trend across the region (Menton 14; Pons 18). As I discussed in my introduction, the distinct, uneven conditions of modernity in Latin America led many critics to question the applicability of new models theorized under the aegis of postmodern politics. Thus, even as historiographic metafiction was readily embraced in some quarters,[10] Colás's claim that Hutcheon's generic appropriation of Latin American texts failed to differentiate between the sociohistorical specificities informing the political conditions separating the two regions was indicative of a greater critical pushback. Colás rightfully exposes holes in Hutcheon's global gaze, though skepticism was also due in no small part to a general equation of postmodernism with the rise of the political right in Europe and the United States. Because the various guises of economic, technological, and cultural globalization were predicated upon a passive periphery's adaptation of homogeneous models from centers of production, intellectuals feared that postmodernism imported from US models similarly signaled cultural imperialism, echoing economic relations in which Latin American governments seeking international financial support during the lost decade adopted neoliberal polices. And since the unsustainability of socialist experiments resisting capitalism was a primary stake, the problematic was explored in Hispanic America first under the purview of the social sciences and cultural studies as opposed to literature (Beverley et al. 6).

Moreover, while North American postmodernism was premised on critiques of democratic society, Latin American governments were still in the process of redemocratization, thus the region's postnational logic emerged via a separate set of contingencies. As a critique of national harmony, many of the contemporary texts that revisit the colonial period do so to explore the painful and artificial conditions under which nations were constructed, additionally using these struggles as metaphors for contemporary forms of state control. Yet this is only one of many objectives for historical fiction, and if Colás ultimately appreciates Jameson's attempts to account for the effects of globalization upon political contexts, Jean Franco dismisses the Marxist critic's narrow reading of the periphery. In her contribution to Veeser's *The New Historicism*, Franco argues that it is one thing to suggest that literary genres are

---

10. See Domínguez, Skłodowska, and Pulgarín.

deeply implicated in the process of national formation and its attendant problems of national and cultural identity and quite another to claim, as Fredric Jameson has recently done, that the "national allegory" characterizes Third World literature at the present time, that is, in "the era of multinational capitalism"—for not only is "the nation" a complex and much contested term but in recent Latin American criticism, it is no longer the inevitable framework for either political or cultural projects. ("Imagined Community" 204)

Noting that Latin America's literary history was founded on hybridized genres, Franco aptly describes the false document when maintaining that totalizing periodization paradigms "overlook an entire culture['s] history in which essay, chronicle, and the historical document have been grafted onto novels" (210). While Franco applauds the emergence of female writers as a greater expression of difference, she cautions against equating this new cultural visibility with actual democratic participation in authoritarian states.

Regardless of whether early proponents of the new historical novel shared Franco's sentiments, they largely avoided the term postmodernism in their diagnoses of cultural production critical of national ideology. Thus, if the cultural studies boom in the 1990s would reveal unequal power relations to be both the principal cause and theme of new historical fiction (Pons; Rivas, *La novela*; Perkowska), Seymour Menton's pioneering study provides a decidedly more benign analysis of the genre's sudden proliferation. A large number of works parodied Christopher Columbus's "discovery" of the Americas in 1492,[11] which he attributed to the imminent 1992 quincentennial celebrations and a desire to spark debates about the ethics of celebrating the conquest's oppressive legacy (27–29). At the same time, Menton also suggests that historical fiction is an escapist genre, and its popularity therefore represented an attempt to turn away from the harsh economic and political realities of the continent during the 1970s and 1980s. These aesthetic approaches, however, gloss over the fact that reactionary fiction did not merely offer an alternative to contemporary social realities, but also was a product of those destabilizing conditions. During the lost decade, in addition to economic crises and external debt, cultural factors also complicated national consensus; long-standing social mores were challenged as women, homosexuals, and other marginalized groups began to openly demand participation in public spheres (Perkowska 30).

---

11. For in-depth explorations of authors who rewrite the accepted versions of the conquest and its romanticized leaders, see López, Lewis, and Hernández.

The region's corpus of new historical fiction fully took shape, then, at least a decade after that of the United States, yet the production from both canonical and emerging writers in Hispanic America during the 1980s was unparalleled in the Western hemisphere, equally in terms of quantity and its inclusive pan-Latin American nature. Texts making up this new canon include Augusto Roa Bastos's *I, the Supreme* (1974) and *The Admiral's Vigil* (1992), Carlos Fuentes's *Terra Nostra* (1975), Alejo Carpentier's *The Harp and the Shadow* (1979), Ricardo Piglia's *Artificial Respiration* (1980), Mario Vargas Llosa's *The War of the End of the World* (1981), Abel Posse's *The Dogs of Paradise* (1983) and *The Long Dusk of the Traveler* (1992), Edgardo Rodríguez Juliá's *The Dark Night of Niño Avilés* (1984), Tomás Eloy Martínez's *The Perón Novel* (1985) and *Santa Evita* (1996), Rosario Ferré's *Sweet Diamond Dust and Other Stories* (1986), Fernando del Paso's *News from the Empire* (1987), and Gabriel García Márquez's *The General in His Labyrinth* (1989), among many more.[12] Social turmoil manifested itself through skepticism not dissimilar to North American apocalyptic parody responding to its own post–Vietnam War government distrust, though the Hispanic American postnational political framework was initially less regional and more introspective. As a reaction to the nationalistic discourse and officially sanctioned "truth" that military regimes had used to legitimize their ideologies, any official communication, national or international, became the target of interrogation (Perkowska 37–38). In other words, what leads to a sense of reexperiencing past conditions in the region "is precisely the disappearance of the nation, its failure to provide systems of meaning and belief that undermines referential reading" (Franco, "Imagined Community" 208). The misgivings in different intellectual quarters regarding the postmodernist project notwithstanding, approximations critical of Hutcheon ended up reaching remarkably similar conclusions about the pedagogical value strategies like parody and revisionism evinced.

Although the term "new historical novel" began circulating immediately after Ángel Rama documented the return of history, Mexican Juan José Barrientos became the first scholar to officially publish the phrase in a 1985 article of the same name.[13] In it, Barrientos examines as counterpoints two Cuban texts written during the 1960s: Alejo Carpentier's *Explosion in a Cathedral* (1962) and Reynaldo Arenas's *Hallucinations, Or, the Ill-Fated Peregrinations*

---

12. Menton provides a prependix of Hispanic American and Brazilian historical fiction written between 1949 and 1992. Additionally, Pons organizes contemporary Hispanic American fiction by country of production (15–16) and Esteves provides an extensive list of Brazil's own contributions during the last quarter of the twentieth century.

13. The article was retitled for inclusion in Mignon Domínguez. Menton and Barrientos had first informally presented the term earlier in the decade (Menton 188n2).

of Fray Servando (1969). Barrientos indirectly criticizes Carpentier's formal distance and over-reliance upon historical exposition about the aftermath of the French Revolution across the Caribbean. By contrast, Barrientos celebrates Arenas's picaresque rewriting of the documented memoirs composed by Fray Servando Teresa de Mier, a Mexican Catholic priest exiled after revising New Spain's religious history in a famous 1794 sermon. Both the latter's irreverence and implausibility represent a break with traditional verisimilitude, giving rise to a series of contradictory approaches that hammer home the new form's transgressive nature: scholarship is displaced by imagination, chronology by anachronism, documented geographical markers are replaced by unreal spaces, and literary characters by mythological characters (50–62). Refraining from making conclusions about the disregard for accepted history, Barrientos ultimately limits himself to identifying a new aesthetic rather than establishing a corpus of similar works.

Crystallization of the critical response to the new trend occurred in a 1991 issue of the journal *Cuadernos Americanos* dedicated to the historical novel, which featured the articles of the genre's three most impactful proponents—Anglo-American Seymour Menton, Uruguayan Fernando Aínsa, and Cuban Roberto González Echevarría—and which would form the basis of their forthcoming benchmark publications.[14] A quick examination of their distinct approaches reveals a similar dynamic between the strategies of outright parody and the pseudo-factualism of false documents that each recognizes to varying degrees. In contrast to Barrientos, who views Carpentier as a standard-bearer of the old regime, Menton coronates the Cuban writer as the originator of new Latin American historical fiction, citing examples dating back to 1949. Menton provides an aesthetic account of the genre, eliding questions of social exclusion prioritized by cultural studies, yet his model continues to have currency for a number of reasons. First, unlike many regional accounts that focus explicitly on Hispanic production, Menton takes the concept of Latin America seriously, seeking to be inclusive of Brazil's own literary revolution.[15] Second, he is the first to attempt to distinguish between new historical forms and the "old" conventions exhibited during the nineteenth and twentieth centuries, as opposed to simply making ungrounded claims about the former. Third, Men-

---

14. Because Aínsa's contribution to the *Cuadernos Americanos* issue, "La reescritura de la historia en la nueva narrativa latinoamerican" (1991), is an expanded version of "La nueva novela histórica latino-americana," published that same year, I cite from the earlier version. Both Menton's and González Echevarría's articles form chapters in their respective *Latin America's New Historical Novel* (1993) and *Myth and Archive* (1990).

15. Esteves does not believe Menton provides equal representation, arguing that more than one hundred Brazilian works could complement the North American's list of a mere seven non-Hispanic texts (62).

ton argues that the new Latin American historical novel has a genealogy distinct from that of iconoclastic literature in the United States (32), and he takes issue with Hutcheon's historiographic metafiction, largely avoiding the term "postmodernism." While Menton notes a spectrum of texts, from the history-dominant to the fiction-dominant, however, he focuses his attention upon the parodic effects of the latter, and his six components synthesized below bear a striking resemblance to those of historiographic metafiction:

1. Traditional mimetic attempts to represent material history are jettisoned in favor of exploring philosophical quandaries such as those popularized before the war by Jorge Luis Borges (the illusion of reality, the cyclical nature of history, etc.).
2. Purposeful distortion of the accepted historical record takes place through exaggeration, omission, or anachronism.
3. Recognized historical figures are utilized as characters, in contrast to the invented protagonists popularized by Lukács.
4. Metafiction is predominant through narrators' reference to the creative process of their own texts as well as questioning their own discourse.
5. Intertextuality occurs through allusion to or explicit rewriting of previous literary works.
6. Several concepts introduced by Mikhail Bakhtin, including parody, dialogism, the carnivalesque, and heteroglossia, are utilized to defamiliarize the reader. (22–25)

Several features of the list speak to a specific Hispanic American context. Lukács serves as a measuring stick for new historical fiction for obvious reasons, though Menton is perhaps the first critic to discuss the importance of "real" (and frequently villainous) historical figures taking center stage as protagonists, which becomes key for reconsideration of Spain's conquest. Additionally, Menton's location of Borges at the top of the list is designed to pay homage to the Argentine's enormous impact upon both Latin and North American fiction. Nonetheless, while he may seek to downplay Hutcheon's influence with regard to the centrality of parody and metafiction, the concepts of heteroglossia and the carnivalesque serve functions similar to the pluralism and apocalyptic humor postulated by North American critics.

If Menton's literary model was largely apolitical, Fernando Aínsa, who arrived independently at the label "new historical novel," explicitly gestures toward cultural studies, revisionism, and poststructuralist linguistic referents. Following Rama, Aínsa notes a renewed interest in history during the preceding decade, though unlike Menton, Aínsa locates the phenomenon of historical fiction within a greater concern across Latin America, that of the search for social and national identity accomplished through interdisciplinary integrations with cultural anthropology ("La nueva novela" 82). Thus, more than a list of characterizations, his ten attributes act as a cumulative series of axioms:

1. The new historical novel is characterized by a critical rereading of history.
2. This rereading challenges the authority established by official versions of history and is capable of overcoming the deficiencies of conservative power by giving voice to those traditionally persecuted by history.
3. The multiple and contradictory perspectives ensure the impossibility of establishing singular truth about historical fact.
4. Through the use of first-person narration and internal monologues, new historical fiction destroys what Mikhail Bakhtin described as the "epic distance" or absolute status of the traditional novel.
5. While referring to real events, this mode purposefully distances itself from historiography through the use of parody, irreverence, and pastiche.
6. Through the use of anachronism, the new historical novel superimposes different historical time periods for the reader.
7. The historicity of fictional discourse can represent opposing extremes, either detailed documentation of historical referents or the pure invention of chronicles.
8. In some works, false chronicles dress up their textuality as historicism, while in others an authentic historical text is cited yet inserted into a fantastical narrative.
9. The critical rereading of history is reflected in parodic writing, which creates a form of self-aware commentary.
10. The use of humor suggests that language has itself become the primary tool the new historical novel employs to demystify the past. ("La nueva novela" 83–85)

From references to Bakhtin to the belief that parody, humor, and anachronism distort accepted versions of historical events in positive ways, there is significant overlap with Menton's model. Yet, in much the same way that Hutcheon claims fiction can better attend to the silenced aspects of the past, Aínsa targets the trappings of "official history" as failing to reveal the human condition, and the processes of creative rereading and rewriting act as forms of revising the accepted record to incorporate this dimension.[16] He understands rewriting as an engaged process that dialogues with the past instead of simply revering its status as set in stone. Equally important is Aínsa's awareness that parody is not the only form through which revision can take place, as he notes in the eighth axiom, an opposing tendency that is frequently overshadowed wherein texts falsely present themselves in the guise of authentic historical texts.

It is precisely this alternative tendency, mentioned in passing by Aínsa, that Roberto González Echevarría, the third critic involved in the themed issue of *Cuadernos Americanos,* explores in *Myth and Archive* (1990). Given that the Cuban scholar wishes to undo traditional literary periodization, as he avoids any reference to postmodernism in taking the modern Latin American novel as his subject, his inclusion may at first seem surprising. After all, what he terms archival fictions are novels about the formal origins of Latin American narrative discourse ("Archival Fictions" 186–87). Yet in practice, the canonical texts generated by this return to and the rewriting of historical documents have since the 1950s frequently taken the form of historical fiction. One look at the corpus of works he identifies reveals it to be virtually identical to the authors and texts claimed by the new historical novel.[17] But there is a caveat. Believing that the most important narratives in Latin America have originated outside of literature, his taxonomy entails an overlap with false documents, for he understands novels as historically having attempted to pretend to be something other than fiction:

> Having no fixed form of its own, the novel often assumes the shape of a given kind of document endowed with truth-bearing power by society at specific moments in time. The novel, or what is called the novel at various points in history, imitates such documents to reveal their conventionality, their subjection to strategies of textual engenderment similar to those governing literature. Through this counterfeit of legitimacy the novel makes its contradictory veiled claim to literariness. ("Archival Fictions" 185)

Forced to compete with nonliterary forms of writing, Latin American narrative has been governed by three primary forms of discourse that provide the novel's origins at different moments in history: legal discourse predominated during the colonial period and dealt with the control of knowledge and

---

16. Although influenced by Hutcheon, Skłodowska provides one of the most comprehensive social historicizations of parody in historically oriented Hispanic American Boom fiction.

17. He identifies Carpentier's *The Lost Steps* (1953) and García Márquez's *One Hundred Years of Solitude* as the paradigmatic examples. Other authors mentioned have been claimed by new historical fiction, including Roa Bastos, Fuentes, Rodriguez Juliá, and Fernando Del Paso.

property; scientific writing by domestic and international travelers became prominent during the nineteenth century; and anthropology and ethnography became the cultural dominants after the 1920s as scientific reports shifted from questions of biology to explorations of language and myth (10–13). In doing so, these texts evince a textuality that is based on relationships with nonfiction documents rather than other literary texts, which in turn alters the authority extended to the discourse of the text.

Gesturing to Foucault's concept of the archive as both a repository of knowledge and a means of controlling access to that knowledge, archival fictions self-consciously reengage these three types of discourse and thematize them through a focus upon written language within their narratives, often through the mediating presence of a diegetic historian who interprets the imaginary texts (González Echevarría, *Myth* 18). The purpose of dividing literary history into three dominants is partially to escape the literary periodization model (romanticism, naturalism, realism, etc.) imported from Europe, although the lack of nonliterary markers as turning points for narrative production means that archival fictions largely downplay any political historicization. Additionally, unlike the feminist bent of intrahistory, the contemporary works from the second half of the twentieth century that González Echevarría explores are almost exclusively by white male canonical writers,[18] and while the model argues for a pan-Latin American narrative by turning to the origins of colonial Spanish writing, Brazil's distinct postwar literary scene is not included for consideration. Nonetheless, the book has been immensely influential, and as a general commentary upon the variety of textual production that constitutes a fundamentally new understanding of history, the thinking behind archival fictions demonstrates how the same canon of texts can be read in ways that run counter to the emphasis upon parody and anachronism alone.

False documents take this thinking to an extreme, for rather than simply pretending to be what they are not, they self-consciously interrogate what function and whose interests documents ultimately serve. If instead of championing the ways in which parody explodes the recognized historical record, we examine the core of new historical novels for what they say about the creation, utilization, and textuality of documents, it is possible to discuss revision as more than a form of rewriting, and instead as a means of actually disputing the authority on which documents are archived. Having remarked upon Brazil's distinct response to the archive, allow us to explore its production during

---

18. I explore the term "intrahistory" in chapter 3, which owes much to Carlos Pacheco's "Historiadores de papel: la metahistoria en la reciente ficción hispanoamericana" (1998).

the same period of political upheaval to further develop the conflict between parody and documentary self-awareness.

THE NEW HISTORICAL AND THE PSEUDO-FACTUAL NOVEL IN BRAZIL, 1976-2000

If Rama first noted the return of history in Hispanic America in 1981, Brazilian cultural critic Silviano Santiago also saw the end of the 1970s as opening a new window on historical awareness in his native land. Writing "Prosa Literária Atual no Brasil" (1979) in response to the waning power of the military regime, Santiago categorizes two overarching literary tendencies; one is creative—a formal anarchy testifying to the malleability of the novel—and the other testimonial—autobiographical accounts designed to document recent political repression during the military dictatorship, blending the past with the present (*Nas malhas* 29–31). The pattern echoes similar tendencies in the United States and Hispanic America, although Santiago had previously recognized these opposing extremes of Brazilian letters under the dictatorship within a different context: magical realism and the parajournalistic reportage novel. By fictionalizing real events, this latter category sacrificed artistic integrity, but could comment on the stories that censored journalism could no longer communicate, therefore more effectively revealing the issues affecting the country than the fantasy employed by allegorical texts.[19]

And yet the false document in Brazil was not only tied to the question of history. A frequent collaborator of Rama, Antonio Candido had also previously explored this dichotomy between realism and antirealism in the country's "new narrative" of the 1970s, in which the incessant blurring of genres resulted in unquantifiable texts, with "books that seem more like journalistic reports; stories that are indistinguishable from poems or chronicles; floating signals and photomontages; autobiographies in the tone and style of novels; narratives that are theatrical scenes, texts created via the juxtaposition of clippings, documents, memories, reflections of all types" ("O papel" 112). As novels of resistance faded with the return to civilian rule in 1985, they were replaced with a desire to reconsider—both critically and with a sense of nostalgia—the country's history. The question of national identity, which had been central to the Romantic historical novel and to political discourse preceding the military coup, returned to the forefront of the popular imaginary (Pellegrini, "A

---

19. See "Repressão e censura no campo das artes na década de 70" (1979), collected in *Vale quanto pesa*.

ficção brasileira" 366). As a consequence, the 1980s became dominated by two new tendencies, theme-based rather than stylistic designations: urban and historical fiction. The former, in the wake of rapid city-growth during the military regime's push for modernization, sought to account for rapidly changing social conditions, frequently focusing on violence. The latter, perhaps the most politicized of all American historical writing, sought to rescue the collective memory of the country, though both groups were ultimately concerned with diagnosing contemporary conditions (366).

Despite potentially exhibiting the most vibrant tradition of false documentation in the hemisphere, however, Brazilian scholars have been less at pains to claim the unique identity of the Portuguese American historical novel, and have instead turned in equal numbers to either Hutcheon's historiographic metafiction or Menton's new historical novel, often critiquing one model and aligning themselves with the other.[20] Nonetheless, in much the same way that the country's classical historical novel emerged distinctly from that of its regional counterparts, new Brazilian historical fiction responded to a different set of criteria. Even though the conditions in Brazil during the 1970s giving rise to national disenchantment shared much in common with those in Hispanic America from a political-historical standpoint, the country's literary and cultural production did not necessarily follow the same patterns. Menton, for example, understands the ten years leading up to the 1992 quincentennial of Columbus's New World arrival as signaling a renewed need to reflect upon the continent's origins, though in Brazil the year 2000 had greater significance, as navigator Pedro Álvares Cabral claimed the eastern coast of South America in the name of Portugal in 1500. Indeed, as the turn of the twenty-first century neared, the number of Brazilian novelists who revisited the early colonial period also began to gain momentum.[21] The flourishing of historically themed works in the early 1990s may also have represented the attempt to rediscover the hope provided by revolutionary heroes during a moment of national crisis (Malard 143) in the wake of President Fernando Collor's disastrous economic reforms in response to the lost decade and his resignation amidst impeachment proceedings in 1992. Yet examples of a radically new form of historical fiction date back to the gradual opening of the military dictatorship during the 1970s and subsequent democratic transition in the 1980s, in essence, responding to a very different type of national crisis.

---

20. Valente (*Viva o povo*) and Sinder openly cite Hutcheon, while Baumgarten and Esteves extend Menton's approach. Weinhardt's descriptive "fiction-history" synthesizes both North American scholars' theories ("O romance histórico").

21. For a discussion of the several texts (largely untranslated) exploring the sixteenth century during the decade leading up to Brazil's quincentennial, see López's introduction.

If the modality in Brazil has been less dominant in comparison to Hispanic America's frenetic production during the 1980s and 1990s, it has been no less important to national reckoning (Esteves 63; Weinhardt, "Outros palimpsestos" 49). Despite this output, scholarly interest in the phenomenon has curiously lagged in Brazil, and even today the field is much less developed than in Hispanic America and the United States. The most significant scholarship was initiated just before the turn of the twenty-first century,[22] yet in tracing the birth of the phrase "new historical novel" to 1996, it has overlooked Inter-American scholar Luiz Valente's foundational contributions at the end of the 1980s.[23] His absence from Brazilian debates may stem from his location within the North American academy, yet it was he who first adopted the term "Brazilian New Historical Novel" to refer to a unique type of antihistory, independent of Menton's and Aínsa's schematics.

It should come as no surprise that Valente believes what he alternately labeled antihistory (alluding to the antirealist bent of other texts) and the new historical novel seeks to redefine the terms of the national debate regarding the country's present. Texts first appeared as the amnesty laws lessened the regime's restrictive cultural oversight and allowed for dissenting voices. The military rule had meant that only a single truth regarding the nation and its modernization had been publicly circulated, and writers questioning all types of totalizing interpretations of reality therefore felt the need to

> distance themselves from anything "official." This attitude is reflected in the novelists' predilection for stories focusing on the marginalized or the forgotten and for characters representing atypical individuals in a social and political space marked by discontinuities and fragmentation, rather than types who embody national ideals. Thus the return to the historical novel can be viewed as a response to the social and historical conditions of the 1970s and 1980s. Faced with the realization that the optimistic definition of Brazil based on harmony and unification, as formed in the nineteenth century and manipulated by military rulers from 1964 to 1985, conflicts with the reality of a society that is fragmented politically and socially. Brazilian writers have turned to the past in search of explanations for the divisions they perceive in the present. (Valente, "Fiction as History" 54)

---

22. Esteves posits Malard's catalogue of the 1990s historical fiction boom as the field's seminal text.

23. Valente first published using the term in 1994, though he workshopped it at conferences dating back to the 1980s (correspondence with the author).

Valente embraces the tenets of both metahistory and historiographic metafiction, yet he also notes evidence of Bakhtin's discourses of carnivalization, heteroglossia, and dialogism in accord with Menton; thus the primary characteristics he identifies in iconoclastic narratives should by now sound quite familiar. Principal among these strategies is the use of parody to subvert traditional historical language and question romanticized characterization of "great men" as heroes. A second goal is to draw attention to social injustice by focusing on atypical groups and individuals not accounted for by Brazil's false discourse of racial harmony, and an attendant concern is skepticism regarding the dictatorship's conservative modernization project. For Valente, the paradigmatic writer in this vein is João Ubaldo Ribeiro, whose historical interests culminate in *An Invincible Memory* (1984), but the critic additionally suggests a provisory corpus that later scholarship has borne out: Márcio Souza's *The Emperor of the Amazon* (1976), Antônio Callado's *Everlasting* (1981), Silviano Santiago's *In Liberty* (1981), Moacyr Scliar's *The Strange Nation of Rafael Mendes* (1983) and *Tropical Dreams* (1992), Nélida Piñon's *The Republic of Dreams* (1984), Eustáquio Gomes's *Fondle Fever* (1984), Dionísio da Silva's *The City of Priests* (1986), Ana Miranda's *Bay of All Saints and Every Conceivable Sin* (1990), and Rubem Fonseca's *August* (1990), among others.[24] The texts cover a wide variety of historical periods and writing styles, yet they are ostensibly linked by the use of parody and intertextuality that is most central to the definition of new narrative strategies, which become more important than the invention of fantastic situations or the inclusion of real historical figures (Esteves 68), though several of the texts also present documentary elements that demonstrate the tension between parody and realism.

At the same time, similar to the previous traditions surveyed in this chapter, the specter of "official history" must also be acknowledged as a critical marker that lends a political edge even to texts whose aspirations are decidedly more literary. New Brazilian narratives not only explore integral events in officially sanctioned history, then, but also actively revise the trajectory of national literary history, inviting a reconsideration of contemporary political and social conditions to demonstrate that fiction shares with history the task of "reconstructing" the past (Baumgarten 170). Many of these novels highlight narrative (inter)textuality by utilizing literary figures as protagonists, although frequently these protagonists are actually representatives of oppression rather than liberation (Malard 145). Their function is ultimately to revise present

---

24. For more titles, see Valente's *História e ficção*. Esteves includes extensive appendices listing both traditional and new historical fiction published 1949–2000. In "Outros palimpsestos," Weinhardt in turn examines the sixteen historical novels written 1981–2000 that won Brazil's prestigious Jabuti Award.

perceptions by telling the story of history's losers, while also providing a platform for female writers in a genre traditionally dominated by men (Esteves 72), especially visible in the increasing number of women writers, such as Nélida Piñon and Ana Miranda, who place female protagonists in primary roles. These themes have brought greater awareness to the cultural myths of racial and social harmony, and while this has resulted in less expression by indigenous, Afro-descendant, and other ethnic minorities than in United States, new voices are slowly, but surely, appearing.[25] In the twenty-first century, Marlene Weinhardt cautions, not all historical fiction is new historical fiction. Nonetheless, she celebrates shifting attitudes that have increasingly been accepted by commercial and experimental texts alike, where distinctions between past and present can become increasingly blurred, the border between representations of original scholarship and appropriated citations has been largely erased, and there is no longer a preference in subject matter between national and foreign historical figures ("Outros palimpsestos" 48). In other words, its association with cultural decolonization has evolved, reaching a postnational consensus in an indirect manner that Fuentes's new Latin American novel of the 1970s could not have imagined. Nor should the new novel overshadow the importance of documentary fiction. Similar to the Hispanic American canon, many of the groundbreaking Brazilian texts listed above also demonstrate the tension between document and fiction simultaneously, from the false diary providing the form of Souza's *The Emperor of the Amazon* to that of Santiago's *In Liberty*, which I will analyze in chapter 6. While the importance of the Brazilian nonfiction-novel peaked in the late 1970s, new works such as Ana Maria Gonçalves's award-winning *A Color Defect* (2006), which presents itself as the forgotten diary of a female African slave discovered by Gonçalves herself, demonstrate that the false document remains both critically and popularly viable.

CONCLUSION

The rest of this book will explore case studies that have been arranged around specific thematic or formal questions related to the theme of primary documents. As I hope is clear at this point, whether understood as a cultural designation or as socioeconomic periodization, North American postmodern trends may have been perceived as a form of intellectual expansionism

---

25. Examples include Ana Maria Gonçalves's *A Color Defect* (2006), Maria José Silveira's *The Mother of the Mother of Her Mother and Her Daughters* (2002), and Lebanese-Brazilian writer Milton Hatoum's *Dois Irmãos* (2000).

in Latin America, but authors and critics across the hemisphere were quick to appropriate similar forms of skepticism for their own purposes, which extended beyond discussions of cultural complacency or consumer culture. If anything, I would argue that false documents temper the radical claims of postmodernism by grounding representation in seemingly conventional forms, although the implications are potentially more far-reaching. Similar to the previous chapter, my trajectory of new historical literature is not intended to be exhaustive. Rather it seeks to demonstrate recurrent, complementary strategies that authors and critics both developed in each respective region, despite operating under divergent political conditions.

At the same time, I have drawn attention to a reflexive pseudo-documentary impulse that evolved in conjunction with its postmodern counterpart, though it has received markedly less attention. Part of this disregard is a consequence of the universal way that the label historiographic metafiction has been applied to refer to any type of self-reflexive text that engages historical questions, though as we have seen, self-awareness does not necessitate parody, anachronism, and conspicuous distortion of the historical record. Indeed, in the case studies that follow, I will analyze several works that have been previously associated with the canon of postmodern literature, though I hope to demonstrate how, rather than privilege rupture, these false documents demonstrate affinity for the historical process and seek to educate by putting the question of form and authority before the reader. In some cases, individual texts contain competing elements of both the iconoclastic and the testimonial, and the model of false documents is not intended to completely displace Hutcheon's prototype, but rather to accentuate the important potential for historical and literary collaboration that has been ignored in favor of disciplinary discord.

Robert Berkhofer finds it paradoxical that literary scholars and the social scientists began to question the possibility of writing history at precisely the moment that historicization became a vital means of contextualizing their own fields (*Great Story* ix). Because of the lingering distrust for postmodernism in historiography departments, parodic intertextuality served a specific purpose when Hutcheon first theorized it as a response, but even then, its criticism of historiography signaled ignorance of the field's debates. The irony of the former's institutionalization as the primary theoretical approach is that its metanarrative of resistance and rupture is perpetuated, even after the "blurring" of such boundaries has ceased to promise radical change. If historiographic metafiction asks whose interests historiography represents, then we must also consider what is gained by such disciplinary attacks, which do not always apply the same standard to literary production. In fact, Berkhofer questions the ultimate value of "de-referentiality" for literary authority, since "literature, like science and history, is demoted to just another text, like films, cartoons, and other cultural objects" (9), although this cannot extend to the status of documents. Literary theory that focuses less on overtly subversive aesthetics and more upon revision—similar to historiography—as a literal rereading of the status of documents, offers a constructive response to exceptionalist critiques that frequently do not attract attention beyond literary spheres.

As I have stated previously, false documents inhabit the same intersectional space within which Inter-American studies can relate to hemispheric areas studies, leading to a final issue observed in the preceding pages: the malleability of the postnational concept. Issues such as democracy, progress, and modernization are analyzed in at times contradictory fashion within the three sociolinguistic traditions. If the endgame is only to deconstruct and therefore revise the national narrative, however, then the state may be reinforced as the central organizing structure, a criticism against some Hemispheric American approaches. Yet analyzed in a comparative or regional grouping, postnational projects gain meaning by thematizing how writers have responded to different national traumas—war, governmental control, colonization, inequality—through shared strategies, and this expanded framework places the representation of nation in a network of cultural confluences and democratic contact zones.

CHAPTER 3

The Ends of Argentine Democracy

The False Memoir(s) and Cultural Hybridity behind Tomás Eloy Martínez's The Perón Novel

> Each one of the facts in this book has a document, a letter, a tape recording, that attests to its veracity. In the uncertain years during which these pages were written, the illusion of truth was the only thing we Argentines could carry around and perhaps the only thing of which we were not dispossessed.
> —Tomás Eloy Martínez, *Las memorias del general*

WITH THIS paradoxical claim, journalist, author, and academic Tomás Eloy Martínez concludes the introduction to his collection *Las memorias del general* (*The General's Memoirs*, 1996). Yet despite initially highlighting the archive of documents contained in the book as a means to authenticate the truth claims of his corresponding articles, in the following sentence, Martínez insinuates that truth may be no more than a utopic construction in times of national crisis. At first glance, it may be tempting to see such epistemological skepticism as an outgrowth of his bestselling novel *Santa Evita* (1995), published the previous year, which "invents facts as if facts were written by journalists" (Martínez, "Truth in Fiction" n.p.). Indeed, the self-reflexive narrative not only ostensibly documents the Argentine military's transnational attempts to hide Eva Perón's corpse, a means of limiting her symbolic value to resistance against the dictatorship that had ousted her husband Juan Perón in 1955, but it also incorporates Martínez's own act of writing, thus cementing his status as a postmodern Argentine author.[1]

Despite the proximity of the publication dates, however, Martínez's fluctuating attitude toward his collection of documents has a much more complex and extensive history. The general referenced in his title is Juan Perón (1895–1974), the definitive figure of Argentina's shift from modernity to postmoder-

---

1. See Davies ("Portraits of a Lady"), Martin, and Perkowska.

nity (Colás 152; Davies, *Projections* 1). Gaining popular support through the socialist programs he enacted as both Minister of Labor and President of the Republic (1946–1955), Perón's cult of personality continued to cast its shadow over Argentine politics for more than three decades, and his physical absence resulting from eighteen years of exile, first in the Caribbean (1955–1960) and later in Spain (1960–1973), only served to further amplify his populist legacy. Martínez was commissioned to conduct multiple interviews with the deposed president in Madrid over the course of four years, and the titular chronicle— Perón referred to them as his "canonical memoirs"—emerged out of these sessions, edited and published in 1970 in *Panorama*.[2] The April 14 edition of this popular weekly journal also mixes registers, its cover promising an "exclusive document," while the accompanying image features Perón in a relaxed and domestic setting in front of his Spanish residence, affably smiling while holding his dog (see Figure 1). The pose is designed to humanize the deposed leader, and noticeably absent from the cover image are two close companions abroad, his third wife, Isabel, and his personal secretary, José López Rega, both of whom would soon play important roles in his short-lived presidential administrative return. One reason for this omission: not mentioned on the cover is the fact that the memoirs only cover Perón's first fifty years of life (1895–1945), and central to his strategic self-portrayal is the constructed narrative of a self-made man at the height of his powers, thus the various sections of the article inside the magazine, starting with Perón's childhood and moving through his military and political successes, are demarcated by personal photos featuring Perón's first-person descriptions as captions, further heightening the article's familial, empathetic angle. Designed to flaunt the magazine's direct access to Perón, presiding over the director's introductory comments on the inside cover is even a photograph of the general and Martínez, side by side, but the journalist would soon do everything in his power to separate their legacies as he attempted to disown the memoirs.

This journalistic criticism would eventually lead to Martínez's self-exile to Venezuela in 1975 because of attempts against his life. Thus the "uncertain years" to which Martínez alludes in his introduction to *The General's Memoirs* are the 1970s themselves, a decade in which Argentina's Dirty War would lead to the "disappearance" of up to 30,000 suspected dissidents and socialist sympathizers at the hands of right-wing death squads. The name "Dirty War" has primarily denoted the military dictatorship's National Reorganization Process

---

2. Perón claimed this during a telephone exchange in the weeks after Martínez published the sanctioned memoirs on April 14, 1970. Under López Rega's influence, Perón refused to speak about Evita on record, but Martínez did publish on April 21 and 28 fragments of their conversations about his second wife without the secretary present (*Las memorias* 12).

FIGURE 1. Juan Perón on the front cover of the *Panorama* 1970 special edition

(1976–1983), yet various accounts trace the origins of state-sponsored terror back to Perón's return to power in 1973 and his subsequent death the following year.[3] As vice president, Isabel succeeded him before being deposed in 1976 by a revolving door of military generals, and the regime would finally collapse as a consequence of social unrest over the failing economy and the military's embarrassing defeat by the British in the 1982 Falklands War. According to Martínez, both the Falklands War and the Dirty War were founded on falsified histories disseminated through propaganda. As he claims in an oft-cited

---

3. See chapters 3 and 7 of Hodges on the origins of Argentina's state terrorism.

interview, "In my part of the world, documents often were falsified by governments. There is almost nothing authentic" (Bach 15).

Martínez's most celebrated response to the falsification of documents for political gain, however, can be traced to *La novela de Perón* (*The Perón Novel*, 1985), an experiment with fiction that later prompted *The General's Memoirs* and anticipates the strategies of *Santa Evita*. The novel not only presents a panoramic view of Argentina in 1973 as the deposed leader prepares his triumphant return to Argentina, but also the memoirs that Martínez helped publish, including what appear to be fragments of Perón's autobiography, play a central role. Yet after each section of Perón's account, the novel inserts excerpts from a special issue of the magazine *Horizonte*, in which a group of Perón's forgotten family and colleagues provide testimony that contradicts the romanticized image provided in the autobiography. The publication *Horizonte* never actually existed, and these "counter-memoirs" are in fact fictionalized versions of documents and testimonials that Martínez amassed during his investigative research after the Madrid interviews (and included in *The General's Memoirs*). Similarly, it turns out that the supposedly autobiographical sections of Perón's memoirs are overtly fictionalized, a fact that Martínez later worried was lost on many readers.

While the variously falsified documents within *The Perón Novel* trace the general's life from childhood through his deposal in 1955, they ultimately provide context for gauging the fragility of democracy in Argentina. The Ezeiza massacre that took place on the day of his 1973 return is the axis around which several different groups claiming to represent Peronism organize. The fictional Perón spends his final weeks of exile reviewing and correcting the canonical autobiography previously published by Martínez, on the one hand, rehearsing it in preparation for the masses and, on the other, "introducing himself into the Memoirs López Rega has written for him" after transcribing the cassette recordings and "doctoring documents" (41). The men's conflicting approaches to the construction of Perón's image are made explicit when their two versions are stylistically juxtaposed on several occasions. Yet the memoirs are not only a convenient device for examining how documents can be distorted, lies told so often that they become truth. Perón seems oblivious of the text's importance to his own failing sense of identity, though he carries them around with him at virtually all times, even in a midnight taxi ride to symbolically bid farewell to the city of Madrid, as if they were a charm to ward off the spirits of history. Sporting an Iberian accent after so many years abroad, the ailing Perón is ultimately too old to embrace the idea of uprooting his life in order to return to Argentina, yet he has become a victim of the doctrine he invented via the multiple groups manipulating his legacy.

Illustrating an obsessive chain of editing and rewriting, *The Perón Novel* enacts on a microlevel the various attempts by Martínez to problematize the power of Peronism in subsequent decades, as we will see shortly. Leftist and rightist presidential candidates with conflicting platforms continued to claim fidelity to Peronism during the 1990s and 2000s,[4] though the timeliness of the novel's publication as Argentina emerged from a dark historical period contributed to its national success, even if the book would only receive greater international attention after the acclaim of *Santa Evita*. Yet while Eva's myth was examined through a variety of media dating back to Andrew Lloyd Webber's 1978 musical, *The Perón Novel* has remained the only work to specifically examine the general (Punte 224). Taken together, the translation of both of these publications led them to be much more closely associated with postmodernism than the Latin American new historical novel.[5]

The objective of this chapter is not to trace histories of the distinct Peronist factions that precipitated the massacre, although Santiago Colás has provided such an account in his important *Postmodernity in Latin America* (1994). Instead, I reconsider the basis of postmodern descriptions in claims that Martínez's narrative demonstrates the "end of history" through the impossibility of its construction (Neyret 203–4). This end is distinct from Fukuyama's neoliberal end to ideologies, whose viability in Latin America Martínez has dismissed, given the increased power of popular protest in Venezuela and cultural nationalism at the lost decade's end (*Réquiem* 351). Having researched and written scholarship about the tradition of merging history and fiction in Argentina dating back to the nineteenth century, it is Martínez, after all, who claims that Perón and his vocal critic Jorge Luis Borges ultimately shared the idea that documents could be fictionalized.[6] Nonetheless, this does not mean that Martínez relativizes history—if his incessant engagement reveals anything about his own politics, it is that he insists upon an ethical distinction between truth and falsity—but rather he attacks Perón's chameleon-like ability to claim multiple and contradictory truths as symptomatic of the manipulation of authority in Argentine politics. Democracy may be a utopic concept for the journalist, but he believes that having such a goal is vital for public and intellectual engagement.

---

4. See Serrafero for a comparative analysis of President Carlos Menem's (1989–1999) neoliberal Peronism and Néstor Kirchner's (2003–2007) alignment with the region's shift toward the left.

5. Neyret is one of the few to analyze the text as new historical fiction, though he views postmodernism as synonymous.

6. See Martínez ("Mito, historia," 7) regarding the ironic comparison of Borges and Perón, while his "La batalla" provides broader analyses of Latin American historical writing.

After being hired as director of the Latin American Studies Program at Rutgers University in 1995, Martínez played with the line between autobiography and fiction by including unnamed narrators who write and teach in New Jersey on more than one occasion. With their interplay of US and Latin American settings, *Santa Evita* and his posthumously published *Purgatory* (2010) are perhaps his most obviously Inter-American works in geographical terms. And yet the history of *The Perón Novel* is both transnational and postnational, based on interviews conducted in Europe, written primarily in Venezuela, and finished in the United States. Indeed, one of the ironies of its depiction of Argentina is that it features an exiled journalist writing about an exiled president, thus what these two dueling figures share most is, ironically, their removal from the national politics they seek to revise. In a special issue of *New Perspectives Quarterly* dedicated to postnational writing, Martínez argues that the "story of your nation as narration transforms the nation into a tale. But that's different from nationalism. Perón personified nationalism, but I don't think that *The Perón Novel* is a nationalistic novel" ("Truth in Fiction" n.p.). Coming from an Inter-American intellectual who employs postnationalism to draw international attention to human rights issues, this distinction has tangible repercussions for recoding the leader's legacy both abroad and at home, for "the Perón that people are thinking of in my country today is the Perón of my novel, not the Perón of history" (ibid.).

Based on an analysis of Argentine Ernesto Laclau, Jon Beasley-Murray's recent *Posthegemony* (2010) importantly critiques both cultural studies and Peronism for their hegemonic foundations. Because I will specifically evaluate the novel's transnational context as a critical response to Latin American postmodernism, however, I turn to a different Argentine scholar contemporary to Martínez: Néstor García Canclini, whose influential *Culturas híbridas* (*Hybrid Cultures*, 1990) is tellingly subtitled "Strategies for Entering and Leaving Modernity." In part an early example of US–Mexico border studies, García Canclini's monograph examines the problematic evaluation of modernization in a region where modernity—much like Peronism within Argentina—has been interpreted in contrasting ways that has led to conflict between different groups vying for power. The anthropologist argues that populism achieves its power by evoking shared culture to provide the illusion of transforming the masses' status as spectators into that of political agents. García Canclini also sustains that the inherent hybridity of postmodern media opens up the past to popular reinterpretation, particularly through the disruptive processes of what he terms "decollection" and "deterritorialization," practices that I will argue are illustrated by Martínez's strategic juxtaposition of the memoirs and counter-memoirs as outdated forms of media.

Concluding that the hybrid intersection of Latin American and the US modernities challenges the concept of geographically bound nations, García Canclini thus provides a productive Inter-American reading of postmodernism as a cultural rather than purely economic phenomenon. Repositioned within a cultural rather than national context, *The Perón Novel* signals the beginning of this historical period in the 1970s through its recognition of the waning efficacy of printed media, for as the book progresses, the various textual artifacts documenting Perón are gradually displaced by the increased reach of television over the masses. In this sense, both the investigator and the investigated become casualties of the populist project.

García Canclini's inclusion here has less to do with his shared national origins than the numerous critical pieces Martínez published about his own fiction. The same year he released *The General's Memoirs,* the journalist made two important claims. First, after the Dirty War, it was no longer possible to evaluate history, in terms of truth, only as culture. Second, it was no longer possible to imagine power in absolute or homogeneous terms (*Réquiem* 351–52). Whereas historical fiction of the 1970s sought to play up the unreliability of all archives, new fiction could no longer totalize, only compete to fill the resulting void, much like the examples of media García Canclini examines. Before analyzing how Martínez employs such strategies for entering and leaving Latin American postmodernity, my path will first detour through the writer's complicated history in his capacity as a journalist, historian, and creative writer while (un)covering Perón. Thereafter, I will contextualize Perón's own Inter-American populism through García Canclini's deconstruction of the modernization project, before finally demonstrating how hybridity provides a novel alternative to North American postmodernism in relation to both Martínez's novel and its protagonist.

"THE MEDIUM WAS REALITY": THE BORDERS OF HISTORY AND FICTION

Writing the novel largely from exile, and launching it on the eve of the much-publicized judicial trial of the military juntas responsible for the Dirty War, Martínez imagines Perón's return as the end of democracy—not history. The general's strategic multiplicity allowed him to cultivate loyalty in opposing ideological factions of the population, from the conservative military establishment to the revolutionary youth movements on the left. Importantly, his novel not only draws from Martínez's own investigative reporting, but also cites liberally from a 1974 Peronist magazine article in which the Montoneros urban guerillas claim credit for the retaliatory assassination of the anticommunist military general who had earlier deposed Perón, intimating that the general sanctioned the violence.[7]

This ideological and political divide tragically came to a head in 1973 on the day of Perón's return from exile. As the largest gathering in national history converged upon Ezeiza Airport outside Buenos Aires, anticommunist military snipers opened fire on the leftist Peronist youth groups and the urban guerillas carrying banners. In the midst of the confusion, the total number of casualties was never verified by authorities, though the massacre marked Peronism's rightward turn as well as initiated the state violence that would pave the way for the Dirty War (Crassweller 387–88). For Martínez, the Ezeiza Massacre acts as a violent fulcrum around which to examine the conflicting images of Perón that various groups had constructed in his absence. Thus, in addition to following Perón and his secretary's creative revision of the memoirs, as well as fictional journalist Emiliano Zamora's interviews in preparation for his magazine's special issue, the novel details radical groups representing both leftist and rightist Peronist factions as they plan attacks upon the other, as the witnesses Zamora gathers to undermine Perón's memoir become unwittingly caught in the middle of this battle over past and present. As the book makes clear, Perón's ability to allow others to project their desires onto him has faded with age. While the fictional reporter Zamora acts as a stand-in for Martínez throughout most of the novel, Martínez also briefly appears as a character when Zamora visits his office to request documents for the *Horizonte* special issue. There he recounts his disappointment upon meeting Perón and discovering a decrepit old man rather than the mythical figure he had idolized on television growing up, a personal disillusionment that anticipates the masses' similar realization:

> I sensed that he always guessed how the other person saw him and immediately projected the anticipated image. He had already been the Leader, the General, the Deposed Dictator, the Macho, You-Know-Who, the Escaped Tyrant, the Boss of the GOU [sic], the Nation's First Worker, Eva Perón's Widower, the Exile. . . . I saw so many semblances that I became disillusioned. He was no longer a myth. At last, I said to myself, he's nobody. He's hardly even Perón. (259)[8]

---

7. Neyret has noted fictionalized elements in the original 1974 article, which was released four years after the assassination of General Pedro Aramburu (206). While Martínez also points out inconsistencies in the document, he anachronistically presents the confession as if it had been prepared back in 1971.

8. All translations of *The Perón Novel* are taken from Asa Zatz's 1988 English translation. After the international success of *Santa Evita*, Helen Lane completed an improved translation,

As an outspoken critic of Perón in his newspaper columns, Martínez had firsthand experience of the uncertain years and the suppression of information that accompanied the 1970s. His investigative chronicle, *The Passion According to Trelew* (1974), was banned by military authorities because of its representation of the state's torture of urban guerillas. As one of several journalists to receive death threats from the Argentine Anticommunist Alliance (AAA) outside his newspaper office in 1975, he was forced into exile in Venezuela and the United States, where he would spend much of the rest of his life as an academic.[9] The Triple-A death squad was secretly presided over by José López Rega, Perón's personal secretary in Spain and later Minister of Social Warfare upon the general's return to Argentina. In *The General's Memoirs*, Martínez includes a 1975 article in which he details López Rega's influence over Perón and ties to paramilitary groups, though the writer complains the newspaper's editors took the liberty of adding entire paragraphs of political statements that he had never seen, let alone sanctioned (147–48). In an act that encapsulates the tension between much of the author's critical and creative production, however, instead of simply reproducing the published article, Martínez anachronistically writes a corrected version that reconstitutes his "original" submission. In other words, Martínez is keenly aware of the beguile of truth discourses such as journalism and historiography, and he experienced how even minor editing could have significant implications for public interpretation. Thus in order to understand the journalist's contradictory approach to primary documents as a substantiating force in his own investigative research and yet a tool of misinformation in the hands of the state, Perón's canonical memoirs must be understood as part of a continuum in Martínez's search for unmasking the man who existed between the lines and behind the mask. Peronism was banned from elections during the 1960s, and Perón himself was not permitted to officially discuss politics from exile; because Martínez realized too late that the ex-leader used him to disseminate a romanticized image to his followers at home, the journalist seems to have operated out of a sense of guilt for his complicity in the statesman's project.

This may explain why Martínez would return to take up misconceptions surrounding the publication at least once each decade over the course of the next thirty years, trying his hand at discrete genres such as biography, exposé, and nonfiction. For even as he first recorded Perón reading the document that the general had dictated to López Rega in 1970, Martínez noted inaccuracies and purposeful embellishment. Additionally, the secretary's own influence

---

yet I preserve Zatz's wording because chronologically its timing has greater bearing on the framework of my project.

9. Martínez worked as a journalist in Venezuela (1975–1983) while writing *The Perón Novel*, and from 1984 to his death he held academic appointments at multiple US institutions (Martin 464).

over the supposedly autobiographical material became clear in multiple forms, ranging from López Rega assuming Perón's identity when the general became tired, to his insistence that he had accompanied a young Perón in military exercises, when in fact he had not yet been born.[10] Confronted by the fact that the memoirs were not "truthful," a combination of Perón's failing memory and his underling's manipulation, Martínez returned home and unearthed damaging documents in the National Registry as well as conflicting accounts from interviews with Perón's previous associates and family members. When he sent the collection of contradictory accounts to Madrid, requesting to publish an annotated version of the memoirs, however, he received the canonical version back without any commentary. In other words, intent on paving the way for his return with a document that endeared him to his electoral base, Perón was more interested in "making his own monument" than in "resigning himself to historical truth" (*Vidas* 128).

Unwilling either to risk Perón retracting the memoirs or to throw away his research, Martínez published them as requested, but he decided to unveil the "truth" by starting work on a biography that he would abandon in 1974. Ten years later, *The Perón Novel* appeared on the heels of Argentina's return to civilian rule and incorporated the failure of the biography into its plot. Credited with "revising" twentieth century Argentine history (Ganduglia 272), the novel itself underwent substantial revisions as Martínez scrapped initial attempts to approach his subject through the realist discourses central to biography and journalism.[11] Alarmed by the fact that historians had accepted the memoirs at face value in their biographies of Perón, and disheartened that his own journalistic attempts to call attention to the misleading document had received little attention, the writer turned to fiction. Juxtaposing a mixture of documented as well as invented texts, he sought to create a duel between the narratives via the character of Perón. His hope was ostensibly that "the falsity of one version (mine) would make clearer the falsity of the version offered by the historical figure. Both could be compared, reexamined, and corrected by historians and critics" ("Ficción e historia" 44). The public reaction he hoped for never materialized.

---

10. See Martínez (*Las memorias* 28) for further details on the interview. Martínez incorporates the spirit of this blatant anachronism into the novel by having López Rega write and edit the updated memoirs as if he were Perón, who is unable to recognize himself in the text anymore, but believes that "the documents don't lie" (*Perón Novel* 42).

11. In his anthology *La otra realidad* (2006), Martínez includes an early abandoned fragment of the novel. The first draft was a journalistic recreation of the recorded interview, the second a novelized biography discarded after discovering contradictory eyewitness accounts, and the third successfully incorporated these earlier failures into fiction format. He first described these three drafts in a 1988 article, although *Las vidas del general* includes a much-edited version that fleshes out his disappointment at historians' uncritical acceptance.

Instead, Martínez lamented that most of the praise afforded him was based on a gross misunderstanding of his project. Literary critics and reviewers lauded the historical fidelity he achieved by inserting sections from Perón's supposed memoirs, personal correspondence between government figures, and archives of witnesses, though these apparent documents were, in fact, largely fictional inventions ("Ficción e historia" 41). Anticipating many of the issues that would resurface in his future criticism, Martínez rejects ties to Argentina's distinct tradition of New Journalism.[12] His purpose, instead, was to reflect upon the process of historical construction, and thus unlike the published memoirs, the novel provides a testament to national decadence and the excesses of military rule (47). In an effort to clear up the misconception of his fiction, he next compiled and published the texts that would appear as *The General's Memoirs* after another ten-year period. This included the complete transcript of the original interviews, the published version of the written memoirs, investigative articles Martínez produced about Perón's ties to Nazism and López Rega's political influence, and finally the archival documents and interviews that contradicted Perón's claims about his origins and military experience.

The ostensible purpose of this return to nonfiction was to force the comparison of the written and spoken forms of the memoirs that had not occurred in response to *The Perón Novel*. Ironically, however, this attempt to set the record straight also led to further misunderstanding. Thus if Martínez imagined the volume would demonstrate the unreliability of the general's memoirs, the phrasing of his title unintentionally suggested the opposite to unaware readers (*Vidas* 11). In 2004 he therefore published the retitled, definitive version of these documents as *The General's Lives*, which features two new chapters and jettisons the published version of the memoirs. Curiously, while the journalist preserves much of the introduction and its account of how he first came to interview Perón, in this updated version Martínez removes the reference to obsessive documentation reproduced in the epigraph I used to initiate this chapter. It would seem that in the meantime he had recognized the contradictory value he assigned to such "illusions" of truth.[13]

Ultimately, as he witnessed how the national public would uncritically read fiction as fact if presented within a form of communication they had been

---

12. Berg (1995) sought to include Martínez within the tradition of nonfiction novel, although the journalist claims to be writing outside any particular national or Latin American genres.

13. After publishing *Santa Evita*, Martínez accepted the thin line separating documents and myth. As he notes, one of the imagined scenes involving Perón and Eva cannot be found in any documents prior to the work, yet the particular exchange has since reappeared uncited in films claiming to tell the "true story" of Eva's death (*Réquiem* 358).

conditioned to accept as truthful, the Argentine author discovered a political variation of Hayden White's tropes of history. Whether official sources or newspaper journalism, the "medium substituted reality; the medium *was* reality" (*Vidas* 125), he would write with dismay in this definitive work. If Martínez had first noticed the phenomenon from the reception of clearly fantastical short stories he published in the newspaper, this was doubly true for the report-like *The Perón Novel*, despite its very title signposting its fictional status. The book initially appeared in weekly newspaper installments that even further complicated its reception by the national public. The entire network of documents, fiction, and history is therefore ineluctably bound by questions of media and reception studies, and the key to the novel's interpretation resides in how the author builds his awareness of these issues into the convergence of narrative threads upon a new political order.

HYBRID CULTURE: BETWEEN THE NATIONAL AND CONTINENTAL, POPULISM AND THE PEOPLE

For Gerald Martin, Martínez may have helped publicize the modernist Boom literature of Latin America during the 1960s and 1970s in his capacity as a journalist, yet *The Perón Novel* becomes postmodern by signaling the transition to the post-Boom era, one critical of the way in which writers were valorized through international Anglophone recognition (464). Martin attributes the novel's comparative lack of recognition to both its narrative complexity and its "generic hybridity"—in addition to fiction the work can be classified as history, journalism, biography, autobiography, and even *testimonio*—decades before other writers would popularize a similar collage of styles. Martin believes the concept of "hybrid writer" (466) has strangely been used to minimize Martínez's creative accomplishments, despite the fact that most of the Boom writers themselves were journalists before gaining fame as authors. Thus while philosophizing about national issues was considered acceptable, Martínez was guilty of denationalizing or worlding Argentine literature "in the way that Ernesto Guevara had Latin-Americanised [sic] Argentine politics" (465), which is to say his particular hemispheric vision did not lend itself to US consumption. In effect, both writers forced the country, which had historically looked to Europe for its social and cultural identity, to recognize its similarity to its regional neighbors. Yet Martin points out that Martínez's location of the leader within a "continental" network of relations echoes the transnational gestures of Peronism itself. The doctrine of Peronism is loosely based upon three principles—social justice, economic equality, and national sovereignty—yet shortly before being deposed, Perón began also advocating for regional alliances.

Believing that his 1970 autobiography had the power to indoctrinate the masses through the example his own struggles provided, Martínez's Perón perceives, "perhaps too late, that the Memoirs were the cross that was missing from the Peronist church" (41). Ascribing such importance to a single document is not poetic fancy on Martínez's part. One of the reasons his false document is so powerful is that the deposed president wrote prolifically during his exile to create propaganda in the form of autobiography and manifestoes.[14] Arguably his most important contribution was *The Hour of the People* (1968), which signaled a radical new chapter in his political ambitions. Much as Martínez's protagonist imagines the memoirs as the crux of his updated doctrine, one of the chapters in *The Hour of the People* consists in its entirety of a 1953 speech to the National School of War about the need for a Southern Cone alliance. Perón justifies the speech's inclusion as a "historical document," previously hidden from the public, which demonstrates the twenty-year history of his continental vision, all the more significant because the United States purposefully misread it to support claims regarding Argentina's imperialism.[15] Now equating national democracy with regional autonomy, the general expands the geographical framework of his previous position, calling for Pan-Latin American solidarity as an antidote to postwar US imperialism. Implicitly referencing the National Security Doctrine, he accuses Washington of usurping Latin American governments and inculcating the heads of the military forces, as well as influencing their economies, trade unions, and social sectors (Perón 268–75). Decrying the global power of the dollar, Perón even calls for the creation of a Latin American common market, although the consolidation of MERCOSUR would only materialize in 1991 as the regional financial crisis concluded. Nonetheless, by targeting Argentina's youth base with his third-worldism, Perón capitalized on post–Cuban Revolution unrest to push his national socialist "third position," an alternative to capitalism and communism.

---

14. *Los libros de exilio* (1996) collects seven individually published works, including Perón's open letter to US President Kennedy, some of which first circulated in serialized form in world newspapers (8). See Davies's *Projections* for a literary analysis of Perón's autobiographies from exile.

15. Perón provides a short introduction contextualizing the speech about continental integration, which he develops to greater degree in subsequent chapters (*Los libros* 277–86).

García Canclini's *Hybrid Cultures* explicates a type of hybridity that is distinct from either Martínez's genre-mixing or Perón's political chameleonism. The anthropological study has become a canonical text within Latin American cultural studies, and repositioning Martínez's novel as a form of popular culture provides a productive framework for entering and leaving the above-mentioned questions of populism and national history within a continental context. Writing at the end of the lost decade, García Canclini's provocative attempt at what he terms "border studies" provides a set of tools for disturbing existing scholarly approaches to geopolitical boundaries as well as social and media borders. The Argentine's central project involves examining the symbolic markets of modernism as accomplices to twentieth-century modernization projects across the region. Ultimately, he demonstrates how socioeconomic and cultural modernism, both of which continued to exercise a disproportionate influence in Latin America in comparison to other regions of the globe, cannot be approached separately or as distinct from the market. Thus he characterizes modernity as a product of "elites and the state apparatuses," a utopian vision that does not represent the reality of Latin America's masses (7).

Given the coexistence of premodern and traditional indigenous groups alongside advanced industrial societies, the concept of postmodernism inaccurately suggests a termination of the modernization project, thus García Canclini unpacks this new historical moment through the concept of hybridity. Because of the religious and cultural syncretism imposed by colonizing Europeans, García Canclini notes that Latin America has a 500-year history of hybridity. Yet the use of popular media for reimagining mass culture inscribes this tension with new political significance. The contact zones where contradictory semiotic and cultural markers populate public space are primary examples of this new hybridity, where the national and the international meet through traditional and technological means. Significantly for García Canclini, while such hybridity characterizes the diversity of peoples in political centers such as New York City, since the 1970s, these attributes are even more formative at the periphery, as is evident where the US–Mexico border separates developed and developing states of modernization, yet fuses their cultures (233). In contrast to contemporary North American literary theories of postmodernism that describe the third world by essentializing it, García Canclini thus demonstrates how heterogeneity or impurity function in a transcultural rather than unilateral sense.

García Canclini's dismissal of postmodern periodization provides a means of distinctly contemplating *The Perón Novel* as an intersection between popular media and written history. Yet the manner in which García Canclini defines modernism is also instructive for our purposes, particularly because the four distinct subprojects that undergird modernization—secularization, the expansion of science and capital, innovation, and democratization—enter into conflict when implemented by competing institutions (12–13). Drawing on Marxist critic Roberto Schwarz's own analysis, García Canclini argues that the practice of Brazilian cultural modernism that emerged in the 1920s in fact facilitated the construction of national identity rather than provided a means for denationalizing, whereas its socioeconomic equivalent largely brought structural changes up through the 1970s via new communication technologies and the commodification of cultural goods (52–55). As an ordering project, modernism sought to catalogue the history of various groups and cultures within rigid categories, with institutions (museums, libraries, official celebrations, etc.) gaining a monopoly on constructing the national past by determining what constituted patrimony, even though marginal groups were frequently ignored by these organizational apparatuses.

In tandem with these boundaries' erosion, García Canclini coins two neologisms to illustrate how cultural hybridity erases the markers of modernism: decollection and deterritorialization. If the construction of specialized collections of high art helped determine class distinctions between the cultured and the masses during much of the twentieth century, the technology of reproduction (photocopiers, video recorders, videos, etc.) has democratized access to such collections and in some cases invalidated the hierarchies supporting classical order altogether. Perhaps even more radically, deterritorialization—understood as both multidirectional migration and the critique of the structuralist bias that underpins imperial studies and dependency theories—challenges the association of the popular with the national. Satellites, computers, and other forms of technology delocalize information and thus "impede our continuing to see the confrontations of peripheral countries as frontal combats with geographically defined nations" (229). The point is not to celebrate such processes but rather document the destabilizing effects of their transgressions.

Another way of approaching the erasure of "referents of legitimacy" involves history, for with no clear means of claiming authenticity, modern ideals become circumscribed by the reproduction of popular culture far more representative of ordinary citizens. Modern history is based on institutions, where museums remove their referents from their original locations and freeze them in time, literally preserving the separation between audience and authority. By contrast, García Canclini argues that cultural history is not a concrete practice but rather an attitude, for it involves public engagement with modern historical markers. Monuments, for example, reify key historical figures, although citizens have increasingly chosen to interact with these sites, spraying them with graffiti to express criticism of social order. Similarly, such monuments' authority can be contested by covering them with publicity announcements contradicting the monumental identity through markers of consumption (222).

As is already apparent, Martínez utilizes this very strategy to question the monumental history that Perón constructs in his falsified memoirs. The memoirs represent a modernist attempt to create a monolithic account of the past, whereas the hybridity central to *The Perón Novel* marks its palimpsest upon the memoirs as publicly engaging with the general's ossified monument. Yet there remains one final term within García Canclini's equation that illuminates the fictional Perón's attempts to indoctrinate the masses, for perhaps the primary target of Martínez's decollection is populism itself. Following his proposition that modernization is an elitist project, García Canclini analyzes three conflicting means through which hegemony has imagined the popular majority as the opposite of cultured. While anthropology has understood "popular" as embodying the traditional or peasant past (folklore), and mass media appeals to popular culture (the masses), politicians attempt to anticipate the will of "the people" (populism). The paradox of Argentine and Brazilian populism in the twentieth century, García Canclini maintains, is that while promising to incorporate excluded sectors of the population through cultural and economic distribution, its failure to make lasting structural changes leads to resurgent oppression of the national majority. In García Canclini's words, "This staging of the popular has been a mix of participation and simulacrum. From Vargas and Perón to recent populisms, the effective revalorization of the popular classes, the defense of labor rights, the diffusion of their culture and their art go together with imaginary stagings of their representation" (191). In this sense, the convergence of the culture industry with populism is vital, because it provides the illusion of meaningful participation through public demonstrations, public rites, and other "performances," although these are ultimately mediated by the press and corrupted by the marketplace. Curiously, because one of populism's strategies evokes premodern values associated with nativism and public protest, the postmodern shift has also compromised the effectiveness of the populist platform. While its authority was eroded by the neoliberal response to the economic crisis of the 1980s, this deterritorialization is additionally a product of the fragmentation of media representation and the substitution of militant participation for marketing (192).

Significantly, García Canclini's claim that the power wrested by the visual is "the staging of a double loss: of the script and of the author" (244) provides not only a description of postmodern hybridity, but it also has bearing on Perón's fictional and nonfictional representation. As opposed to reviving Barthes's death of the author, García Canclini demands the public's agency in choosing their historical symbols. As I will argue for the remainder of this chapter, the loss of the script (the memoirs) and the author (both Perón and Martínez) are the two determining tragedies of *The Perón Novel*. If the novel is ultimately postmodern, it is through the illustration of the localized practices of decollection and deterritorialization. Similar to García Canclini, Martínez does not valorize these processes, for he fully recognizes the futility of writing a novel or presenting journalism given the increased resonance of visual culture. In an attempt to present a means of engaging the past with the present through the memoirs and the counter-memoirs, both the author and his characters ironically end up constructing relics of the past.

DECOLLECTION, DETERRITORIALIZATION, AND THE LOSS OF THE SCRIPT

Martínez applies deterritorialization to the Peronist phenomenon from the outset, confusing the center-periphery tension of nationalism, particularly through the irony of the leader's unwilling return from the margins of power to a location that is marginal to Europe. When Perón receives telegrams imploring him to return to his fatherland, he notes with cynicism, "The only home in Argentina is exile" (*Perón Novel* 5). As the novel opens, Perón, López Rega, Isabel, acting President Cámpora, and the rest of his entourage of over one hundred governors and congressmen are flying over the Atlantic Ocean to Buenos Aires, where throngs of supporters are gathering in welcome. As Perón is disoriented by how few of the statesmen he recognizes, it becomes clear that a majority of them represent López Rega's own political networking. Martínez inserts symbolic details, making this figurative turbulence literal when the airplane weathers a storm crossing from one hemisphere to the other. When informed that the flight has reached land over Brazil, Perón refuses to celebrate in the cockpit, noting, "All I ever got from Brazil was trouble and bad luck" (10).

Indeed, the disorientation is not only geographic but also temporal. On multiple occasions Martínez returns to the plane's symbolic arrival to the southern hemisphere on the shortest day of the year. Yet it is a seemingly innocuous statement by Isabel regarding the plane's flight plan as "contrary to the direction of time" (9) that takes on greater implications when Perón discovers thirty-year-old documents on his seat showing routes from Aerolíneas Argentinas and national railroad networks long out of service. Martínez intimates that Perón is stuck in time; his return to Argentina is predicated on recuperating the persona and politics of the man who was deposed in 1955. It is precisely for this reason that the memoirs, which claim to represent his life up until he first took office, are so important, serving as the imagined bridge between Perón's past rule and the present, mythological credentials for a man losing the battle against time.

Whether left or right, young or old, one of the most notable features of the novel is how remarkably conscious every character is of history as a philosophical concept in which they must participate or accept the consequences of others constructing it to their own benefit. Unsurprisingly, however, it is the general and Martínez's stand-in, Zamora, who have the most power to affect the creation of national perceptions about the past, thus their opposing conceptions regarding history's hybridity and its public engagement circumscribe the novel's politics. For as much as Martínez foregrounds the active distortion of the historical record, he does not pretend that investigative journalism is an ethical panacea. It is clear that Zamora does not relish his assignment to interview Perón's forgotten family members and military associates. His editor believes they need to dig up hidden truths about the general in order to compete in the market with other tabloids—"exhibiting history," as he puts it, by bringing these witnesses to Ezeiza to publicly greet and perhaps compromise the general—although Zamora detests this tack as "cesspool journalism" (31–32). In contrast to the monolithic or monumental status that Perón imagines for his autobiographical history, the counter-memoirs are postmodern in the sense that they are polyphonic, fragmented, and contradictory, although they are never presented as harbingers of truth that cancel out Perón's lies, merely hybrid products of the market that corrupt its subject in the process of competing for public attention.

Exemplifying this duel of narratives in alternating chapters, in between extended excerpts of the memoirs that are presented in chronological order, each subsequent chapter features an equally extensive passage from the counter-memoirs consumed by one of the witnesses, who by turns write notes in the margins of the page or use the interviews to reflect on their own disappearing livelihoods. Chapters 4 and 5, for example, demonstrate this dialectic and the loss of both script and author that Martínez revisits under multiple guises. The former chapter finds Perón reading the memoirs alone in his Spanish home, unable to distinguish what he has written and what López Rega has since added to his account of his family's origins. After starting with a "real" excerpt from the published autobiography,[16] Perón begins to write (fictional) marginalia to temper some of what he believes to be López Rega's excessive writing

---

16. Both the recorded interview and the published memoirs begin with the Perón family's arrival in Argentina, and the novel at times cites the original faithfully, as the very first line of the memoir reread by Perón reveals (*Perón Novel* 42), with other faithful fragments continuing thereafter (45–47).

style. In the following chapter, Montoneros guerilla members read the first section of the *Horizonte* counter-memoirs, which provide a substantially different account of Perón's forefathers and upbringing, and the device allows the newspaper narrative to be reproduced as a document for the reader. As a subsequent military report reveals, a copy of the counter-memoirs is confiscated from the Montoneros' hideout, with a prosecutor's note claiming that the satirical marginalia written by the leftist urban guerillas is proof of their extremist ideology (220). Echoing García Canclini, postmodern history is not a stage but rather an attitude, a means of interacting with or defacing monuments, which is precisely what the group does with the memoirs. This consumption is nonetheless bound up with the act of reception, for neither socioeconomic nor cultural modernism can be uncoupled from the marketplace.

As a particular encounter between López Rega and Perón demonstrates, the commodification of the past is not lost upon Perón; to the contrary, he welcomes it in no uncertain terms. The secretary plays a cassette recording of Martínez's interview to demonstrate how Perón contradicted an earlier version of the story, explaining, "Documents can be erased, destroyed. That doesn't worry me. What I want is for you to choose one version of the story. Just one, whichever" (182). Although López Rega is clearly manipulating Perón, the general's own duplicity is perhaps best encapsulated by his response:

> The reason I've been a leading figure in history time and time again, is precisely because I have contradicted myself.... History is a whore, López. She always goes to the one who pays the most. And the more legends attached to my name, the richer I am and the more weapons I have to defend myself with. Leave everything the way it is. I'm not after a statue, but something bigger. To rule history. To fuck her in the ass. (182)

Of course, Perón is after a monument of sorts through his self-aggrandizing testimonial. The problem is that the technologies that he has utilized to orchestrate his ascendance to power—radio and tango propaganda, written manifestos and journalism—have had their public influence wrested away, replaced by newer technologies that ultimately expose the illusion of his attempt to revive the myth who was deposed in 1955.

As print journalism, the counter-memoirs are equally susceptible, and the fate of these contrapuntal texts demonstrates Martínez's awareness of the shift in media technology across Latin America as television eroded the power of the republic of letters. Zamora's editor's plan to ship the witnesses to Ezeiza Airport backfires when they are discovered by some of the military personnel responsible for masterminding the massacre. The group of elderly is quickly forced onto the rented bus, driven out into deserted fields beyond the city, and abandoned as darkness falls. Each of the members clings to his or her copy of *Horizonte* in much the same way Perón has clutched the memoirs as a sign of validation, though this desire is frustrated. The reader of Martínez's novel has largely gained access to the counter-memoirs through the device of the witnesses discussing and reading the newspaper serial, yet the documents both literally and figuratively disintegrate in the midst of Perón's emblematic arrival in darkness. Some find that pages have been ripped out during the group's rough treatment, others can no longer make out the letters on the page, while another finds that his copy has disintegrated in the rain. Not only are the witnesses left without any physical traces of their participation in the journalistic exhibition, but it is unclear how many readers—if any—have been swayed by tabloid material, despite the powerful collection of voices it contains. In other words, this modernist "exhibition" of print history has failed to break down the barrier between culture and audience. This is made all the more explicit when Zamora, who is stranded in traffic, realizes he has missed Perón's arrival and decides to leave the taxi, entering the blue-collar neighborhoods around him. "I see history through a keyhole," he concedes. "I only know what appears on television." He feels fear upon stepping out into the crowds, for it "is easy to write history. Plunging headlong into it could relocate the meridian of feelings" (350–51).

Curiously, it is at this point that Zamora also becomes figuratively absorbed by the very masses that Perón hopes to inculcate with his memoirs. As Zamora discovers, however, nobody remembers the autobiography or has read the special issue; instead they gather at windows to stare into homes with television to visually participate in Perón's staged return. Significantly, while Perón's status as a puppet of López Rega's may be largely undetectable in the written memoirs, the visual medium of television reveals the ruse. Spectators begin to perceive that the secretary's lips anticipate the words that Perón uses to welcome the nation, as if prompting him. Yet once again the medium proves to substitute reality. Rather than accept Perón's deception, the peasants refuse to believe that the man on the screen is the general, alleging a state hoax as they disband. Symbolic of the death of the nation, the book's epilogue takes place one year later on the day of Perón's funeral, and it is once again television that mediatizes the event for the poor in shantytowns unable to join the thousands of mourners who follow his casket through the city center. In death, Perón has been returned to his mythological status, his body, visible in the coffin for the television, in military uniform after eighteen years of civilian dress. While radio commentators report on the wakes held by workers' unions, it is ironically the masses that are excluded from accompanying the body into the Congress building, as the doors shut and television screen gives way to static. In the novel's final image, a shantytown inhabitant embraces her television as if it were a surrogate for Perón's body. Referring to him in messianic terms, she feels "enveloped" by the departed man's smile and holds out hope for his resurrection. This is the reaction that Perón might have hoped his memoirs would produce, although he never has a chance to circulate the new version, since this textual document is supplanted by the immediacy of his visual reality that compromises his ability to reach "the masses." Thus if Martínez's 1970 print interview in *Panorama* helped bring the general back to life, the image of Perón's death secures his immortality.

CONCLUSION: AFTER PERÓN

Given the central role in García Canclini's account that institutions have for exhibiting and classifying history in the modernist sense, how paradoxical it is that *The Perón Novel* helped contribute to the very mythology it seeks to problematize. After publishing *Santa Evita* and *The General's Memoirs*, Martínez learned that plans to open a museum dedicated to Eva Perón included the inscription on plaques of phrases attributed to the First Lady. Yet he noted that one of the engraved popular sayings was in fact his own invention in *The Perón Novel*, meaning that his character had modified the historical record, as subsequent popular cultural references solidified the apocryphal saying's place within the public imaginary.[17] Thus, however this false document is periodized, García Canclini's insistence upon the coexistence of both modern and postmodern conceptions within hybrid cultures remains a constructive paradigm for scrutinizing the novel's contradictory explorations of power and the popular, or the national and the regional for that matter. And Martínez is very aware of the paradox. What is left after the cultural turn, he rhetorically asks during Argentina's subsequent financial crisis: "Those who can buy books continue to accumulate them in their libraries—the libraries remain elegantly adorned—but almost nobody reads them anymore. The few intellectuals who remain write in the void" (*Réquiem* 254). By this point he harbors no illusions what the implications of this trend are for the impact of his recently published novel, although this should not discourage public intellectual engagement.

---

17. On more than one occasion, Martínez's Perón remembers the words with which Eva supposedly won his heart (which were to be inscribed on the museum plaque): "Thank you for existing." In *Santa Evita*, Martínez's narrator falsely claims to have glossed this expression by lip-reading old documentaries, though the journalist later revealed that he actually invented the phrase for *The Perón Novel* (*Réquiem* 345–66).

Martínez believes that unlike those of its hemispheric neighbors, Argentine intellectuals and political power have historically ignored one another. Yet Perón's rise to power indelibly altered this relationship, for he fashioned himself as a military historian and an intellectual in the numerous monographs he published domestically and from exile. At a moment when the reflection of national models and structural challenges has given way to attempts by the neoliberal wing of Peronism to erase its dirty history, this public stance against the grain takes on even greater implications (251–54).[18]

Martínez writes *The Perón Novel* as a starting point for understanding how the opposing political factions and the exhausted promise of populism helped generate the perfect conditions for the Dirty War and the end of democracy that precipitated the lost decade. He published the book as the nation was attempting to find resolution via the 1985 trials of the military juntas responsible for covering up the torture and disappearance of uncountable citizens, and his narrative of failure proved prescient; the general public was disappointed by the light sentences that were handed down to a majority of the generals (Hodges 279–80). Yet Martínez destabilizes the populist response to the Reorganization Process equally in his novel and his journalism, arguing that the state is not alone responsible. The middle class and the masses provided passive social consent to the violence, initially supporting the Montoneros in 1973, which led to the state's repressive response, as well as accepting the coup in 1976 and López Rega's death squads (*Réquiem* 134).

The nation had not healed, despite the transition to civilian rule, and the armed response of urban guerillas continued throughout the 1980s. Thus Martínez's decision to move away from fiction and return the following decade to "true documents" in *The General's Memoirs* suggests a reaffirmed need for establishing the lines separating fact and mythology confused by the poststructural turn in the previous years. As much a literary critic as an author, Martínez is the first to suggest that the poststructural theories popularized by Foucault, Derrida, and Hayden White have passed out of fashion, and that critiquing the pretense of power is no longer enough to sustain historical fiction. This is because the abuse of power is not unique to the right; the 1980s revealed the failure of the leftist revolutionary projects in Cuba and Nicaragua. Instead, fiction is part of the larger project of cultural history that concerns itself with examining the habits and obsessions of historical "characters" that would never otherwise enter into social or political history (*Réquiem* 351–52).

---

18. In 1991, Martínez accused President Menem of having lied about his campaign promise to prosecute members of the military for their roles in the Dirty War. "The past has already taught us all it can teach us," Martínez cites the Peronist disciple as saying. "If we don't learn to forget, we will turn into a statue made out of salt" (*Réquiem* 35).

Extrapolating from García Canclini, the loss of the script and the author in *The Perón Novel* does not signify the impossibility of history, then, but rather the need for increased ethical representation that counters empty visual signification and marketing campaigns that have distanced historical myth from reality. In this sense, far from representing a disingenuous hybridity, the journalist's desire to read documents both ways in *The General's Memoirs*—as trustworthy evidence and corrupt invention—represents his own popular gesture. Decollecting the documents from his personal archive, he places them directly in the hands of readers and allows them to draw their own conclusions. If for García Canclini postmodern history is a question of attitude rather than a concrete practice, Martínez's own attitude has clearly evolved, and his basis for reconstruction is less postmodern than it is democratic. To revisit Perón each decade was to revisit his own exile, the end of national democracy he witnessed from abroad. And to remind the public of the global and regional ramifications of Perón's own exile was thus to remind that same public that the medium is not reality, whether that medium is history or the general himself.

CHAPTER 4

The "Dialectics" of Feminist Caribbean History

Laura Antillano, José Martí, and the Venezuelan Lost Decade

IN 1946, US officials hailed the election of Venezuela's Constitutional Congress as a "demonstration in democracy for all America" ("Betancourt Party Seems Winner" 6), yet the country's recently established Democratic Action Party would have little time to enjoy its victories. Its center-left platform of agrarian reform and labor rights protection became a Cold War casualty two years later when the military overthrew the popular government and initiated a decade-long dictatorship.[1] The two Democratic Action presidents who briefly served before the coup, Rómulo Betancourt and novelist Rómulo Gallegos, went into exile in the United States and Cuba, returning only when civilian power was restored in 1958. The political importance of popular protest and the return to democracy for hemispheric relations, however, was quickly overshadowed by the 1959 Cuban Revolution. As policymakers looked on to see if the country would follow the Cuban model or one more conducive to cooperation with the United States, Venezuela entered into a largely stable period at precisely the time that much of the rest of Latin America experienced increasingly authoritarian shifts.

---

1. The military's motives in 1948 were somewhat unclear, given its participation in a 1945 coup that overthrew the previous dictatorship and led to the first democratic elections in the country's history. Military leader Marcos Pérez Jiménez's assumption of the presidency may have capitalized on US suspicions regarding the earlier communist ties of President Rómulo Gallegos (Hellinger 65–66).

On the eve of the thirtieth anniversary of the nation's successful revolt against the dictatorship, however, its democratic principles were again under threat, this time as a consequence of the economic lost decade. Black Friday in 1983 marked the start of a protracted crisis that exhausted Venezuela's national reserves, as oil prices collapsed and the currency become devalued. In 1988, when President Andrés Pérez returned to office, the average labor wages were less than they had been during his first presidency, fifteen years earlier. The establishment of the multiparty Committee for State Reform (COPRE) produced a comprehensive report advocating for direct elections and decentralization of the government in 1986, yet the ruling parties failed to implement any of these recommendations, fueling disaffected citizens' increased alienation and resentment toward political corruption. After President Andrés Pérez announced an austerity plan complying with the International Monetary Fund, violent university campus protests signaled a turning point in the hegemony of the governing elite and the rioting in Caracas spread across the country (De la Cruz 188; Hellinger 174–78, 189). Fears that the military would intervene during this period of social instability, after remaining on the sidelines for several decades, proved to be correct when Hugo Chávez claimed responsibility on television for the failed 1992 coup that would later launch his political career.[2]

Importantly, while popular unrest became the most visible symbol of national disaffection, members of COPRE had been attempting to accomplish democratic structural reforms by appealing to both lawmakers and the general public. Importantly, while social and economic prescriptions formed the core of their proposal, the committee also dedicated space to the importance of democratizing access to culture and education. And key to envisioning what the body termed "cultural democracy" was the gestation of a Latin American spirit, in recognition of the increasing importance of regional partnerships to national sovereignty (*La reforma del estado* 369). After releasing a series of bureaucratic documents and statements by committee members in 1986, the committee also launched its own quarterly magazine, *Estado & Reforma*.[3] Several of its thematic issues sought to make the various juridical aspects more accessible to the general electorate, going so far as to publish a 1987 special issue under the title "Heterodoxy and the State" (see Figure 2). In contrast to its usually dry combination of documents, the special volume features inter-

---

2. Chapter 11 in Tarver Denova and Frederick contextualizes the consequences of the government's incompetence and corruption during the 1980s.

3. In 1986, COPRE published the multivolume *Documentos para la reforma del estado* to address questions of governmental leadership and access to education, which was followed in 1988 by the more culturally integrative perspective of *La reforma del estado*.

FIGURE 2. The cover of COPRE's 1987 special issue of *Estado & Reforma*

views with five individuals outside the government, including sociologists, talk show hosts, and television directors, and clearly targeted a popular audience through its culturally oriented perspectives. This is all the more apparent from the cover, which, in contrast to the sparseness of previous issues, splashes the images of the five recognized figures across its front and back. At the same time, these photographs of male authorities also made visible an implicit public trend: whether in COPRE or *Estado & Reforma,* women were ironically almost entirely excluded from the debate over how to make the state more inclusive in its representation.

As a journalist, professor, author, and screenwriter, Laura Antillano has revisited these key democratic shifts in post–World War II Venezuelan history through a variety of genres. During the 1980s, she interviewed historians and adapted ex-president Gallegos's short stories for television. After becoming the first woman to win the Caracas newspaper *El Nacional*'s short story competition in 1977,[4] her ensuing second novel *Perfume de Gardenia* (*Scent of Gardenias*, 1982) fictionalized a personal quest to learn about her father's imprisonment during the military dictatorship, and it marks the first time she began incorporating both real and invented documents into literature to access an era where official history remained under tight control (Interview).[5] Yet it is her third novel, *Solitaria solidaria* (*Alone but Committed*, 1990) that emerges in direct response to the Inter-American lost decade.[6] Here Antillano inserts supposed archival documents to locate the country's economic woes of the 1980s in a historical context—illustrated by its description of public support for COPRE's unheeded recommendations—but also to consider the existential crisis provoked by the erosion of Venezuela's patriarchal society during the 1970s, when the number of women entering the workforce and participating in politics doubled (Hellinger 150). By following a female academic historian who negotiates the pitfalls of personal and public politics from 1974 through 1988, the prolific Venezuelan author establishes the period as one not of loss but of transition, both in terms of gender and critical national identity. Beyond exploring the disjuncture between female agency and postdictatorial Venezuelan history through women's cultural production, *Alone but Committed* is particularly noteworthy for foregrounding both the role of history as a concept and the everyday reality of historians who struggle to record the past with few resources—all while resituating the country within a larger regional network by subverting discourses of national consensus.

The autobiographical overlaps between Antillano, a literature professor at a university in Valencia, Venezuela, and her protagonist, who teaches in the Department of History in the same location, have been noted (Rivas, *La novela* 216). Yet more revealing of the novel's politics is Antillano's engagement with famed Venezuelan historian, journalist, and politician Rámon Velásquez, who served as president of COPRE for several years. Shortly after *Alone but*

---

4. "The Moon is Not Oven-Baked-Bread," the short story for which she won the 1977 installment of the award, would become the basis for her subsequent historical novel *Scent of Gardenias* (1982).

5. The novel tells the generational family story of three women whose lives span a century of Venezuelan history through the Cold War military dictatorship. Its stylistic innovations—fragmentation, collages of multiple forms of popular cultural expression, and multiple female narrators—provide an earlier indication of Antillano's interest in cross-temporal female dialogues.

6. To my knowledge, no English-language research has been published on the text. The only reference I know of is by Menton, who translates its title *Alone and Committed* as part of a list of works he does not consider as new historical fiction, although I have slightly modified the wording based on correspondence with Antillano in which she discussed the title's origins in French student slogans during the 1968 civil unrest. All translations are my own.

Committed was published and Andrés Pérez was impeached, Velásquez would step in to serve as president of Venezuela (1993–1994). Antillano has pointed to the interview she performed with Velásquez in the early 1980s while she worked as a journalist as one of the factors that shaped her subsequent novel. She learned from the historian about his resistance during the military dictatorship, when he was imprisoned for collaborating on an indictment of the regime, *The Black Book of the Dictatorship* (1952). During their discussion, Velásquez referred to the nonfiction book that had landed him in jail as proof that there existed "no greater literature than the history of Venezuela" (Socorro 8). Antillano's representation of history's "literariness" thus stems not from postmodern iconoclasm but rather a concrete awareness of the danger critical writing about the past poses to discourses of modernization, and she makes this explicit by including Velásquez in the novel, when her protagonist—much like Antillano herself had done—interviews him about links between nineteenth-century and contemporary democracy.

To follow the trajectory of its recently divorced protagonist Zulay Montero from her arrival in the university's history department in 1974 to her receipt of tenure in 1988, the novel utilizes chronological flashbacks, locating her political awakening in her college years as a protest organizer in the late 1960s. Indeed, the novel's title poetically adapts a slogan from the French student demonstrations of 1968 (Interview). Montero's academic trajectory through the country's increasing disaffection subtly suggests parallels between the general public's desire for greater autonomy from the government and women's parallel search for autonomy within patriarchal society. At the same time, Antillano uses the historian's research to engage a separate thread of Venezuelan history and place democratic challenge under a microscope, for the novel hinges on Montero's discovery of a forgotten nineteenth-century archive containing a woman's diary entries under the autocratic rule of the self-proclaimed "Illustrious American," Antonio Guzmán Blanco. Comprising documents related to a woman identified as Leonara Armundeloy during the 1870s and 1880s, the archive includes letter correspondence and newspaper clippings, all of which are inserted into the present-day narrative in the form of the historian's own edits as she works to prepare a book for publication a century later. The effect of this temporal juxtaposition is to recalibrate the conventional framework of history. Far from championing modernization, Antillano's portrait of shared female experience questions the myth of progress, drawing attention to the continued need for greater labor and social equality despite evident improvements in women's general standing.

While the novel initially appears national in scope, Antillano's transhistorical strategy bridges separate historical geographies as well as periods, as evidenced by her incorporation of Caribbean intellectual José Martí into the diary narrative. Making use of Martí's documented journey from the United States to Venezuela in 1881 to establish the *Venezuelan Review,* Antillano presents him as an influential figure for the female diarist, taking advantage of Martí's symbolic capital to act as a bridge between regions within the hemisphere. As I will demonstrate shortly, Martí's "Our America" has been central to Latin American and Inter-American models of the engaged intellectual as well as self-determination against US aggression at the turn of the twentieth century, and echoes of this defiance are evident in the attitudes of Antillano's academic community in the contemporary setting as well.

Although a few collections have united research on female writing of historical literature across Latin America (Cunha-Giabbai, Weldt-Basson), women's contributions remain undertheorized, despite the fact that they have occurred parallel to literary shifts associated with male writers. Doubly marginalized in comparison to contemporary Mexican and Caribbean female authors, Antillano's fiction has not been widely analyzed outside of a Venezuelan context, which is ironic given the cultural alternative she provides to national history. With the exception of Luz Marina Rivas's Inter-American comparative framework ("La novela," *La novela*), virtually all scholarly engagements focus exclusively upon female subjectivity via the diaries as intimate writing. My argument in this chapter builds on Rivas as well as José David Saldívar to consider instead the tension created by the temporal dialectic at the heart of the false document, particularly evident in the novel's dialogic structure between two time periods, a question of form that has so far eluded sustained attention. Before undertaking a close reading of the text, I will first examine the importance of Martí's concept of separate Americas for the revival of Inter-American studies contemporary with the appearance of Antillano's book. Next, the chapter examines the existing body of feminist literary criticism on Antillano and her contemporaries, including Marina Rivas's compelling location of the author's work within an intrahistorical, regional Caribbean framework.

Recuperating the role of the contemporary historian as the novel's lynchpin reveals the importance of historical process, one that destabilizes the national frameworks under which both women are subjugated to instead examine common experience. Ultimately, Antillano does not negate history so much as create a self-deterministic model for bridging the gap between the "two histories"—dominant political historiography and peripheral history—that recalls Martí's own call for a historically based model of geographical identification. Thus far from parodying antecedents or maintaining an ironic distance from events, Antillano interrogates national referents from the position of a protagonist alienated from society because of her gender. Creating emotional affect by examining daily life experiences, she demonstrates how micro- and intrahistories—products of cultural and feminist historiography during the 1970s—can cumulatively provide a picture of the general population rather than reinscribe the consensus narrative dominated by a patriarchal, European logic. In the process of creating a parable of revisionist history, Antillano uses the past to demonstrate how the complex stakes of democracy are not only dependent upon national factors but also respond to challenging social questions introduced by hemispheric figures such as Martí (that remain relevant today).

FROM MARTÍ'S AMERICA TO THE INTER-AMERICAN FEMINIST DIALECTIC

As demonstrated by the breadth of contributions to Jeffrey Belnap and Raúl Fernández's *José Martí's "Our America": From National to Hemispheric Cultural Studies* (1998), the cultural capital of Latin American revolutionary figure José Martí has been appropriated by various twentieth-century models of hemispheric political resistance. Most famously laid out in "Nuestra América" ("Our America", 1891), Martí's call for a pan-Latin American solidarity contained an attendant critique of US imperialist expansion in the wake of the Mexican-American War, the country's incursions into Central America, and its impending intervention in the Caribbean. Keenly aware of hemispheric politics in the context of the Monroe Doctrine, the Cuban poet and essayist both admired and distrusted the United States, where he spent much of the last fifteen years of his life establishing the Cuban Revolutionary Party and organizing the island's War of Independence from Spain. During his travels across the Americas, he helped professionalize the field of journalism, founding literary magazines and blending genres in his reports about US and Latin American social issues. Yet if in "Mother America," a speech he delivered to the delegates of the first Pan-American Conference in 1889, Martí presents a poetic vision of Latin America's violent history as a means of forging a usable past, in "Our America" he strikes a more aggressive stance, categorically distinguishing the history of North America from conceptions of "our" (by which he means Hispanic) America based upon divergent social histories (*Our America* 75). Martí extends the latter concept to ethnically encompass "Mestizo America," celebrating Latin America's indigenous heritage, negating the logic of prejudice toward Afro-descendants, and advocating for local political leadership, all while demanding limits on foreign influence. It is no accident that echoes of these concepts, which Martí had actually first developed in Central America during the 1870s (Martí and Foner 24), find their way into Antillano's postnational portrait of Venezuela during the lost decade.

Yet not only does Martí anticipate many of the categories that have somewhat paradoxically come to shape new American Studies, but his cautionary rhetoric also provides a template for Latin Americanists' distrust of the field's recent global designs. Thus, while he acknowledges that competing political interests historically challenged national stability in postcolonial Latin America, Martí worries that the region is beset by a new colonial threat, namely "a risk that does not come from itself but from the difference in origins, methods, and interests between the two halves of the continent, and the time is near at hand when an enterprising and vigorous people who scorn or ignore Our America will even so approach it and demand a close relationship" (*Our America* 93). North American "madness and ambition" prompt Martí's famous call for continental unity through a recognition of shared history, for the "pressing need of Our America is to show itself as it is, one in spirit and intent, swift conqueror of a suffocating past, stained only by the enriching blood drawn from hands that struggle to clear away the ruins, and from the scars left upon us by our masters" (93). The above allusion to slavery gestures to a shared condition that extends beyond ethnic and class lines to yolk US and European roles in the continent's conditions of inequality.

As one of the most influential early Caribbean intellectuals to both position the region as a central component of the Americas and question the discourse of hemispheric Manifest Destiny, Martí's self-deterministic model for cultural engagement became a cornerstone reference of post-revolutionary Cuban intellectuals. Indicative of the cultural turn, Roberto Fernández Retamar notably reframes Martí's master-slave dialectic in *Caliban* (1971) by reinterpreting European and Latin American adaptations of Shakespeare's *The Tempest* (1611). Retamar dislocates Martí's "mestizo America" from the colonial legacy of miscegenation to argue for *mestizaje* as an active strategy of cultural hybridity. In similar fashion to Silviano Santiago's contemporary characterization of peripheral intellectuals' "space in-between" (see chapter 6), Retamar rejects the role of Latin America as an imitation of imported European bourgeois culture, exploring the practice of cultural anthropophagy as a form of political resistance. In contrast to Uruguayan writer Enrique Rodó's *Ariel* (1901), also written in response to the threat of US imperialism, Retamar argues that it is in fact the figure of Caliban that best expresses the identity of "our America" because the figure rejects European thought, mastering his oppressor's own language in order to threaten colonial domination. Arguing that the United States used the 1898 Spanish-American War to convert Cuba into its first "neocolony," the Cuban cultural critic utilizes Martí's literary history to define an oppositional paradigm to continued issues of political dependency.

As perhaps the most recognized revivalist of the divided America metaphor, Retamar has contributed greatly to Martí's association with an exceptionalist school of Latin American thought, albeit a reactive sentiment created in response to North American designs. Nonetheless, the new wave of US-based scholars starting in the 1990s recast Martí as a potential symbol of hemispheric unity, recognizing that his dialectical theorization could be synthesized to rectify critical breaches in propounded methodologies and thus reconnect the two area studies regions through a self-conscious historical framework. Important examples of this include Laura Lomas's *Translating Modernity* (2008), an exploration of how the metaphorical translation of Martí's message and history as a migrant writer made him into a hemispheric spokesperson, as well as Ricardo Ortíz's "Hemispheric Vertio" (2002), which highlights the underexamined place of contemporary Canada in Martí's North American gaze.

Most notably, José David Saldívar has repeatedly propounded Martí's disruptive politics as a necessary component of any American cultural studies, whether through the prism of border studies (*Border Matters*, 1995) or an innovative literary approach to world-systems analysis (*Trans-Americanity*, 2012). Yet it is the critic's first work, *The Dialectics of Our America* (1991), the first chapter of which is featured in Firmat's seminal collection, that resituates Martí and Retamar within an Inter-American historical dialectic aimed at revealing the power of the regime, notably by harnessing White's metahistory and Doctorow's "false documents." In conversation with Retamar, Saldívar believes Doctorow's work "can be seen as part of the general negation by the American *nueva narrativa* that seeks to break down the distinction between the novel and history as institutions" (*Dialectics* 160n31). For Saldívar, linking opposition to the US ruling "center" inherent in both new Latin and ethnic North American writers echoes the role of Martí, complicating the prevailing tendency to consider these groups as peripheral recipients of global cultural flows rather than producers. Conceiving of Martí as an early "cultural anthropologist," Saldívar thus demonstrates how oppositional critical practice results in comparative cultural studies that can remap the geopolitical borders of American studies, centralize foreign relations, and expose hidden histories of imperialism—not to further fragment the cultural imaginary, but to make the field "whole" again (*Dialectics* 5).

In an interview after receiving an award for *Alone but Committed,* Antillano highlights her keen awareness of Martí's symbolic currency as scholar and military tactician, explaining that the book served as a pretext for her to peel back his constructed revolutionary legacy to recover his humanity (Socorro 8). In other words, Antillano performs in fictional terms the postnational fusion of history and the peripheral that Saldívar concurrently wills upon US studies. Though if the Inter-American scholar imagines Martí challenging the concepts of nation and canon central to US identity, Antillano reconsiders Venezuela's positivist narrative of progress by establishing women as producers of history rather than as peripheral observers. Put another way, by reframing Martí's geopolitical dialectic, Antillano explores a temporal dialectic, juxtaposing the lives of two women from distinct historical milestones unacknowledged by the official record. Additionally, Antillano explicitly sets the construction of these private histories—which constitute a Pan-Caribbean female identity—in opposition to the public acceptance of the androcentric political historical record. In the novel's final section, Montero has received research leave to complete her book analyzing Guzmán Blanco's private correspondence, and she relocates to the very Caribbean port town where diarist Armundeloy lived to reflect upon the continued challenges involved in confronting new forms of patriarchal control. "The history of the battles for power: is this perhaps the history of men?" (*Alone* 319) she rhetorically asks, though her materialist approach to political history is clearly designed to articulate an alternative focusing upon creating new forms of social solidarity at odds with nation-based models of progress. Both alone and committed, as the novel's title suggests, Antillano's female characters also conceive of history in dialectical terms, as the author distinguishes between History with a "capital H," as she puts it, which constitutes the publicly circulated discourses about "great men," and a form of history that characterizes the majority of Latin Americans: that which is never recorded because it "pertains to those who always reside outside circles of power, those who stay behind, making food, taking care of children, learning [indirectly] about what has happened through the press, rather than because they are protagonists of events" (Socorro 8). Outside the lens of political history, this domestic sphere represents a longstanding periphery that remains undertheorized because of its continued invisibility, though fiction has the opportunity to partially address this space of forgetting. In this sense, Antillano imagines the possibility of unifying both dominant and peripheral forms of history, a synthetic process that is less a form of radical feminist politics than an alternative to the tendencies of new historical fiction to privilege fragmentation, the dissolution of the subject, and a lack of referentiality (González Stephan 33).

ANTILLANO'S MARTÍ, ARCHIVES, AND THE SPECTER OF NATIONALISM

The gendered terms of the novel's original title, *Solitaria solidaria*, capture a female subject, referring at times separately to Montero and Armundeloy, but also to the women's eventual relationship across time. The title also establishes an invisible dialectic between exclusion and belonging immediately visible in the opening chapter, as Montero divorces her husband and relocates to Venezuela's third-largest city, Valencia, arriving with no family or contacts. Newly appointed at the university, Montero discovers a misplaced file in the library archives containing the diaries and correspondence of a nineteenth-century female adolescent, Leonara Armundeloy. The confessional writing documents the latter's life over the course of two decades (1877–1896) and reveals her gradual transformation from a passive member of a well-connected bourgeois family into a feminist labor organizer, a process of transgression all the more impressive because of the lack of resources available to her in comparison to her eventual biographer Montero. Although Armundeloy participates in musical programs such as the "Bello Sexo Artístico," outgrowths of the Guzmán Blanco's extension of mandatory education to women in 1870 as they began to be incorporated into the social and economic life of the nation, the era did not permit social or intellectual independence (Luengo Comerón 894). Armundeloy is aware that there are few alternatives to marriage, having seen her younger cousin forced into a convent against her will. While Montero will later associate battles for power with male historiography, an outraged Armundeloy complicates such a reading by comparing her aunt's domination of her cousin's body and mind to Guzmán Blanco's hegemonic control over the country: "They will say that one thing doesn't have anything to do with the other, but both are determined by the same measuring stick: the exercise of power" (121).

If, as Antillano suggests, the novel serves as a device for her to gain proximity to the historical figure of Martí, he in turn acts as a device for legitimizing Armundeloy as a journalist and engaged intellectual. Antillano thus takes advantage of Martí's documented visit from the United States to Venezuela in 1881, when he founded the *Venezuelan Review*, to imagine a chance encounter with Armundeloy and her father on the very day he is recorded to have arrived in Puerto Cabello. The shipping port is a center for industrialization of the country, signaled by Armundeloy's father's recent order of printing presses from Europe and the impending construction of a railroad to Valencia. The young woman's political consciousness begins in great part through her contact with Martí, his facilitation of her introduction into literary society, and her subsequent involvement in printing and disseminating his literary journal, all connections that lead to her involvement in a host of male-dominated activities, including journalism and state-funded cartography projects. In a diary entry from 1883, she reflects on Guzmán Blanco's lavish lifestyle in Europe and the United States, noting, "I, for my part, discover every day a larger country that is full of terrible calamities, and the purest feeling of generosity in its people, at the same time, a country of the silent, of the weak. . . . My friend José Martí had the subtlety to make me see things that I was unaware of, certainly painful, but nonetheless extant" (137).

Thus it is Martí who takes Armundeloy to visit the aging lawyer and social activist Cecilio Acosta, who lectures her on the growing role of literature in social and political education, his assertion of literature's unavoidable artificiality reflexively nodding to Antillano's own narrative linking device. Shortly thereafter, Armundeloy's diary briefly recounts the well-documented fallout Martí had with Guzmán Blanco when the very real Acosta died and Martí paid homage to his legacy in the second issue of the *Venezuelan Review*. Incurring the Illustrious American's dissatisfaction, the Cuban is banished from the country, halting Armundeloy's involvement in the printing project. Nonetheless, the platonic yet suggestive relationship established between the public orator and the private diarist during his brief stay leads them to maintain contact over the course of the next decade while he organizes against the Spanish in the United States. This bond is attested to by the correspondence also preserved in the archive, as the two journalists collaborate on articles and political consciousness-raising until an 1895 Cuban dispatch reports Martí's death during the conflict. As a hemispheric citizen who speaks against the effects of neocolonialism, Martí comes to signify a negation of the Illustrious American's use of literary and painting competitions to transform art into state-sponsored propaganda.

Martí thus serves as a counterpart to Armundeloy's cousin Sergio, with whom she shares a brief romantic encounter before he leaves to pursue his education in Paris. As she faithfully waits his return, correspondence between the two reveals Sergio's embrace of European cultural standards and his conservative support for Guzmán Blanco, and he even suggests she desist from adopting positions on national politics about which she knows little (80). Under Martí's tutelage, however, Armundeloy ceases to accommodate Sergio and instead pursues community engagement, and given her increasing experience as a newspaper editor, she soon shifts from mapping out her personal life to obtaining a job as a cartographer and designing a map of the nation. The task requires archival research to redraw currently ambiguous political borders (138), a process of revision similar to Montero's own public lectures at her state institution. As such, both women must work within the context of men's battles for power, and while they cannot ultimately reject the conditions of the state, they can outline a common female experience that finds solidarity across geopolitical boundaries.

In fact, Antillano is at great pains to situate this experience in a larger context that consistently echoes Martí's political concerns. Once Armundeloy gets involved in the mapping project, for example, she becomes increasingly aware of international politics. Thus, she soon learns about the Monroe Doctrine when the Venezuelan government discovers the British have arrived at the mouth of the Orinoco River with the intent of installing a telegraph line. After sending Guzmán Blanco as a foreign minister to London, the government calls for US military support to rebuff the English invasion under the conditions of the Monroe Doctrine. The industrious Armundeloy even reproduces a section from the drafted memorandum, an ostensibly legitimate document whose source is cited cryptically in a footnote.[7] In the end, however, the state physically imposes itself, for Armundeloy's generation of women has much less room to dissent from normative gender roles than does Montero's network. As a consequence, her attempt to organize workers to promote social equality leads to her own downfall. After the death of her husband during a police raid on a public demonstration the couple organizes, Armundeloy's final, inconclusive entries reveal that she herself has been tortured before release from custody.

The dialectic between neocolonialism and national sovereignty is not limited to the historical narrative, however. In one of the few lighter moments in the text, Montero's colleague from the history department, a politically engaged priest involved in liberation theology, playfully appropriates the sentiments of Martí's "Our America" and Retamar's anthropophagic reinterpretation to describe the cultural role of colonial-era food. He is scheduled to provide the welcoming remarks at the opening of a new "traditional" restaurant, but his celebration of gastronomical hybridity quickly turns into a discourse on transculturation and cultural anthropophagy. If his generation should be labeled "in transition," a reference to the movement for decentralization of the government, he argues tongue-in-cheek that alimentation "is the act that stops us from eating our fellow men," and to "share food is sublimated cannibalism" (207). The priest recognizes the paradox of referring to hybrid food as traditional, given the longstanding existence of indigenous customs before the European arrival to the Caribbean. Like Martí, though,

---

7. A footnote provides the source of the memorandum citation (The Archives of the Venezuelan Ministry of Foreign Affairs), though it is not entirely clear if this is supposed to indicate Montero's scholarship or Antillano's own attempt to notate documented historical events.

he sees common identity between these groups, as the greatest threat to this transcultural mixture of influences comes from North America. He therefore hyperbolizes the historical sentiments of "Our America" by suggesting the influx of fast food restaurants has mounted an economic and cultural challenge to the sanctity of national autonomy, as citizens "have been the object of a new invasion and conquest, just as, if not more, devastating than that of Pizarro or Cortés" (206). At the same time, the sardonic critique suggests that the same questions of national and regional solidarity continue to exist in different forms in contemporary society. The emphasis upon the shared historical identities of marginalized groups becomes clearest when Latin America is viewed in the context of racism across the globe. In a speech given to delegates from the National African Congress about the suppression of human rights in South Africa, Montero's university chancellor links Latin America's political struggles to those of imprisoned Nelson Mandela: "The historical debt of our university, demonstrated through concrete deeds such as its solidarity with the fight of the people in their devotion to liberty; a democratic and anti-imperialist fight in the case of Chile, Argentina, the Caribbean and Central America; solidarity with the peoples of Sahrawi and Palestine" (255). Increasingly, the novel creates larger circles of geographical awareness that additionally decenter the nationalist referents initially institutionalized in each narrative thread.

The frequent repetition of terms related in meaning to "solidarity" and "loneliness" take on multiple meanings throughout the course of the text. Armundeloy's isolation stems from her inability to accept social codes. She rejects the institution of marriage as a means of gaining social stability, and when she does finally marry it is out of practicality, as she discovers solidarity with a union leader and their shared revolutionary activity. By contrast, Montero's divorce initially leads her to reflect upon her involvement in student movements in the late 1960s when there was great solidarity in the sentiments of various groups against the government. When she arrives in Valencia, the vestiges of this activity appear in the guise of clandestine liberation theology meetings. Yet by 1988, when students again begin violently protesting corruption and austerity measures on campus, much to the shock of her colleagues, she no longer feels the same way about masked resistance, arguing that it provokes needless student deaths and its efficacy is limited by partial media coverage. This is because both her concepts of national-scale revolution and history have eroded, leading to an existential crisis when she questions the fact that social researchers merely produce "words and papers" rather than effect any meaningful social change (287). She is only able to make peace with her profession at the novel's end when she embraces the concept of intrahistory and its documentation of local-level change.

The uncertainty of Armundeloy's fate compels Montero to move beyond the fragmented and incomplete personal record to search out burial records. Montero's own story follows a similar pattern, and it is no accident that the last two time periods of the novel take place during the height of the backlash in response to the lost decade. In 1984, the government attempts to curb economic and political problems stemming from mismanagement, with the formation of COPRE as a means of creating a bipartisan evaluation of the state's infrastructure. The commission's controversial suggestions for increasing democratization through direct popular election, however, would only begin to be seriously considered by political parties in 1988, even if they were not fully implemented until the political unrest of the 1989 Caracazo riots forced the issue. While Montero's engaged friends become involved with promoting the Commission for State Reform, she instead feels paralyzed by her continued romantic and social isolation. In an attempt to inspire her participation, the women argue that the personal and the national do not exclude one another, for if their feminist activity successfully decentralizes power, this union will lead to an establishment of more proximate human relations. Montero is initially unconvinced at such "feminine" logic, although when she emulates Armundeloy and rewrites traditional history from an intimate, female-oriented perspective she effectively internalizes this strategy. Antillano's message is simple: we share more than heritage with our predecessors, and Montero makes an effective foil precisely because her profession as a historian is not merely symbolic but is also explored as a response to the challenges of daily life.

FEMINISM AND PAN-CARIBBEAN INTRAHISTORY

Antillano has justified her approach to political history within the broader context of Latin American narrative, noting that epistolary correspondence has been incorporated into literature from its inception and need not be associated with female expression alone. This is especially true within a Latin American context, for she points out that Columbus's own diary is read today as a form of foundational literature.[8] There is thus little if any postmodern intent in her experiment to suggest the actions of principal national male

---

8. Antillano privileged personal documents because correspondence and private diaries highlight the subjective, poetic nature of traces of the past that we read as fact. "Of course," as she puts it, "I'm not inventing anything, letters have always been incorporated into literature, and even Christopher Columbus's dispatches [from the Americas to the Spanish Royal Court] are today read as a type of fiction" (Socorro 8).

figures of the nineteenth century be read like those of characters in a novel (Socorro 8). As a testament to the male-dominated account of political historiography, the nineteenth-century diarist and her family are fictional, while a majority of the male figures who influence her social network, including cartographers, social activists, public musicians, and botanists, are recognized historical agents. At the same time, as the constructive influence of Martí and historian Velásquez demonstrates, Antillano privileges a dialogue between literature and historiography over the simple negation of androcentric historical models.

As further proof of Antillano's distinct politics, her novel trades in the playful irony of iconoclastic new history for the sincere introspection of socially isolated protagonists. Instead of subverting the agreed-upon record, she establishes the theoretical grounds for female historical novels to uncover an "other" history. While a primary tactic of the new Latin American historical novel is to demythify famous historical personages—conquistadors, despots, revolutionary leaders—few studies within this framework have focused attention on the contributions of recognized female historical agents, partially because of their general exclusion from the political record but also through ignorance of the growing body of contemporary women's writing (Rivas, *La novela* 400–401). Led by Luz Marina Rivas, analyses of Antillano's work have tended to view it in concert with that of two other contemporary female Venezuelan writers, Ana Torres and Milagros Mata Gil,[9] casting them as exemplars of a particular subset of the genre: the intrahistorical novel.

The term intrahistory, first coined by Spanish author Miguel Unamuno in 1895, the year of Martí's death during the Spanish-American War, designates the need for minor histories of everyday individuals—not institutionalized in books, registers, or newspapers—to more accurately portray the greater historical record. Within recent decades, this evocation of asymmetrical power relations has been appropriated by Hispanic American scholars, echoing Antillano's distinction between dominant and ex-centric history.[10] Such intrahistorical texts, which dialogue with the voiceless victims of history, along with the common citizens and marginal witnesses to events, assist subaltern subjects to explore history "from below" as a means to speak for a disenfranchised collective group identity (Rivas, *La novela* 87–88), therefore representing the postmodern fictional counterpart to the Latin American *testimonio*

---

9. For analyses comparing the three authors' historical fiction output, see Rivas ("La perspectiva," "La novela," and *La novela*), González Stephan, and Zambrano.

10. For accounts of intrahistory's evolution, see Pacheco, and Rivas (*La novela*, 60–66).

genre.[11] Because female voices have been excluded from official archives, these perspectives must be drawn from informal sources including private correspondence, oral testimonies, and visual registers. While not restricted to women, because the intrahistorical novel privileges domestic spaces and intimate confessions, its greatest advances have come through writing about the female experiences of or resistance to domesticity. At the same time, critical analyses have tended to gloss over the effect that racial and social differences have upon any claims to a singular female experience, a fragmentation made much more explicit by the witness-anthropologist dynamics informing the creation of many canonical Latin American *testimonio*.

The fictional focus upon quotidian experiences from anonymous individuals, as opposed to sweeping political panoramas of formational events, has also led to comparisons with cultural historical practices such as microhistory that began to receive greater attention during the 1980s.[12] Rivas maintains that the particular strategies these female authors share—the use of collages, diaries, photographs, popular music, graffiti, and representations of publicity to construct autobiographical texts—have the quality of counterliterature that always remains marginal to the historical record. By contesting official historiography's dependence upon institutions such as schools, the function of civic monuments, the use of historical figures on money, and the creation of national holidays (*La novela* 73–74), intrahistorical texts would thus *rewrite* history, although it should be pointed out that the new mentalities regarding once-marginalized sources signaled by new history and new historicism provide a means for interdisciplinary dialogues between intrahistorical expressions. Many of these distinct typologies for a unique feminist writing are compelling, though many critics continue to see parody and intertextuality as the predominant strategies of this marginal history. Moreover, in Antillano's case, satirizing male writing is not the primary goal, as the important place of Martí and Velásquez attest. Instead, she considers how the concept of what constitutes legitimate or orthodox eyewitness accounts depends upon what institutions have alternately archived or ignored.

Antillano's choice to explore the final decades of the nineteenth century is ideologically significant for Venezuela, but not only as a measuring

---

11. While *testimonios* share with postmodern skepticism "the rejection of master discourses" and the valorization of the marginal, the two projects' approach to marginality is distinct, for *testimonios* encourages affective rather than ironic rupture (Yúdice, "Testimonio" 21).

12. Rivas provides a list of female intrahistorical work that preceded Antillano's during the 1970s (*La novela* 18–19), foregrounding that Mexican historian Luis González y González's intrahistorical research both preceded European interventions and established a female-subject focus (107).

stick to gauge how women's social roles have shifted over the last century. They are also a key episode in the country's modernization under Guzmán Blanco, whose contradictory set of national and foreign ambitions Armundeloy breaches through her inclusive community-based organization (Fernández, "Guzmancismo" 81). Paradoxically, despite his authoritarian tendencies, Guzmán Blanco also imported democratic European ideals, made literature and science priorities, established universal education, and sought to reform the country's social conditions through economic progress (Fernández, "El Guzmancismo" 74–75). It is no accident that the first historical novels appeared in Venezuela, decades after many of its neighbors, during this period of nation-building.[13] It is also no accident that the genre has traditionally been studied through canonical male practitioners of the twentieth century,[14] and the continued obscurity of female precursors complicates establishing any genealogy that contextualizes the evolution of female historical writing as a process (Cunha-Giabbai 12). Acknowledging twentieth-century intrahistorical production therefore offers two constructive advantages. First, it contextualizes literatures of resistance in the wake of 1968 student movements and feminist-guerilla accounts after the decade of military dictatorship.[15] Second, it provides a paradigm for understanding women's writing in a regional rather than purely national context, one that more appropriately matches the shared postmodern goals of subaltern representation and postnational literature.

Rivas has made an interesting case for understanding intrahistorical works within a Hispanic Caribbean framework by expanding the geopolitical association of the region with the Caribbean islands to include the surrounding coastlines of Venezuela, Colombia, Central America, and Mexico based on shared traits of migration, exile, histories of slavery, and popular cultural production ("La novela" 108–10). Seen in this light, the comparative corpus of Caribbean female authors is much more robust, yet while several of these authors have written texts that feature women acting in informal capacities

---

13. While both scholars agree the Venezuelan historical novel served to construct a national mythology after the wars of independence, Márquez Rodríguez traces the genre's origins to Eduardo Blanco's *Zárate* (1882), while Lombardi instead points to Romanticist Juan Vicente González's *Biografía de José Félix Ribas* (1861).

14. Márquez Rodríguez's coeval utilization of "new historical novel" is distinct from Aínsa's, instead detailing the modernist male vanguard prior to Alejo Carpentier.

15. Zambrano traces the female historical novel to the pioneering work of Teresa de la Parra in the 1920s, which paved the way for the literature of violence, a trend during the 1950s and 1960s in which female narratives provided testimonials of guerila warfare. Like the intrahistorical novel, these texts utilized informal sources such as diaries and autobiographies to explore social and political consequences of such involvement (243–44).

as witnesses to events and organizers of information,[16] Antillano's *Alone but Committed* is unique within this group, as its female historian is a representative of institutional history. While critical interest has highlighted what Armundeloy's nineteenth-century diaries reveal about the social era, the novel in fact turns on the figure of the historian, whose contemporary access to resources allows her to rescue the diarist's experiences from obscurity.

Despite her increasingly active engagement in local politics, Armundeloy remains an anonymous figure to the historical record. Because she is part of the social elite, she is able to speak freely about the politics of dictatorship as well as the symbolic male violence that transcribes her private and public duties through the confessional space of her diaries and letters, though her writing only takes on contemporary significance through its fortuitous preservation and Montero's subsequent recuperation. In other words, to minimize the historian's contribution to feminist historiography by highlighting only the rescued past is to ignore the consequences of such practices for twentieth-century revisionist conceptions of democracy. Through the tension created by the double narrative, Antillano not only provides an example of feminist history but also thematizes the process of feminist cultural historiography through Montero's research.

THE HISTORIAN AS SOCIAL AND TEMPORAL DEVICE

For the remainder of the chapter, let us turn our attention to the essential role that the occupation of history plays in Antillano's gender/temporal dialectic, which the critical tendency to privilege Armundeloy's tragic fate has overshadowed. I previously mentioned Antillano's interview of Rámon Velásquez as one stimulus for the novel, for the author fictionalizes her own journalistic encounter to include Velásquez as a secondary character. This allows the president of COPRE to link the two time periods, as he speaks about both the necessary political reform of the 1980s and its difference from nineteenth-century military factions. In much the same way that Martí influences Armundeloy, then, Montero views Velásquez as a professional mentor to the extent that she

---

16. Rivas ("La novela" 110) provides an extensive list of female authors linked by Caribbean geography and thematics, including ethnic heritage writers in the United States. In addition to Venezuelan authors Antillano, Mata Gil, and Torres, then, she incorporates Colombian Fanny Buitrago; Dominican Aída Cartagena; Dominican-American Julia Alvarez; Cubans Marta Rojas and Margarita Sánchez Gallinal; Cuban-American Cristina Garcia; Puerto Ricans Ana Lydia Vega, Rosario Ferré, and Magali García Ramis; and Nuyorican Nicholasa Mohr.

acknowledges his influential research on Guzmán Blanco when she begins writing her own diary in 1988.

In this final time period, she has solidified her position at the university through a decade and a half of service, and she has the honor of delivering the graduation ceremony address for departmental students and their families in attendance. Her goal is to inspire these new historians to reflect on the purpose of history, thus it is telling that she begins her talk by citing Velásquez and then ruminating on the discipline of history; in suggesting that humans create history to define their own identities, it is clear that she is extrapolating from her own experience, claiming equal status for female identities within national and international paradigms. Describing historiography as both a form of education and literature, Montero pleads for graduating students never to forget that "history, in the conditions that we live today in Latin America at the end of the twentieth century, is a bottle thrown into the sea, a sea full of trash, this bottle can become caught in the sandy bottom and forgotten, but all of us are here to rescue that bottle, to read the message it contains and share it with everyone, to make it our flag in the battle for justice and the fulfilment of our destinies as nations" (312). After rescuing Armundeloy's message in a bottle, Montero reconciles her sense of political impotence within academia through her embrace of cultural methodologies, realizing that the historian's gift lies not in advocating large-scale or revolutionary change but rather in inspiring empathy by examining incremental improvements through intrahistorical means.

More than simply a career that provides convenient allegorical opportunities, then, historiography and the less glamorous aspects of its daily practice are just as much Antillano's focal point as are the microhistories she invents. Whether linked to intrahistory or new history, *Alone but Committed* resituates historical revisionism as a personal act that requires a complicit reading audience to collectively reconsider outdated models. Having explicitly politicized the practice of history as a form of rescuing from oblivion individual cries for help to create a collective form of solidarity, Montero leaves the thunderous applause of her graduates and begins to write her own individual story by starting a diary influenced by Armundeloy's example. This is the final step in her dialogue with the nineteenth-century writer, yet the question becomes how that dialogue is established for the reader's participation.

The presentist approach understands history's value through its interpretation via and communication with the present, a credo that Antillano extends to demonstrate continued ignorance of women's contributions to society. While the reader gains chronological access to Armundeloy's archive, also interspersed between the documents are fragmented accounts of the contemporary historian's own trajectory over fourteen years (1974–1988). Moreover, the arrangement of the two narratives reveals that Armundeloy's paradoxical embodiment of solitude and commitment has a profound effect on Montero's private and public attempts to come to terms with her own disconnections from conventional lifestyle choices. Because she arrives at Carabobo University in Valencia recently divorced, Montero is immediately able to relate Armundeloy's marginalization to her own experience. In restaurants, waiters openly reveal their surprise at serving an unaccompanied woman, while in departmental curriculum meetings she has no opportunity to participate in decisions with her male colleagues. The university administration claims her role as instructor is fundamental for the development of the nation, yet Montero muses that its bureaucratic language communicates nothing beyond statistics (19–20). When she does participate in planning community presentations and attempts to engage the audience through accessible narrative rather than data, she is accused of being sentimental (144).

Unable to discover a sense of professional or emotional solidarity with her coworkers, Montero retreats to Armundeloy's diaries as a means of discovering a meaningful language, one that aims for affect over statistics, the process of which encourages the power of freedom over the discourse of the regime, to return to Doctorow's distinction. And since the diaries make Montero aware of her relative privilege in comparison to her female predecessors in the nineteenth century, she gains strength from the example of individual resistance to patriarchal models. Disseminating Armundeloy's challenges within and contributions to her era, Montero's act of feminist recuperation is motivated by both public and private goals. The complex nature of this dynamic is apparent from the first moment that Montero discovers the forgotten archival folders and steals them from the library. Antillano clearly sympathizes with Montero's alienation, and one of her primary strategies for effecting communication with the reader in line with the historian's own sensibilities is to eschew the statistical focus of social history and reveal instead the subtle intersection between the two time periods through everyday experience.

Antillano's most noted strategy involves a comparison of the women's daily experiences through overlaps in content, whose continuities and divergences illustrate shifting technologies and sociocultural attitudes. In an early letter, Armundeloy reveals her emerging politics to Sergio by excitedly confessing a dream wherein she was transported to the twentieth century and saw a local university that both admitted women and featured female instructors (59). This blatant reference to gender discrimination is undoubtedly the most forced example of temporal connection between the two time periods, and while it is out of character with regard to the novel's more subtle use of affect, it suggests how central this interaction is to the narrative's attempt to synthesize two individual women's stories as a collective female experience. Some of the biographical similarities suggest why Montero would identify with Armundeloy when reading her letters—both of them have relied upon strong and liberal father figures, for the teenager lost her mother at an early age, while Montero's Chilean mother chose to leave the family and return to her homeland—yet Antillano typically provides a much more understated form of convergence that allows an engaged reader to actively make the connections and recognize differences. In essence, the reader must assume the historian's role to analyze and decipher the authenticity and the sources of the documents. While the notion of past and present individuals seeing their own stories in one another is a central device utilized by other intrahistorical writers, as the case studies analyzed in other chapters of this book demonstrate, the act of editing communication between past and present individuals is not unique to women's historical writing. Antillano's utilization of a historical professor, however, generates this exchange in a creative manner, so that the dialectical experiences become largely a function of the novel's structure, for it is not only the form of the false documents that provides an eyewitness account of the past but also how the documents are read that generates contemporary identification with social disparity.

The novel consists of fourteen chapters, though each chapter follows a distinct structural logic. The first one details Montero's arrival in Valencia after her divorce, her difficulty adjusting to the new conditions, and her discovery of the archive. Chapter 2 consists entirely of the first year and a half of Armundeloy's diaries, beginning with her initial romantic encounter and ending with her dream of a more egalitarian society in the twentieth century. Subsequent chapters, however, break down the structural boundaries between the two narratives to reveal increasing overlap and emotional identification, shifting back and forth between one episode in Montero's life and one document from Armundeloy. After the young bourgeois girl provides an account of her household duties in washing and ironing clothes, Montero takes the diaries with her when she visits the laundromat to wash her own clothes, demonstrating how technologies may have changed, but basic human chores have not. When Montero reads in the newspaper that Salazar's dictatorship in Portugal has been overthrown, Armundeloy's cousin includes in his 1879 correspondence a letter to a North American newspaper written by Guzmán Blanco in which the leader takes issue with the paper's depiction of his return to power as an insurrection rather than a popular mandate against the previous president (82–83).

Up this point, the two time periods are distinguished by distinct fonts as well as the dates associated with the documents. By chapter 5, however, the markings have disappeared and the two texts literally blend into one another with no gaps, revealing the degree of identification—an embedded example of "women's writing"—Montero has begun to experience. Armundeloy narrates her experience participating in the small-town processions of the Afro-Venezuelan San Juan Festival, and this is juxtaposed with Montero's own trip to the same town with a new romantic partner. Their experiences bleed into one another, for both women are invited by one of the black dancers into the circle, lose themselves in the hypnotic rhythm of the drums, and become aware of a man's desirous gaze. Yet despite these similarities, the event marks a divide between female public spaces, for Armundeloy, unlike her twentieth-century counterpart, is not able to cross racial lines, remaining a spectator to the cultural demonstrations of black participants (115–18).

Several footnotes included by an unidentified editor reference texts written during the 1980s as if the scholar were fact-checking the narrative. Logically, Montero must have read the archive of documents in her first year at the university, yet the juxtaposition of certain diary entries with events in her own life over the subsequent decade and a half suggests that she sees these historically narrated facts as reference points around which she organizes her own experiences. For example, immediately after a later account of Armundeloy's involvement with labor movements details her husband's murder and her capture, police abruptly enter Montero's apartment in order to enquire about her relation to a friend killed in a supposed narcotics deal. The montage of home invasions reaffirms the state's continued surveillance powers, just as the historian's discovery that the female revolutionary may have committed suicide coincides with Montero's professional and existential crisis. Thus, during a lecture about the country's foreign debt crisis, she learns a student from the countryside has just lost her entire family in a flood, and, struck by the disconnect between the recitation of statistics and the concrete experience of human loss, is unable to continue the class.

This identification highlights another gap in the record—one in time—which leads Montero to investigate Armundeloy's future, or "the part of history that emerges in the gap between her diaries and the letters" (250). Deciding to move beyond the text, Montero adopts an increasingly materialistic approach to her subject, attending conferences around the country in order to come into direct contact with historical spaces so that the names of famous leaders cease to be anecdotes and take on concrete characteristics. As she admits to her friends after she conducts interviews and peruses burial registers in the town of Puerto Cabello to determine Armundeloy's place of rest, "It is a necessity to connect myself with something physical of her, even though I could say that I can almost see her through the truth of her words" (305). Truth, however, should not be taken for granted in Montero's account of her historical research, for Antillano has quietly undermined the authenticity of some of the documents that the reader may easily take for granted. Montero's own inserted documents appear at different moments in the archive, although just as Montero's and Armundeloy's aesthetics blend into a single narrative, Antillano does not alert the reader by marking the moments that Montero invents texts. The only clue is that the narration occurs in third person rather than first. Utilizing newspaper accounts, for example, Montero narrates what Armundeloy could not: the day of police ambush that led to her husband's death and her own incarceration. The historian also imagines the diarist's suicide once she is able to establish the date of her burial. Yet she does not limit herself to filling in the "gaps" between the existing documents at the end of Armundeloy's life. When Martí is exiled for his part in honoring deceased activist Sergio Acosta, the information is revealed in an "unsigned text" that is clearly not the voice of Armundeloy. In essence, Antillano challenges the reader to distinguish between the "real" document and the historical reconstruction that has been inserted by Montero and presented as part of the preexisting archive.

The historian is thus involved in much more of the narrative's construction than the reader can initially understand. Not only are the documents presented within the implied context of Montero's interpretation, but it is unclear how much of the diaries contain elements of her clandestine in(ter)vention. Perhaps most important in terms of the dialogic relationship Antillano establishes between temporal periods is not Montero's recuperation of Armundeloy so much as Armundeloy's recuperation of the historian, which is highlighted by the academic's decision to write a diary "in the style" of Armundeloy's own confessional writing, leading to the ultimate form of identification through the union of content and form. While much of the second half of the novel consists of Montero's participation in professional presentations, class lectures, interviews, or graduate ceremonies, what is most telling is how the novel ends with a rejection of this public dimension in favor of private reflection. Immediately after the honor of speaking to the graduating class, the historian leaves the urban setting of the university to begin her sabbatical in Armundeloy's place of birth, a small beach town where she initiates her own diary in solidarity with the forgotten activist. This act of writing also creates a form of structural resolution where Armundeloy ceases to be a subject and instead becomes an example, speaking to Montero's present. The historian's inspiration to recuperate her own personal space becomes the clearest sign that the nineteenth-century feminist's legacy will live on, even if her revolutionary acts will never be celebrated nationally in the manner that Martí's political engagement has been.

RECOVERING THE LOST DECADES

Disappointed in the federal government's lack of response to the COPRE reports in 1988, Montero turns away from national unrest to preserve her personal health. It is telling that in the midst of the country's democratic and economic instability, the historian ultimately flees the politics of the university and urban life for the country's Caribbean coast, where she can still participate in the illusion of a forgotten era. In order to finish her revisionist research project about democracy under Guzmán Blanco, which she believes can inform the contemporary democratic crisis, Montero begins her sabbatical in a small house on a quiet stretch of coastline near Armundeloy's home. Her goal is not to simply organize information for her academic book but to "create" a type of writing that brings the information to life (318), and she is accompanied by a new lover, a mechanic from whom she has unsuccessfully attempted to hide her profession for fear that her social class will alienate him. Their relationship provides mutual company, but not too much proximity, for she has come to realize that she requires a sense of isolation in order to—like Armundeloy—become a producer of written history (317). Away from any distractions of the city in this isolated location, she thus discovers the perfect blend of solitude and solidarity, as she not only examines the work of Guzmán Blanco but also starts her own diary in which she records the peace she finds in the simplicity of a sunset reflecting upon the water, natural occurrences that have not changed since Armundeloy's lifetime.

Indeed, the two forms of writing are intricately related, for she applies a similar analysis to Guzmán Blanco's personal writing as she did to Armundeloy's diaries. This leads Montero to reconsider her own interpretation of the Illustrious American, discovering in letters to his wife a delicate consideration of domestic aspects of life mixed with his reflection upon international conflict and national economics (316). Antillano's decision to end the novel on this very specific evocation of the controversial national figure suggests the generative nature of her project of history, one that does not reject the official record in the process of propounding a feminist revision but rather seeks to imagine the historical record, much like Saldívar's American dialectics, in a holistic fashion that synthesizes both the official and the unrecorded. Feminist recuperation in Montero's context becomes both a means of self-preservation and a springboard into a form of historical solidarity that utilizes strategies pertaining to both political and microhistory to generate a form of writing that brings the information to life, just as Montero does with regard to her subject.

Antillano's privileging of the role of official history through her academic protagonist does not preclude the work from serving as a form of intrahistorical novel. It simply recognizes that the literary genre's origins in new history signify that historiography is as pluralistic as the female and Caribbean identities subsumed under the umbrella of Latin American intrahistory. It is all too easy to essentialize "official" history, despite the great variety of approaches such as microhistory that have worked in tandem to create new forms of presentist reading and critical audience participation. The Pan-Caribbean identity that intrahistorical female critics have described is still primarily Hispanic, but through Inter-American comparison it has room to grow, with increasing access to French and English language women writers who recast the region's varied history. In *The Other America* (1998), Michael Dash worries that Cuba's cultural production overshadows awareness of the Caribbean's diverse traditions, though intrahistory can help draw attention to noncanonical writers and stories by challenging the grounds on which identitarianism is theorized in the first place. The dialectics of historical experience in Antillano's *Alone but Committed* provide a blueprint for avoiding binary classifications or reductive indeterminacy. Montero recognizes that the act of historical revisionism has subconsciously led her to reject national conventions and gender rules. Reorganizing her own life "parallel" to Armundeloy's also signifies the beginning of a "new battle" in an equally new geographical location (319).

When she finishes a few lines later, then, with the rhetorical question, "The history of the battles for power: is that perhaps the history of men?" her remark does not ultimately target Guzmán Blanco but rather the exclusive way in which the modern nation has been and continues to be documented. Power divides, yet she will instead seek solidarity, in effect claiming collective experiences as a means of belonging, one that is not exclusive to expressions of power, gender, or citizenship. The unstated goal is to deconstruct the myth of the Illustrious American in much the way that Antillano seeks to demythify Martí and the contemporary Venezuelan crisis—not through parody or satire, but by creating opportunities to move from statistics to human compassion. Montero's address to her graduating class is equally a message from Antillano to the reader regarding responsibility to actively discover and disseminate individual contributions. Like the microhistory created by Armundeloy's diary, *Alone but Committed* is a textual act thrown out to sea that requires the bottle to be found and the message to be shared. The protagonists' production of undervalued primary and secondary documents, respectively, represents one of many possible female experiences that does not appear in any national archive yet which also offers a means of transcending physical frontiers through the basic shared experiences they recover. Claiming Martí as a migratory subaltern subject, Saldívar asks, "What are the limits of our modern notions of citizenship, identity, and residence for activist intellectuals involved in intense processes of deterritorialization?" (*Trans-Americanity* 31). The rhetorical question is equally applicable to Montero's subjectivity and Armundeloy's subalternity, for neither figure is accorded status as an intellectual whose work circulates across gender lines, let alone transnationally. The question here is not of modern or postmodern identities but rather how Antillano has created a fictional intrahistory to accompany national economic and social debates while relocating academic debates about institutionalized peripheries, making postnational critique accessible to a committed, yet divided democracy.

CHAPTER 5

History at the Periphery

Postdictatorial Literature and the Abandoned Generation of Ana Maria Machado's Tropical Sun of Liberty

BY SEVERAL ACCOUNTS, the 1970s arrived in Brazil before the rest of Latin America. Between 1968 and 1974, the Brazilian military dictatorship (1964–1985) initiated an ambitious modernization project by developing national infrastructure and infusing foreign capital into an increasingly free market system (Edwards 66). Nonetheless, this "Economic Miracle," however central to the regime's political and discursive rhetoric for building the future, was not the catalyst for the early transition to the next decade. Instead, 1968, branded "the year that never ended,"[1] marked the period when the regime, after a period of consolidating power by targeting political opposition figures, turned its attention to civil society as a whole and ushered in its most repressive period (Cosson 15). With the insurgency of the Cuban Revolution a recent memory, the Brazilian military coup initially responded to conservative fears regarding the populist discourse of then President João Goulart. As increasingly vocal student mobilizations and labor strikes—capped by the "March of One Hundred Thousand" in Rio de Janeiro in June 1968—responded to the government's violent suppression of public protests, however, the regime responded by passing the most sweeping of its seventeen institutional acts. Unveiled in December of the same year, AI-5, colloquially known as the "coup

---

1. The phrase was popularized by journalist Zuenir Ventura's 1989 book of the same name.

within the coup," dissolved the national congress and suspended virtually all political and individual rights, paving the way for the legitimization of torture as a means of ostensibly protecting the state from guerilla threats (Dassin, "Testimonial Literature" 169).

Ana Maria Machado's second adult novel, *Tropical sol da liberdade (Tropical Sun of Liberty,* 1988), utilizes the viewpoint of a recently returned journalist to reflect upon these key historical events that led to her exile, including the police murder of student Edson Luís de Lima Souto at a peaceful 1968 Rio protest, for the protagonist is forced to return to her peripheral role in activist history in order to address a psychological ailment now censoring her ability to write. In an analysis of post-1964 literature challenging representation under the dictatorship, Regina Dalcastagnè contends that Machado's novel is the most documentary-like of responses written about traditionally female domestic spaces during the era (130).[2] This is not intended as criticism, though the book has not been as well received as the author's other work, in part because the novel has been interpreted as veiled autobiography but also because Machado's psychological reflection eschews the brutal sensationalism of torture foregrounded in many testimonial texts, reactions that suggest how powerfully literary conventions had conditioned popular response (Umbach and Vargas 267).

Even when associated with the post-1964 literary canon, *Tropical Sun of Liberty* was generally interpreted on its release in light of contemporary genres of truth literature, not as a work of historical fiction, which has resulted in a limited understanding of its ambitious scope. This is all the more ironic because Machado both anticipated such criticism by subjecting her protagonist's writing to the same denunciation and explicitly signaled the limits of the testimonial trend. In order to move beyond associations of the novel with autobiography and conventional realism, this chapter aims to reconfigure its apparent "documentary" nature through the framework of false documents. My aim is to demonstrate how the work's categorization as a form of "transition" literature ignores the critical assessment of contemporary genres of realism that Machado embeds in the text from the vantage of the redemocritization period. Instead, I will argue that its metafictional commentary upon how the 1970s was (mis)represented in Brazil exemplifies a particularly vibrant Inter-American example of what Idelber Avelar has since termed "postdictatorial" literature. The reception of Machado's redemocratization novel demonstrates the difficulties of flouting the expectations for national reconciliation within the literary

---

2. Under this subcategory, Dalcastagnè also examines Lygia Fagundes Telles and Salim Miguel.

market, one whose infrastructure and influence had notably expanded as a consequence of the dictatorship's capitalist push toward modernization.

SHIFTING MARKETPLACE: FROM TRUTH LITERATURE TO THE REDEMOCRATIZATION NOVEL

The 1970s in Brazil has been labelled a "cultural void" or alternately a series of "empty drawers," the latter a metaphorical reference to the official repositories where censored texts were presumably kept (Pellegrini, "Brazil in the 1970s" 57).[3] As these distinct descriptions suggest, both the repressive conditions and the presumed lesser quality of produced work contributed to bleak cultural diagnoses. In addition to suspending voting rights and banning all political gatherings, for example, AI-5 also institutionalized various forms of censorship, from the soft power of intellectual cooptation to the more visible effects of systemic suppression of freedom of the press. Critics were slow to characterize the aesthetic consequences of censorship on literature, for the relationship between artistic and economic, political, and social factors of the 1970s required temporal distance to analyze its tendencies from a comprehensive perspective (Pellegrini, *Gavetas vazias* 5–6). Yet as scholarship commenced in the latter half of the 1980s—Machado's novel may be read as a creative contribution to such debates—the verdict remained out regarding the viability of the frequently parajournalistic function that authors adopted during the latter years of the dictatorship.

One point of intersection generally agreed upon, however, was that the evolution of literary strategies provided a barometer for gauging how public attitudes were shifting in regard to the dictatorship's power. Despite the specter of censorship, which extended beyond the political realm to encompass forms of popular cultural production such as music and television, the literary market was comparatively less affected by the new protocols than other modes of production. Thus, even as the simultaneously emerging logic of capitalism began to influence which topics were published for separate reasons, oppositional writers turned to prose to fill in the cultural vacuum, and this engagement can be visualized in five-year responses.[4] In rather oversimplified terms,

---

3. In an interview with Vartuck (1978), film director Carlos Diegues argued that the Brazilian "cultural void" was less a consequence of censorship than it was a consequence of intellectuals' failure to produce quality work. The interview gave rise to the phrase "ideological patrols," Diegues's critique of leftist intellectuals' policing of creative processes to assess that they met oppositional expectations.

4. For a description of the literary market's resilience during the period, see Cosson (29).

the first half of the decade witnessed a tendency toward allegorical parables and fantastic narratives that camouflaged their political commentary, while a radical shift toward concrete referentiality characterized the latter half, providing a more open indictment of dictatorial excesses via "real-life" stories based on fact.[5] If the political allusions within the former dominant were not always accessible to the reading public and therefore limited their consumption to other intellectuals, the direct writing of truth literature turned the concept of censorship itself into a character either directly or indirectly present in its practitioners' narratives.

Corresponding to the *distensão* period of the national political system that began under President Ernesto Geisel (1974–1979), in which the regime began to gradually loosen its restrictive policies, the evolution of literary strategies that privileged documentary representation acted as a barometer for the changing relationship between the dictatorship and civil society. Despite the initial period of growth stimulated by the rise of consumerism, for example, by the latter half of the decade, middle-class support for the regime eroded as the economy was beset by fallout from the global oil crisis and left in near collapse by rising inflation (Cosson 18–20). Investigative journalists once again began to explore questions of political corruption, although this was not without its risks, as the secret police's attempt to cover up its torture and murder of journalist Vladimir Herzog in 1975 demonstrated (Sussekind 37). Instead many writers from the field of communications sought to create engaged literature through what came to be known as the *romance-reportagem* or the Brazilian nonfiction novel, in which authors paradoxically blended literary and newspaper codes by taking documentable current events and purposefully narrating them via the conventions of fiction (Cosson 11).

Tending toward sensational stories of crime and sexuality, such truth literature's surprising popular success as a hybrid genre generated mixed responses. Because its fragmented style provided a means of effecting social critique and circumventing newspaper censorship, it was readily accepted within journalism circles. By contrast, while a few literary critics in the early 1980s such as Manuel Antônio de Castro attempted to legitimize these bestsellers as an early postmodern challenge to the primacy of language (qtd. in Cosson 52–53), most public intellectuals paled at the overt sentimentalism and lack of aesthetic quality.[6] In fact, rather than inviting response from their readership, the

---

5. See Santiago's "Prosa Literária Atual no Brasil" (32) in *Nas Malhas da letra*, which served as a benchmark for critical reinterpretations of 1970s literature from Sussekind's landmark *Literatura e vida literária*, first published in 1985, to Pellegrini's *Gavetas vazias*.

6. Cosson's chapter 2 provides a detailed exploration of the distinct journalistic and literary receptions of the *romance-reportagem*.

works' categorical treatment of good and evil led to a narrow valorization of the journalists' roles as investigative truth seekers. Tânia Pellegrini has countered these aesthetic arguments, noting there was little incentive for authors to engage in linguistic experimentation, for there was greater "urgency" at hand: literature took on the parajournalistic function of resistance through documentation of what had not been documented (*Gavetas vazias* 21). In her account, postmodernism is a product of capitalism, not a critical reaction to it, for the emergence of a new economic order impacted social relations and therefore determined choices available to consumers in the first place (177).

Popular success of the *romance-reportagem* was ultimately short-lived. In conjunction with social and political shifts, the market would also help determine the next evolution of truth literature as the decade ended and a period of transition toward civil rule commenced (1979–1984). If the 1970s began prematurely, then they also effectively ended early with the revocation of AI-5 in 1978 and the subsequent passage of the Amnesty Law in 1979, along with reestablishment of the multiparty system. The Amnesty Law served two very different purposes of national importance. On the one hand, it permitted the safe return of political activists exiled during the regime's most draconian period. At the same time, however, the law also provided protection for members of the regime against persecution for their part in human rights abuses and systematic torturing. Returning exiles initiated a wave of autobiographical accounts labelled as testimonial or "memorialist," though unlike the *romance-reportagem*, the strategy of this truth literature was not to sensationalize social critique through a focus on criminality, but rather to describe the authors' experiences as part of resistance movements as well as victims of torture. Testimonial writing also became a bestseller phenomenon, in part because the public increasingly sought to make sense of the conditions that led to the dictatorship in these years, but also because these brutal narratives of violence provided a symbolic means of holding torturers publicly accountable since the legal system could not seek justice. Within their writing, authors frequently reproduced documents, both governmental and private, as a means of supporting their claims to authenticity and veracity.

Corresponding to another key shift in the country's history, these autobiographical accounts helped facilitate the conditions for democratic dialogue in which history according to average citizens was made accessible. Much of this literature revisited the period of 1969–1973, with the most common topics being the narration of demonstrations, the formation of guerilla groups, and the practice of political kidnappings (Dassin, "Testimonial Literature" 164–67). The most well-known example of this narrative arc, for example, is Fernando Gabeira's bestseller *O que é isso, companheiro?* (What's This, Comrade?, 1979), which details Gabeira's governmental opposition through urban guerilla warfare, most notably his involvement in the 1969 kidnapping and subsequent release of US Ambassador Charles Elbrick. The catharsis such texts produced notwithstanding, there were also legitimate criticisms of the nature of the genre. From the creation of shallow one-dimensional characters to the reductive binary representations of guerillas and the military, the author-protagonists turned their largely failed engagements into heroic narratives in which they took central stage, though curiously the authors provided "virtually no profile of Brazilian society and little systematic analysis of the Brazilian political situation. They do not take on even the most pertinent question of what the armed struggle meant in general for the Brazilian political process" (Dassin, "Testimonial Literature" 78).[7]

While the *romance-reportagem* and testimonial literature may have been derided as mediocre forms of literature, these two trends served similar functions in recovering the country's collective history—paradoxically, through the act of testifying *against* and condemning the country's past (Pellegrini, *Gavetas vazias* 175; Sussekind 74). In terms of archival documents, as Silviano Santiago surmises, future historians of the era would only have military versions of events upon which to draw (*Nas malhas* 34). As I discussed in chapter 2, the concurrent emergence of the new historical novel during the distension period also signaled an attempt to recuperate a censored past, though its hallmark was self-awareness that blended both parodic and documentary tendencies through a return to aesthetic experimentation. Yet far from attempting to heal the nation, this new generation of writers called the limits of nation-state itself into question. Once the transition period had successfully initiated the redemocratization process, one of the central questions facing authors became how to react to the critical-popular disagreement of truth literature and its legacy.

MACHADO'S REJECTION OF TRUTH LITERATURE AND THE LOST DECADE'S RETURN

Former journalist and professor Ana Maria Machado, whose long list of accomplishments includes serving as president of the Brazilian Academy

---

7. Santiago was one of the first to critique the potentially harmful aspects of testimonial publications (*Nas malhas* 33). For analyses of the role of heroism in Gabeira's popular work as well as the numerous texts that followed, see Sussekind (73–81) and Pellegrini (*Gavetas vazias* 33–60).

of Letters, is acutely aware of the literary lineage informing the relationship between democracy and memory in her native Brazil. The same year she published *Tropical Sun of Liberty*, Machado spoke at a conference in the United States in which she elaborated on the evolution of fiction during the dictatorship, noting that the "hyper-valorization of journalistic texts" in the 1970s meant that "to speak of the imagined, the invented, of the fictitious (to create fiction, in other words) remained entirely out of fashion at the start of the redemocratization period" (*Contracorrente* 23).[8] She argues that a double sense of shame informs much of post-1964 literature—both reticence to explore aesthetic questions (or embrace artistic quality in the face of important issues such as resistance) and guilt at potentially feeling emotion on an individual level rather than attempting to speak truth to power as a collective unit. As she reveals, this amounts to a form of self-censorship potentially as limiting as earlier state methods of cooptation and intervention.

From the vantage of the transition in the 1980s, then, *Tropical Sun of Liberty* explores the country's most repressive period of the dictatorship as an antidote to both these fears of expression. While she recalls the experience of the generation of students that gave the most important period of their lives to combatting the dictatorship, her message is not one of triumph in the face of failure. Instead she channels uncertainty, for while the 1980s may have offered the return to history, it also saw a return to the economic and political conditions of the 1960s—campaigns for reform, uncontrollable inflation, and the continued threat of dictatorship—posing similar challenges to the future of democracy (*Contracorrente* 28).

Domestically and internationally, Machado may be most closely associated with her prolific writing of children's literature, yet the representation of history has been a recurrent preoccupation spanning both juvenile and adult texts throughout her career, a particularly self-aware designation leading several of her works to be catalogued as examples of historiographic metafiction.[9] Despite Machado's initial presentation of *Tropical Sun of Liberty* as a critical reexamination of recent literary strategies, however, the novel has not been analyzed in this reflexive vein or included in the canon of new historical fiction. Instead, the tendency has been to treat the work in autobiographical terms as a continuation of the truth literature initiated by testimonial

---

8. The presentation is titled "O trânsito da memória: literatura e transição para a democracia no Brasil" and is included in Machado's nonfiction collection *Contracorrente* (1999).

9. For more on the recurrent theme of history in Machado's works, see Pinto-Bailey ("Memory") and Gonçalves Vieira.

accounts and *romance-reportagem*.¹⁰ There is legitimate basis for this confusion, for in addition to starting the novel in 1982 during the testimonial boom (Umbach and Vargas 269), there is notable overlap between Machado and her female protagonist Helena Maria, a journalist who returns to her childhood home during the democratic transition to convalesce from both a physical injury and a psychological affliction that has left her suddenly unable to write. Like Lena, Machado was a student activist during the 1960s, and like her protagonist, she was arrested though luckily spared torture, and upon her release fled the country. Additionally, both women's brothers, as members of the MR8 guerilla group, participated in the kidnapping of US Ambassador Elbrick (central to Fernando Gabeira's influential testimonial novel). Yet these personal echoes are ultimately details that must be contextualized within a larger metanarrative structure, one that parallels Machado's novel itself, for the author emphasizes the importance of creative imagination over the creation of a narrative epic. Upon return from exile, the journalist receives requests to write about her experiences, and the novel thus reveals her attempts to write a fictionalized account of her exile as a stage play to be unsuccessful. Despite her profession, it is telling that she believes fiction allows her to more "truthfully" communicate exilic suffering than nonfiction discourse.

Since the turn of the twenty-first century, more attention has been paid to the novel's imaginative dimension, although the primary means of locating its contribution to Brazilian recuperation of memory has been an examination of the journalist's emotional and physical paralysis as an allegory for the ailing nation and its need to reconstitute collective memory.¹¹ While both national allegory and confession play important roles in the novel, insistence upon this approach runs the risk of reproducing the very documentary bias that Machado underscored in international conferences upon the novel's publication. Exercising a controlling effect on the production of creative fiction ultimately diminishes the novel's philosophical components, for while the book references unofficial documents, this is not as a device for supporting Machado's truth telling claims. Instead, the documents act as vehicles for transporting the protagonist, her mother, and the reader back to decisive historical moments

---

10. To my knowledge, Vecchi is the only critic to discuss the novel as a metadiscursive reflection upon memorialist fiction (257–58). Virtually every critical treatment of the novel responds in some form to the alleged autobiographical overlaps in the text, although Pinto-Bailey ("Memory") notes through personal correspondence that Machado denies that the book should be read under this paradigm (184). Ernst argues the novel's historical component has been largely ignored, while the work itself has been mistakenly read as a late example of *romance-reportagem* (351).

11. Pinto-Bailey ("Memory"), Ventura, and Forster each view Lena's body and the house where she convalesces as expressions of national allegory.

in the evolution of regime censorship. Within Lena's family home, numerous personal archives—photographs, depositions, interviews, diary entries, and letters—prompt both the protagonist and her mother to reflect upon the events in 1968 that led up to the creation of AI-5, the journalist's arrest, and her subsequent exile. Indeed, while she recalls the events that ushered in the long 1970s through a form of documentation, the details of the subsequent decade in Brazil—an empty drawer—are conspicuously absent, since Lena was in exile during this period. Machado thus uses fragments from contemporary popular culture—samba music and tropicalist lyrics, political poetry and ruminations on exile—not only to document cultural forms of resistance that provided a voice to exiled artists but also to demonstrate that the period was anything but a cultural void.

Indeed, although the novel's subjects anticipate many of the issues that journalist Zuenir Ventura would explore in his 1989 narrative history *1968, The Year That Never Ended* (Dalcastagnè 130), a documentary engagement does not automatically equate to autobiography. While at first glance, Machado provides some of the telltale signs of *romance-reportagem* and exilic confessional literature, a closer inspection reveals that all of these elements do not emulate but instead expose the inherent failure of both genres to address the issues of individual memory and suffering. Thus, while the plot revisits the key formulaic issues central to contemporary testimonial literature, from the formation of resistance groups to the kidnapping of political figures, it does so from within the purview of fiction where poetic language and self-reflection are central rhetorical devices, just as there is no attempt to verify the events narrated as either factual or authoritative. In fact, while the novel incorporates numerous references to documents such as depositions and personal writing, this has little to do with constructing authenticity for the reader, but instead serves to create a device for exploring affective questions through a personal prism as opposed to seeking to make a collective political statement.[12]

Second, while Machado and her journalist-protagonist exhibit biographical parallels, the author avoids the trap of creating a heroic epic in an attempt to valorize the resistance movement. Far from it, her effectively paralyzed protagonist is a product of a dysfunctional nation that, without being able to seek justice against the regime, has not yet come to terms with its past wounds. Finally, although Machado's narrator is a journalist by trade, the concept of an investigative *romance-reportagem* is quickly compromised, for the narra-

---

12. Dassin maintains that one of testimonial genre's shortcomings in Brazil was its privileging of the political at the expense of the personal, reducing social commentary to generalizations and shocking images rather than creating emotional connections with readers ("Testimonial Literature" 173).

tor fails in her attempt to create a fictionalized version of her experiences in exile. Machado ultimately refuses to embrace the sensationalism of crime or guerilla warfare, push an ideological agenda, or create categorical portraits of perpetrators and victims, and in this sense, the understated work shares counter-market characteristics with Silviano Santiago's *In Liberty* (Umbach and Vargas 268–69), which I will analyze in the following chapter.

The reflexive component of the novel is vital for understanding the work's overall premise, for Machado creates an example of what her own protagonist refers to as "peripheral" history. While I will return to this concept shortly, it is worth noting here that "periphery" in this instance has less to do with Machado's feminist considerations than describing marginal characters who were not active agents in resistance movements and therefore had not had a platform on which to narrate their experiences.[13] And while the dictatorship foregrounded the nation as an all-encompassing framework, it has been duly noted that Brazilian production during the 1970s must be contextualized within the larger Latin American network of responses in order to be fully comprehended (Pellegrini, *Gavetas vazias* 25–26).

If the categorization of *Tropical Sun of Liberty* has proven tricky, then we may do well to approach redemocratization novels as a category of fiction distinct from *distensão* and transition texts while subjecting them to both regional and extranational examinations. To accomplish this, in what follows I propose that Machado's undervalued fiction benefits from being examined as part of what Idelber Avelar has productively termed "postdictatorial" literature. Avelar's foundational criticism within Latin American memory studies has been mentioned in relation to the novel in passing (Pinto-Bailey, "Memory, History" 185), though I want to suggest an in-depth look at his classification of postdictatorial texts as a paradigm that not only accurately characterizes the powerful strategies that Machado employs but also helps resolve the confusion her mixture of fact and fiction has generated. Postdictatorial literature is inherently historical and Inter-American, while concerning itself with negotiating the failure of literature to provide a pathway to reconciliation, yet it does not therefore dictate that the past cannot partially be recuperated. Metatextual intervention demonstrates how failure can paradoxically be employed to positive effect in rewriting the lost decade of Latin America's exiles, a strategy not dissimilar to the constructive use of failure Updike envisions in *Memories of the Ford Administration* seen in chapter 8.

---

13. Pinto-Bailey ("Sincronicidades") and Dalcastagnè have provided feminist readings of the novel in which women are able to create history from within spaces normally associated with gendered domestic tasks. I do not seek to contradict this, but rather explore the specific use of the concept "periphery" as the novel's protagonist evokes it.

COMMODIFYING HISTORY: POSTDICTATORIAL
LITERATURE AND MACHADO'S INTER-AMERICAN RUINS

Machado is not considered in Idelber Avelar's influential first book, *The Untimely Present: Postdictatorial Latin American Fiction and the Task of Mourning* (1999), though her focus upon the attempt to simultaneously forget and preserve the memories of Brazilian and Hispanic American dictatorships exemplifies the very tension at the heart of Avelar's thesis. A brief unpacking of the three referents that constitute his title—"untimely," "postdictatorial," and "Latin America"—in fact reveals a project correlative to historical representation within an Inter-American paradigm. By "untimely present," for example, Avelar describes the cohort of authors whose act of distancing themselves from dominant literary forms of prose makes them "foreign to their present" (20). In the process, such authors not only give voice to the trauma of the recent past, but more importantly reveal the way that popular literature, whether bestselling postmodernism or naive testimonial realism, has not adequately resolved the trauma of the recent past but merely exploited it. Avelar is clearly dismissive of 1970s popular fiction across the region, though he is equally critical of theories claiming to represent a single, coherent continental identity, thus rather than offering a pan-Latin American diagnosis of South and Central American dictatorships, Avelar focuses specifically upon southern cone democracies—Argentina, Brazil, and Chile—that emerged from authoritarian regimes during the 1980s. Indeed, the comparative political framework he employs to trace regional confluences between the respective intellectual shifts displays quintessentially Inter-American methodology.

With regard to the questions of memory and mourning, Avelar believes that the transition to democracy had less of an effect upon the past than is generally surmised. He argues instead that the most substantial and lasting transitions occurred under the dictatorships themselves, for it was during this general period that national focus shifted from the state's central economic role to an embrace of the free market, the latter as a response to perceived underdevelopment from foreign powers. Although the respective dictatorships thus conflated civic political freedom with the economic freedom of capitalism, newly elected democratic governments in the 1980s did not abandon this developmentalist attitude so much as sustain it by adopting neoliberal policies. Redemocratization was accompanied by a return to national canons, partially because "the dictatorships, by submitting unconditionally to *international* capital, turned the *nation* into the critical battlefield for all political action" (36, emphasis in original). As Avelar reads the modernization policies of the era, the dictatorship was just as interested in securing power as it was maintaining it through forms of ideological consumption, purging both so-called urban terrorists and others who could offer resistance to multinational capital.

One collateral consequence of this new market logic was that that memory, and by extension, the concept of national history, also became commodified. The overwhelming contemporary focus of competing new narratives representing both governmental discourse and popular new literatures of resistance contributed to the "erasure of the past as past" (2). While Avelar levels particular criticism at the Hispanic "Boom" in Argentina and Chile for having sold aesthetics as a surrogate for politics, within Brazil he calls out two primary forms of protest literature—the *romance-reportagem* and the testimonial-autobiographical novel—as responsible for facilitating the anesthetization of the population to the deeper emotional consequences. While these parajournalistic texts ostensibly sought to create a counterhistory that challenged the dictatorial purchase on truth, Avelar argues that both genres' attempts to create identification with heroic figures, far from recovering the past, served to commodify memory as information for popular consumption (61–68).

Proposing an ethical imperative for authors to renounce heroism and to instead explore a "topology of defeat" (15), he therefore defines postdictatorial literature as a transnational corpus of texts that emerged primarily during the redemocratization processes of the 1980s. Including canonical authors such as Argentine Ricardo Piglia, Chilean Diamela Eltit, and Silviano Santiago from Brazil, this cohort of writers is united by the need to reevaluate the (inter)national legacies of terror more than any specific stylistic or formal elements. Yet unlike their earlier journalistic and autobiographical counterparts, postdictatorial texts do not embrace the logic of the market, and because they offer complicated insight into the period without hiding the conditions of their production, they avoid perpetuating the cycle of commodification that represents the past as a product. Cultural studies critics might view this assertion of aesthetic innovation over mass fiction as running counter to poststructural blurring of high and low culture, yet it should be noted that the novelists Avelar gathers together do attempt to decenter fixed notions of justice. Their strategy, however, involves denying closure. Instead, they reveal the ruins and fragments of the state in an attempt to engage the past through active mourning (2). Paradoxically, such authors must admit that the task of mourning is impossible to conclude, yet this intrinsic failure also assures that an unresolved remainder of past catastrophe is not only introduced into public discourse, but also left to haunt collective memory.

Viewed through the lens of the three above concepts informing Avelar's analysis of postdictatorial literature, *Tropical Sun of Liberty* too imagines a "topology of failure," in this case, through Lena's unsuccessful attempt to produce a collective document of her generation's grieving. With regard to the untimely, not only is the novel's impetus historical (rather than a fictionalization of the present), but its entire narrative, composed of a series of flashbacks extending back to the emergence of the student resistance movement in 1968 and the passage of AI-5, hinges upon the inability to articulate the pain suffered by an entire generation of people. Lena's ultimate powerlessness to create the testimonial narrative requested of her would seem to be an admission that Machado does not pretend to offer such a document either, yet the ruins of this failed text have positive consequences for establishing public debate in postdictatorial Brazil. Additionally, the novel expressly rejects the popular discourse of its contemporaries in favor of an estrangement from the present through poetic language and symbolic experimentation. Finally, Machado questions the possibility of any cohesive hemispheric identity, yet nonetheless gestures toward the necessity to consider intersecting Inter-American experiences. Indeed, the tragic selection of personal depositions from Latin American exiles, in addition to serving as a primary source for Lena's creative writing, provides for the reader fragments and metaphorical ruins that haunt public discourse because of their irresolution.

The novel's postnational focus is most clearly enunciated in the latter stages of the novel when a discussion about the National Security Doctrine between Lena and her pacifist mentor, Luís Cesário, illustrates a dialectic at work between an exceptionalist nationalism and regional confluence. Lena suggests that much of the current repression stems from foreign pressure, for Brazil's generals studied in the United States and returned with ideas equating guerrilla resistance with terrorism. Because her interlocutor never left Brazil, he views the issue more narrowly as a uniquely historical national crisis: "Our soldiers have had an obsession with imitating foreigners for much longer, back when the United States was still in its diapers and hadn't grown up. . . . The rest of Latin America is the rest of Latin America; it is not Brazil. We may have a few things in common; we're brothers, we suffered some of the same things together, we were similarly bloodied by colonizers, but we have different histories" (316–17). Lena's ideological perspective has been shaped by her suffering abroad, however, thus she is not convinced by the artist's refusal to understand Brazil in tandem with neighboring dictatorships. She thus highlights the ironic shared autodetermination of Latin American democracies that emerges from their opposition to US political and military strategies:

> But now, the means through which the different countries are slowly heading towards redemocratization shows that they are also similar, don't you think,

Luís Cesário? I mean, Chile still remains under the control of violence, Paraguay as well, there are various others. But Argentina, Uruguay, Peru . . . as well as us . . . you don't think this corresponds to a different moment in American politics for the continent? You don't think that Somoza only fell in Nicaragua, Baby Doc in Haiti, because the United States let it happen? That now their strategy is different, and they continue treating us in a single bloc, that we're all the same? (317–18, my translation).

Luís Cesário stresses Brazil's agency within its own downfall, whereas Lena believes that the types of student protests and guerilla movements that have evolved across the region constitute an important political confluence that unites, rather than separates the resistance. On the one hand, the argument locates the history of military repression within a larger context, while on the other it suggests the dangers of understanding Latin America as a stable, definable entity that erases difference. In the process, Machado reveals that her own project of recuperating Brazil's exiled generation cannot be neatly located within national discourses. If the experience of exile extends beyond geopolitical borders, the extranational ruins become all too apparent when Lena reflects on the fates of the exiles she interviews while in Europe.

The archive of individual and family texts that Lena has preserved from her college years and her subsequent escape from the country provides the means for modelling the fragmentary nature of memory. In some cases, family photos recall the beginning of governmental crackdowns, while in others specific articles and interviews act as conduits for revisiting the trauma of key events that were subsequently whitewashed by official accounts. The saddest ruins of a generation have been catalogued in one of Lena's many notebooks through interviews she conducted with other political exiles. As Lena randomly reads through the informal depositions, the spectrum of fragmented experiences reveals a series of broken dreams. Whether Uruguayan, Chilean, Bolivian, or Brazilian, the interviewees express a complex resentment for their adopted country while struggling with their inability to ever fully return to Brazil. Several individuals not only recount their own struggles but also reveal the paradox of their limbo by referencing other exiles who gain international recognition for their political writing or scientific work yet face hostile resentment at home when they attempt to return, ironically from intellectuals who see them as traitors for having left in the first place. A Chilean bookshop owner whose Parisian store serves as a center of cultural resistance and caters specifically to exile literature is criticized for profiting off the sorrow generated by national disaster. When the Latin Americans who comprise her primary readership begin returning home and her business fails, she accepts that she must be left behind, telling Lena that the loss of the communal space her store provided will force her into a second exile (170). While many of these individuals harbor a desire to return to an imagined space of national belonging, for most it is no longer a possibility. A journalist colleague of Lena's is senselessly killed by the police after returning to Brazil in a case of mistaken identity, while at the opposite extreme a torture victim rejects her Brazilian name and heritage to remain in Europe, discovering that she can only be a tourist when she travels back with her German husband and children a decade later.

In most cases, Lena has no knowledge of what has become of the individuals she met in hotels and public spaces, and it is precisely this lack of closure that resonates with the reader. The memory of these marginal, disembodied figures survives only within the confines of her collection of notebooks. Inhabiting a space between Latin America and Europe, they are united in the postnational exercise of nostalgia. In many ways, Lena's own personal epiphany stems from recognizing that she has been given the opportunity to come back not only physically but more importantly emotionally, and therefore cannot reject the task of coming to terms with her past. Yet this must come, as she discovers through the collapse of her own testimonial project, on a personal level within the confines of her home, not a memorialist outpouring to a reading public. Shortly after publishing the novel, Machado conjures up the above lesson by starting a talk she gave in the United States with a disavowal: writing is a solitary act—if the written text finds an echo in a larger audience or historical moment, thus expressing a collective imaginary, then it becomes divorced from the original purpose (*Contracorrente* 11).

CULTURAL HISTORY, PRIVATE DOCUMENTS, AND MACHADO'S RHETORICAL STRATEGIES

Within the novel, documents play the role of cultural reference points instead of testaments to authenticity. While the reproduction of Lena's collection of dictatorship-era photographs, notebooks, journalism, and her creative writing represents one form of documentation, a second documentary layer is subtly achieved through Machado's paratextual framing devices. The chapter epigraphs play a central role in the novel's politics, not only because a majority of the poem and song fragments are taken from production in the wake of the AI-5, but also because they act to thematically determine the content of each untitled chapter, suggesting that Machado's narrative is tied to the cultural dimension of the period rather than merely to its protest movements. Machado does not highlight the publication dates of each work—the fragments are cited without titles or any additional identifying information—though they are recognized enough by national audiences to resonate. Lyrics about exile from the principal tropicalist singers Caetano Veloso, in "London, London" (1971), and Gilberto Gil, from "Back in Bahia" (1972), for example, precede the chapter in which Lena's thinly veiled autobiographical play about her exile in Europe is presented. The lyrics of Maurício Tapajós and Paulo Cesar Pinheiro's song "Nightmare" (1972) proved to be a danger to record and eventually became an anthem for the country's guerilla movement, thus an excerpt precedes the chapter detailing Lena's brother's own clandestine involvement in guerilla movements. And while poet and diplomat Vinicius de Moraes wrote "Pátria Minha" in 1948 stationed in the US, after being forced to resign by the Brazilian regime and go into exile, he began publicly reading the poem as a critical response to the passage of AI-5; fragments from his complex description of homeland preface multiple chapters whose central themes relate to exile and democracy. As a member of what she terms the generation "abandoned by God" (272), Lena is absent from Brazil during much of the 1970s, yet while she watches events from afar that physical marginality also provides insight into the conflict. In a poignant memory, she recalls watching on French television close-ups of liberated prisoners whose bodies have been broken in different ways as a result of torture, and she realizes that those back in Brazil have no access to such images. Thus while her own personal archive cannot inspire national memories of the period, artists' contributions provide a snapshot of contemporary cultural production that both challenges censorship and descriptions of the period as a cultural void. Additionally, as opposed to public narratives documenting torture, they provide a model for poetic responses to the regime.

In fact, in the same way that de Moraes infuses his poem "Pátria Minha" with new meaning by rereading it in the context of repressive political shifts, presentist reinterpretation of cultural markers is key to locating the overarching self-reflexive framework of *Tropical Sun of Liberty*. Most obvious is the novel's title, which is drawn from the first stanza of Brazil's national anthem wherein the "sun of liberty" shines on a heroic people and their homeland.[14] If taken out of context, such lines would seem to reinforce the nationalism of regime discourse, though the reference takes on ironic proportions within the context of the novel, for heroism and freedom are both suspect within the confines of erased memory. Machado signals this shift through the opening epigraph to the novel—lyrics from a 1946 samba performed during Carnival

---

14. The anthem was first composed by Francisco Manuel da Silva in 1831, although the official lyrics that accompany the music were only established in 1922.

in celebration of the end of the Estado Novo dictatorship (1937–1945)—which dialogues with the national anthem: "The sun of liberty shined again," the first stanza begins, ending with a less figurative message: "Tyranny has been defeated by democracy."[15]

There is little ambiguity to Machado's attempt to position her book as a similar response to the return to democracy. In a subtle metatextual layer, however, many of these cultural markers can be found in a single document from the text: a letter that Lena writes to her brother while he is in hiding, in which she promises to preserve the true "history" of his life that had been publicly misrepresented by state-controlled media (193–95). In essence, this letter is a microcosm of the novel, which represents one woman's heartfelt letter to an entire generation. "Sun of liberty" takes on additional connotations as both a symbol and an organizing device, bookending the novel as the narrator basks under the sun's rays in an effort to heal her body and spirit. Prefacing chapter 1 is an epigraph taken from Caetano Veloso's song "Strange Force" (1978), which reinforces the question of life's relation to art: "Life is a friend of art / It's the part the sun taught me / The sun that traverses that road / That it never went down." The natural setting of Lena's family home reveals another contrast to urban testimonial or guerilla truth literature.[16] As such, the sun symbolizes both a universal and spiritual phenomenon that extends beyond cultural and religious borders, evidenced by Lena's memories at the ruins of the Pyramid of the Sun from her visit to the ancient Mesoamerican city of Teotihuacan outside Mexico City. She also recalls her childhood reading of the Bible in which history is viewed in similarly universal terms as a life force: "The same History that flowed uninterrupted, linking up everything that happened under the sun" (321). The dialectic between collective and individual, national and international, propels much of the protagonist's wrestling with her past. One of the chief forms of history that Lena maintains from her period of exile in Europe, the document upon which she intends to base her stage play, is a collection of depositions of other political exiles from Latin America—Uruguayans, Chileans, and Brazilians, as well as Bolivians and Peruvians—most of whom have since suffered tragic fates and whose stories would otherwise be lost. Lena's goal is to preserve these mournful fragments, saving them from obscurity by translating this transnational suffering into art that can meaningfully communicate a shared experience of displacement that extends beyond the national.

---

15. Information on the song "Depois Eu Digo" and its relation to the Carnival of Peace accessed via the "Galeria do Samba" website.

16. See Ernst regarding the book's rejection of questions central to urban literature.

THE PERIPHERY OF HISTORY AS CRITIQUE OF CONSUMERISM

If the forced migration experienced by the exiles that Lena interviews illustrates one type of periphery, the role of postdictatorial ruins in the novel is most coherently illustrated by the concept of "historical periphery" developed by Machado's protagonist upon her return to Brazil. It is through a dialogue in the second chapter that her critique of contemporary truth literature is established. The epigraph excerpts Ferreira Gullar's poem "To Translate Oneself" (1980), from the exiled socialist poet's first collection upon returning to Brazil. Creating a dialectic between the narrator's two impulses—one part of his identity represents the crowd, the other loneliness; one part represents everyone, the other nobody—Gullar asks, "To translate one part / into the other part / which is a question / of life and death / would that be art?" (Gullar lines 25–29) which thematically underscores both the chapter and the entire novel.

In a subtle metafictional turn, then, Lena and another returned exile maintain an extended conversation about the merits of transition literature and whether it constitutes art. At this point in the early 1980s, neither individual knows whether the improving political conditions will continue to hold, thus educating the public about the conditions under which exiles lived has pressing political implications. The last time Lena saw Honório, the two exiles were wandering Europe, lost without a sense of place. Honório confesses that since returning to Brazil he no longer shares any connection to those members of his own generation that never left, only younger groups that have not been anesthetized by the repressive conditions. Because Lena is a journalist, he suggests she should use her writing ability to publish a testimony of her own experience abroad. Lena, however, argues that confessions are for prisoners, and that her job is to communicate facts to the public, not engage in sentimental personal journeys:

> My profession is journalism, not writing personal testimony. I don't believe that exists. I think it's more honest therefore to assume that this concept of personal testimony is a fiction, it belongs to the genre of fantasy, if this does indeed exist in literature under that name. Which is to say, an invented way of telling things, pretending in the story that events happened a certain way, even though they didn't. (32)[17]

---

17. All translations of the novel are my own.

When her interlocutor points out that writing must ultimately follow existing conventions and that all histories must be inherently selective because it is impossible to recreate every detail, an infuriated Lena presses the issue on the grounds of ethics. Anticipating Avelar's critique of misrepresentation in *romance-reportagem* and testimonial literature, the journalist insinuates that "there are people playing the role of hero, attaching epic deeds and charm onto the actions of others to avoid talking about more serious things. . . . If you can't tell the truth [in order to protect the identities of other guerillas], then don't. But don't tell lies pretending that it's the truth, pseudofactual confessions to give fuel to historians in the future" (32). While both activists agree that fiction is more "honest" in this regard because it openly embraces invention and can inspire readers to seek out the facts for themselves, Honório counsels that anything Lena produces will be judged as a form of autobiography because of her identity as an exile. Such dialogue suggests that Machado knew she was taking a risk with the novel, and the irony of this self-awareness is precisely that the charge of autobiography was leveled at *Tropical Sun of Liberty* upon publication.

Yet when Honório repeats that she has an ethical obligation to share her story with the nation, Lena criticizes the pressure to collectively speak for the memory of others, a position Machado would reiterate for her own "solitary" work when speaking to US audiences the year of the novel's publication (*Contracorrente* 11–12). Instead, Lena maintains that hers would constitute the history of the periphery. Misunderstanding this ambiguous remark, her friend responds with disdain that this project isn't about following the current vogue of narrating the story of the favelas as alternative cultures, but rather telling the story of middle-class women. Lena, however, is not interested in following popular trends. "I'm not talking about the geographical periphery," she rejoinders, "I'm talking about the historical periphery" (33–34). What emerges from her explanation is that during the shift from the 1960s to the 1970s she felt that she was somehow always at the margins of groups and events, placed in danger by her guerilla brother's actions, yet never herself an agent in organizing protests. While some individuals were "sucked" from the margins to the center (34), she feels guilt for not having participated in resistance to the same extent as either her brother or Honório, even though she too ended up needing to flee the country clandestinely. In essence, she considers herself the antithesis of the heroes who populate testimonial literature, as she instead embodies the multitude/solitude binary that Gullar creates. Once he understands her interest in personal over political history, Honório encourages Lena, because hers represents the average experience of their generation precisely because of her marginal relation to major events. Nonetheless, he disagrees with her proposal to simply unite other people's testimonies from the periphery as if a report, an apparent reference to the interviews of other Latin American exiles she has collected. He brings the discussion full circle by highlighting that intimate stories would not have an emotional impact if framed as nonfiction or other discourses of truth: "You know better than anyone that the newspaper is the biggest fiction in the twentieth century" (35).

Both exiles make important points. Lena's marginal status in relation to the narrative of history is both social and geographical (as an exile), and it raises vital questions about the line separating mere documentation of history from art that inspires change. Honório's reference to the effects of state censorship on media argues to the same end and is duly supported by Lena's personal archive of documents. For instance, as she recuperates from the mental breakdown that precipitates her symbolic return to her predictatorship childhood home, Lena is unable to completely disconnect, obsessively reading the newspaper, feeling that something is missing or that she is "marginalizing" herself by leaving her career behind. Noticing how the media has stopped speaking about the economic crisis, she recalls how her own newspaper responded to censorship during the dictatorship, at times publishing cooking recipes or sections of the poem *Os Lusíadas* in place of the rejected article so that readers would at least recognize that suppression of information was taking place. As she examines articles she has saved from the period, Lena remembers that editors used ambiguous headlines, outdated photos, or allegorical references to indicate days featuring multiple arrests of dissidents, at times even literally writing between the lines of obituaries (203–4), though her own editor became increasingly complicit with the regime.

Chapter 6 ends by reproducing an article from an unnamed colleague who was refused publication, despite having been written during the redemocratization period, over fear that repressive controls might return in the near future. The article exposes the hypocrisy of the government when an interrogation room is discovered and various federal employees pretend not to recognize the instruments of torture, cynically suggesting harmless alternative uses for the devices and blocking state inquiry into the space. It quickly becomes clear that despite the collapse of the dictatorship, those responsible for torture will not be held accountable and that unconcealed censorship continues across all modes of expression. While Lena once believed that she could help others through her journalism (260), disillusionment reinforces her perceived need for the type of truth that only openly fictional accounts can provide. While she therefore accepts that the "Brazilian rhythm of making history truly is quite slow," the transition to democracy seems to have lasted as long as the dictatorship itself, thus although she "understood that historical time was something else, for her own lifetime these years were too much, it was something being robbed from her without the possibility of return" (155).

It is perhaps not surprising that she chooses to write theater rather than a prose novel. By working with multiple characters, she hopes to avoid creating an epic of heroism, though more importantly, she remembers her own capture by the police as if it were a scene from a play (290). Nonetheless, since she soon realizes a form of self-censorship is necessary in order to avoid damaging either her country or her loved ones, she begins with the most obvious point of marginalization after her capture: her absence from Brazil. In different chapters, several sections of an unfinished play about exiles in Europe are presented to the reader as part of Lena's personal archive. At first, the dialogues and domestic scenes of everyday life appear to have little to offer, though when read later in conjunction with a series of preserved letters and other forms of correspondence between Lena and her family, the play illustrates how the fear and distrust of the government continues to erode any sense of Brazilian security even when she is supposedly free abroad. One woman believes she sees her torturer in the Paris metro, and she begins to slowly unravel, while a vicious rumor that the protagonists are informers leads to their ostracism from expatriate circles. Lena wonders to herself whether she should have included a character's suicide in the play, since she was in contact with expatriates who continued to be tormented by the violence they suffered and took their own lives. In fact, while Lena claims pure fiction is the antidote to fantasy, the play is ironically revealed to be a thinly veiled testimonial account. Indeed, both Lena and her mother at different points recognize how aesthetically poor the text is. Yet, instead of finishing or editing the work, Lena begins to realize that she may well never be able to write again (325), a symbolic vestige of the silencing effect that her exile accomplished.

It is bitterly ironic that Lena, unable to actively write, is thus consigned once again to the status of passive reader on the margins. As she attempts to creatively document her generation in response to Honório's challenge, the writer suffers the sudden onset of a mysterious psychological disorder that renders her unable to write coherent sentences, let alone practice investigative journalism (45). Despite being the perfect candidate for using literature as a pedagogical tool for contextualizing the lost generation, her dream of constructing a written record of the abandoned generation must itself be abandoned. If Lena's ailing body allegorically represents the nation during the 1980s as it sought to heal itself—with her foot condition, she remains virtually paralyzed—then her sudden dyslexia embodies the lingering effects of self-censorship that Machado highlighted within testimonial literature when speaking of the recuperation of national memory.[18] Lena seeks professional help, wondering if her reaction is a side effect of medication for her depression, but fear of what she must deal with prevents her from rejecting her treatment until a breaking point prompts her to return home. Beyond allegorically representing the return of exiles, Lena's escape from the city to her family home represents the first time that she is able to psychologically understand the extent to which the regime has damaged her. She literally returns to her own history, including indirect suggestions that she suffered a stillbirth during exile, for the pain of raking through old memories is necessary to heal. An unstated consequence of her guilt at the periphery of history is Lena's intense fear of failure, which ultimately becomes a self-fulfilling prophecy. When she finally accepts the possibility that her writing capacity may be permanently affected, she begins to reformulate her anger over the lack of national justice. Rejecting the collective and instead taking shelter in her own personal mourning for the epoch lost to her, she literally is able to get back on her two feet again.

In the final pages of the novel, as she rereads and summarizes several angry sections of her aborted play not presented in the narrative, she asks herself a question: "Was it worth it to persist in this? To attempt to retrieve, narrate, and prepare it all so that somebody could experience it in a theater?" (326) Instead of revealing her decision to abandon or continue the project, however, she transitions from the rhetorical query into a childhood memory in the forest. Her grandfather, who has had a recurring role in her recollection of the house, overrides the other male family members' objections to her participation in a hunting excursion, and she does justice to his belief in her, as she proves more daring than her male cousins who are too frightened to cross a potentially dangerous river. Figuratively indirect, the memory provides a subconscious example of her overcoming her peripheral status, and it seems that it unblocks a psychological barrier. Suddenly resolving to quit her medication and reinitiate contact with her estranged husband, she packs her bags and checks availability on the next flight back to Rio de Janeiro. In doing so, she signals her readiness to move beyond the past, and, for the first time, look toward the future from an accepted peripheral position. In this final turn of events, Machado brings the entire novel full circle, for the song lyrics to Veloso's "Strange Power," which precede chapter 1, narrate the very memory Lena relives: "I put my feet into the brook / And I think I never removed them / The sun still shines on the road / And I never left it." Aside from the sense

---

18. Machado roots the problems of literature's parajournalistic function in the divisive infighting that occurred between leftist intellectuals during the 1970s (*Contracorrente* 21–22).

of purpose the lyrics communicate, they also privilege the path forward on individual—not collective—terms.

DEMOCRACY AND THE POSTMODERN PERIPHERY

In a sense, to write within a postdictatorial context is always an admission of the periphery's failure to reconstitute the center, whether a period of history or a generation of individuals. One of the definitive traits of postdictatorial fiction evoked by Avelar is that writing is paradoxically no longer possible, and thus "the writer's only remaining task is to account for that impossibility" (232). This is partially a response to literature's loss of status after postmodernism, understood in Jamesonian terms as a historical moment initiated when the threshold for the global dominance of capital was reached. Whatever this may have meant for the flow of international capital from the United States southward, within Latin America, Avelar argues, the military dictatorship shepherded in this new economic stage. As a result, the task of mourning in its aftermath was confounded through the confusion of cultural and political referents. If literary representation after the civilian transition no longer enjoys the privilege that it had within the paradigm of modernism, then how can it productively enter into the process of resolving the absence of representation during the various dirty wars? In this sense, Avelar hopes that postdictatorial discourse responds directly to the dehumanization of ethics that occurs in developmental models for consumerism-as-democracy. If nothing else, the decline of literature—not only its low readership within the region, but the general turn away to "culturalism"—will itself come to constitute a form of ruins whose documentation will help spotlight ethical injustices. This is the value of "untimeliness," its rejection of the marketplace and theoretical frameworks that come to determine intellectual production in favor of experimentation.

Machado's insistence upon the writer only speaking for herself represents just such a rejection of the market, and the untimeliness of *Tropical Sun of Liberty* explains its uneasy relationship to transition literature in Brazil. If at once a literal example of "nationalism by subtraction," to repurpose the title of Roberto Schwarz's landmark Marxist critique of cultural imitation, the novel also locates exilic trauma in a regional network that obeys no national boundaries. Moreover, Machado's strategy lends itself to discussions of nationhood and belonging beyond the context of redemocratization. But perhaps most importantly, she reveals that the recovery of collective memory must begin with either personal or regional relationships or run the risk of becoming trapped by the very discourses of nationalism that returning exiles sought to destabilize.

Organized by exiled sociologist Herbert Souza, *Democracy: Five Principles and a Purpose* (1996) gathers together contributions from five of the most influential Brazilian writers of the decade, along with Mexican Carlos Fuentes, each of whom is tasked with exploring a different aspect of democracy through fiction. Machado's section examines the issue of diversity. It is telling, however, that she recycles the very strategy that undergirds the novel under examination. Instead of telling a story, she narrates her failure to create a narrative-on-demand by explaining the shortcomings of various abandoned attempts. Yet she draws attention to her process not as a form of metafictional parody, but because she claims dialogue is the principal foundation of universal democracy. For this reason, she justifies turning her contribution into an extended dialogue about her failure with "whomever reads me" ("Diversidade" 63), Brazilian or otherwise. The breakdown of communication lies at the heart of the ideological battles between intellectuals during the 1970s that she reconsiders in this nonfiction text. At the same time, it puts into perspective the transformative role of the trope of failure within *Tropical Sun of Liberty* as a form of dialogue, the imperfect return to democracy toward which it gestures, and the postnational necessity of personal reconciliation in which national models may paradoxically force individuals to mourn through conventions commodified by the literary marketplace.

CHAPTER 6

Allegorizing Brazilian History

Silviano Santiago's In Liberty, *Invisible Texts, and Ideological Patrols*

IT WAS SILVIANO SANTIAGO who first drew attention in 1979 to the return of Brazilian history during the decline of the military dictatorship. In contrast to Hayden White, however, in his subsequent Jabuti Award-winning novel *Em Liberdade* (*In Liberty,* 1981), he characterized the burden of the peripheral historian not as a question of creative obligation but as a "thankless task" wherein artists must educate the public about the erosion of public "truth" accomplished through the exhaustive repetition of "invented facts" (219–20).[1] Throughout his career as a cultural critic, Santiago has obsessively returned to two interconnected questions: what is the relation of the peripheral intellectual to social justice and in what different settings can cultural hybridity act as a form of social transgression? Much like his alternation between scholarly essays and creative fiction, the above themes mutually inform one another in his oeuvre. Thus his most recent novel, also a Jabuti Award recipient, *Machado* (2016), is part fiction and part literary criticism, and its focus on the foundational Brazilian author Machado de Assis provides an example of the national framework Santiago outlined in his turn-of-the-century discussion regard-

---

1. The title of Santiago's untranslated novel has most often been transcribed as "At Liberty," though I adopt the rendering of Ana Lúcia Gazzola, one of the translators responsible for the only English-language collection of Santiago's essays, *The Space In-Between* (2001). All translations of *In Liberty* are my own.

ing the "amphibious" nature of popular literature.[2] Conversely, the analysis of European and North American influence upon Latin America in *As Raízes e o Labirinto da América Latina* (*The Roots and the Labyrinth of Latin America*, 2006)—whose title references the foundational works by Brazilian Sérgio Buarque de Holanda and Mexican Octavio Paz analyzed within—echoes his earlier fictionalized biography *Viagem ao México* (*Journey to Mexico*, 1995), which follows modernist French playwright Antonin Artaud's madness-inducing trip to Cuba and Mexico in the 1930s. Yet all of these national and regional frameworks, as well as even the scholar's global-oriented theory of the twenty-first century, epitomized by *O cosmopolitismo do pobre* (*The Cosmopolitanism of the Poor*, 2004), are ultimately adaptations of his earliest and most-cited model of intellectual hybridity, "O entre-lugar do discurso latinoamericano" ("Latin American Discourse: The Space In-Between") (Leal Cunha, "Entre-Lugares" 10–11).

Conceived for a Canadian symposium in which he presented alongside Michel Foucault in the early 1970s, "The Space In-Between" was written in French while Santiago was teaching in the United States, and it drew on the energy of the countercultural movements sweeping universities across North America at the time. He next translated the work into English before finally publishing it by the end of the decade in Portuguese in his collection on cultural dependency, *Uma literatura nos trópicos* (*A Literature in the Tropics*, 1978). As his most regionally inclusive theory, the multiple versions and languages marking the transition of the "space in-between" into the canon of Brazilian letters appropriately echoes the project's Inter-American scope. Indeed, despite the title, Santiago not only addresses Hispanic American and Brazilian intellectuals as members of the periphery but also gestures to Francophone Canada when placing into relief the asymmetrical hemispheric dynamic anchored by the United States. As Santiago has explained, because of the marginalization of Brazilian culture, he felt obligated to structure the essay around Hispanic American authors and French critics so that academics would be able to relate (Leal Cunha and Melo Miranda 181). In effect, the essay proposes a means of counteracting political flows from cultural centers through recourse to an "invisible" text, a false copy that reveals subtle contradictions in the logic of hegemonic models. Gaining traction in postcolonial criticism,[3] this subtle response to cultural imperialism contrasts with the more overtly "cannibalistic" forms of parody long favored within the Brazilian modernist tradition.

---

2. See the essay in Santiago's *O cosmopolitismo*.

3. For examples of the concept's deployment regarding transculturation and third space, see King and Browitt, Mignolo, and Lomas.

His second novel, *In Liberty*, appeared on the heels of *A Literature in the Tropics*, and in addition to its focus on history, it resituates the latter's critique of international dependency theory to address the need for Brazilian intellectuals to apply the same criterion to the current national dictatorship. Producing an apocryphal version of modernist writer Graciliano Ramos's missing 1937 diary, Santiago establishes a historical link between Brazil's two twentieth-century dictatorships, Getúlio Vargas's New State (1937–1945) and the military regime (1964–1985) that was unraveling as he wrote. Significantly, the book provides the cultural critic's most sustained meditation upon intellectual resistance toward authoritarian models, effectively demonstrating the applicability of the space in-between to distinct forms of postnationalism. Whereas Santiago's famous essay deconstructs the standard of colonial purity and unity in response to subordination by cultural and economic centers, the postnational resistance central to *In Liberty* oscillates between discourses of national unity and self-destructive leftist politics, a relationship shown to be equally germane to contemporary authoritarian regimes across the continent.

Indeed, Santiago has confirmed that while the novel ostensibly represents a modernist writer's resistance to authoritarianism, it is in fact a thinly veiled allegory regarding the imperiled state of creative freedom during the Brazilian military's most repressive period of the 1970s (Leal Cunha and Melo Miranda 186). The urban guerilla response had been neutralized earlier in the decade, though by including Ramos's research of historians' accounts regarding the most famous failed opposition in Brazilian history, the eighteenth-century Minas Gerais Conspiracy, Santiago establishes a pattern of historical repression. For one of the apparently historical documents Ramos reproduces in his journal in fact draws verbatim from a 1975 Brazilian military report that denied responsibility for the death of jailed journalist Vladimir Herzog. And while the text is openly critical of censorship and the cooptation through which the government limited cultural resistance, it also reserves harsh judgment for the complicity of Santiago's progressive colleagues who failed to organize against the military.

In her influential study released the year civilian rule returned to Brazil, Flora Sussekind examines why truth literature became the dominant form of production during the late 1970s and early 1980s, challenging the claim that censorship was the determining factor limiting aesthetic contributions. Before the oppressive decade under AI-5, for example, she points to the dictatorship's effective cooptation of intellectuals—strategies similar to those enacted during Vargas's New State, as Santiago has demonstrated—which limited their public audience by employing the newly accessible spectacle of television to commodify middle-class viewers and national history (23–24). Additionally,

Sussekind explains how two issues during the 1960s fractured the political left by pitting Marxist scholars against artists who did not view literature as a vehicle expressly for political ideology. The first was the surge in nationalism encouraged under the dictatorship and the second was the perceived assault on literature by the rise of structuralist theory, as the left's petty infighting began to receive coverage in a variety of media. In a 1978 interview with Pola Vartuck, filmmaker Carlos Diegues coined the phrase "ideological patrols" to characterize the damaging effects of cultural policing—censorship of the moderate left in this case not by the state but rather by hardcore liberals and the Communist Party. Not coincidentally, Diegues cites Graciliano Ramos as an example of how intellectuals creatively experimented under previous dictatorships without aligning themselves with either group (Sussekind 60). Thus, Sussekind argues, the destabilizing effects of these intellectual debates ultimately provided the conditions for the privileging of testimonial/documentary literature and biographical depositions as exiles took advantage of the 1979 Amnesty Law to return home. Yet by this time, the establishment of a new form of control further complicated intellectual collective identity: the governing logic of the market. Sussekind provides a wide panorama of works falling into the popularity of the "documentary trap," yet one text stands out as an anticonfessional work that purposefully disappoints readers expecting heroic descriptions by instead creatively highlighting the limitations of the testimonial trend: Santiago's *In Liberty* (91). Unlike its counterparts, which traffic in sensational depictions of torture and guerilla warfare, Santiago's work largely describes the banal routine of a historical writer who refuses to transform his experience into a public document to serve ideological interests.

Santiago published the novel at a crucial moment in Brazil's history, as citizens were unsure whether the government's controlled liberalization would continue or return to more oppressive policies, yet he allegorically links the freedom of writing amidst ideological patrols to the intellectual censorship that occurred during the modernist period. Not by coincidence, he announced the end of Brazilian modernism in 1982,[4] an important contextual marker for understanding the numerous postmodern threads he weaves together in the false document. At once biography, literary criticism, fiction, and a form of autobiography (Miranda 90), *In Liberty* has been defined by Santiago himself as a "false diary" that presents itself as Ramos's personal journal upon release from political imprisonment in 1937, the objective being to identify new forms of cultural transgression (*Nas Malhas* 116). A pastiche of referents, the work is presented as a critical edition of Ramos's discovered manuscript, featuring

---

4. See "Fechado para Balanço" in *Nas Malhas*.

an editorial introduction by Santiago authenticating the work; Ramos's diary entries, marginalia, and later additions on undated sheaves of paper; newspaper and pamphlet clippings; and excerpts from historical manuals.

While the mimicry of Ramos's voice seems to have confused some critics who believed the work was nonfiction (Avelar 17), Santiago's appropriation of Ramos's identity is neither a hoax nor a lampoon of the writer—who had himself been a vocal critique of the modernist movement[5]—but rather an attack on the political and literary conventions of modernism that exercised hegemony over Brazilian production for six decades dating back to its 1922 origins. Ultimately, Santiago does not so much plagiarize his predecessor's style as pay homage through what he terms postmodern pastiche, although his definition is based on a specifically Brazilian tradition that runs contrary to US models, as we shall see shortly. Given Santiago's own paratextual commentary in response to Fredric Jameson's negative characterization of pastiche, it is not surprising that critical explorations of *In Liberty* have approached the novel primarily through a Euro-American postmodern prism.[6] Echoing Santiago's own affirmation, it has been read as emblematic of the pastiche novel, a product of intertextual translation, and a poststructural example of Jean Baudrillard's simulation and simulacra and Jameson's prison-house of language.[7] Nonetheless, while the novel may be "postmodern" in terms of providing an alternative to modernist discourses of rupture, in Brazil the term engages both a distinct sociopolitical history and a different set of strategies in relation to the market than North American traveling theory, for the act of parody had already played a central role in modernist cultural production.[8]

Decentering cultural dependence has additional implications for geographically peripheral spaces where unequal modernization facilitated the coexistence of distinct stages of development. In fact, a brief analysis of Santiago's characterization of postmodernism reveals significant overlap with the oppositional strategy first defined in "The Space In-Between." Although he did not adopt the vocabulary of poststructuralism, Santiago's earlier advocacy for intellectual resistance from the periphery antedated similar discussions

---

5. In contrast to his colleagues, Ramos claimed the modernist movement had done nothing for prose, but instead "gave a chance to the stupid and mediocre," running its course by the early 1930s (qtd. in Nist 106).

6. The transcription of Santiago's live question-and-answer session included at the end of "Fechado para Balanço" describes postmodern pastiche.

7. Franco (*Critical Passions*) and Avelar examine the work as a pastiche novel, Miranda as intertextual translation, and Jackson as a simulacra.

8. Coutinho (1997) provides a helpful analysis of Brazilian postmodernism's distinct periodization, given the country's modernism anticipated North American postmodern strategies (327–29).

among Hispanic American scholars by two decades.[9] In other words, while Brazil is typically marginalized both within the Americas and in Latin American studies, its approach to postmodernism has much to teach neighboring traditions. For Santiago, modernists conflate the difference between product and medium ("Postmodern Reception" 200), and it is this essentialism that *In Liberty* exploits.

By collapsing the temporal distance between present and past in this false testimonial, Santiago paradoxically attempts to liberate Ramos from being remembered as a political symbol of the left to humanize the author and his aesthetic contributions. Indeed, "liberty" in the novel becomes a private space for Ramos to meditate on the role of the Brazilian intellectual quite literally as a space in-between fiction and history, the freedom of self-expression and the imposition of the state. Caught between government decrees and pressure from the communist and literary establishments, Ramos's tenuous position in the middle of opposing institutional agendas exemplifies how the correlation between power and censorship is not a reflection of any singular ideology. Thus, in addition to commenting upon the recurrent state of oppressive Brazilian politics, Santiago utilizes his false document to interrogate the authority extended to forms of writing—including journalism, historiography, and realist literature—that rely on truth claims to represent the past from a monolithic perspective. Drawing on his own experience producing state-commissioned articles, the fictional Ramos ultimately rejects discourses of realism as "fascism" to instead promote creative fiction as a means of opposing the mediated facts that have been canonized through uncritical repetition. His unwillingness to rubberstamp state interests, despite his paradoxical dependence upon the government for work after his imprisonment, demonstrates his greatest act of intellectual resistance, and Santiago clearly holds this example up to his contemporaries.

My goal in exploring *In Liberty* as a false document that corresponds to a Brazilian conception of the postmodern—accentuating the product rather than the medium, the artifact rather than the artisan—is thus to draw attention to the various academic debates and forms assumed by ideological patrols during the return to history, for Ramos's rejection of truth literature is emblematic of his forger's critical attitudes to contemporary schisms. In order to trace the two intertextual strands that provide the key for unpack-

---

9. A 1993 special issue of *South Atlantic Quarterly* dedicated to the tension between center and periphery in postmodernism unites well-known representatives from the Americas, including Fredric Jameson, Nestor García Canclini, George Yúdice, and Nelly Richard, the latter of whom describes a strategy of "countermimesis" that pretends to share the dominant vocabulary in order to later subvert and appropriate those same terms (Richard 458).

ing *In Liberty*, the remainder of this chapter will first briefly detour through a contextual overview of Ramos's testimonial fiction via Santiago's scholarship on the modernist paradigm and its authoritarian tendencies. This will in turn provide the basis for interrogating Santiago's correlative approach to postmodernism—namely, democratizing the production of meaning while activating readers to become critical participants in public debates—as a local revision of his hemispheric claims in "The Space In-Between" regarding impersonation via an "invisible" text. After understanding how these heterogeneous concepts are tied together through the act of intellectual resistance, I will turn to how the novel establishes an obligation for intellectual responsibility through critique of truth literature's ahistoricism. Finally, examining how Santiago allegorically utilizes history to assail both conservative and "progressive" sources of censorship at the start of the 1980s demonstrates a creative form of cultural hybridity that reveals the unexpected and invisible forms authoritarianism can take during times of political turmoil.

RAMOS, THE PRISON OF MODERNISM, AND TESTIMONIAL FICTION

As Antonio Candido first demonstrated in *Ficção e confissão* (1956), and countless other critics have further elucidated in the decades since, the blend of first-person narration and fictionalization that characterized Ramos's memoirs was also the hallmark of his most important novels, including *São Bernardo* (1934), *Angústia* (1936), and *Vidas Secas* (1938). This challenge to the referentiality of first-person testimony makes Ramos the perfect vehicle for Santiago to bridge political and intellectual eras. In the previous chapter, I outlined the abundance of testimonial literature that appeared as political exiles began returning home after the 1979 Amnesty Law, and the timing of Santiago's false confession is not coincidental. While memorialist fiction was a central genre of modernist writing, Santiago is clear that contemporary representations of firsthand experience such as Gabeira's cannot be considered postmodern, not only because of their claims to reproduce reality but also the inherent mythification of their narratives' participants as martyrs.[10] This explains why, in much the same way Ramos refused to portray himself as a hero in his prison memoirs, Santiago's fictional journal entries reveal the pressure that the political detainee withstands in order not to martyrize himself

---

10. See the titular essay of Santiago's *Vale quanto pesa* (1982) as well as others in the collection.

for the political left. Writing early in the diary about censorship and torture as part of the "long and fastidious monologue that is our History," he wonders why Brazilian society cannot accept opposition as a vital necessity to improve the political enterprise (*In Liberty* 34). While the Vargas regime is the subject of this rhetorical query, the mention of torture clearly applies to the contemporary military regime. Additionally, Ramos recognizes this same intolerance for dissidence in the communist party, whose insistence upon social realism and political ideology lead to similar forms of ideological patrolling (159), a similar complaint to that of 1970s intellectuals who were not considered progressive enough by their more militant counterparts. Thus for Santiago and Ramos, there are multiple conservative and liberal institutions that promote unanimity, obliging him to choose a path in-between to preserve his integrity.

At the same time that he wrote the novel, Santiago had begun reflecting on the origins of modernism as more than simply an artistic movement. From its symbolic beginning during the Modern Art Week in 1922, one hundred years after Brazil gained independence, the modernists' avowed goal of progress rested on two interrelated aesthetic and political tasks: the updating of art through culturally elite production and the modernization of society through an authoritarian government (*Nas Malhas* 76). In the decade following *In Liberty*, Santiago devoted multiple critical collections to the analysis of modernism, casting doubt upon innocent interpretation based on two particular counts: institutionalization and totalitarianism. First, the cannibalizing creed of Brazilian modernism exerted more extensive influence over popular cultural production during the twentieth century than did its Hispanic analogue, evidenced by the resurgence of its anthropophagic irreverence in poetry, theater, and cinema as well as popular protest music before and during the dictatorship. By virtue of gradual institutionalization, however, its originally transgressive parody gave way to mere ceremony and repetition, thus in Santiago's analysis, postmodern strategies offer an alternative to stagnation rather than simple negation.

The second issue concerns how critics have minimized the totalitarian thought of the movement's originators, for the modernist manifesto of rupture represents a closed system; rather than facilitate literary or political exchange, it articulates a monolithic logic of progress, making it a potential accomplice to political control. This lack of plurality meant that the line between resistance and complicity was often blurred. Or as Santiago puts it, the "principal modernist novelists and poets managed to coexist with the New State . . . because ultimately there was no essential difference between the two groups' approach to power" (*Nas Malhas* 79–80). Both grew in reaction to the Old Republic overthrown in the 1930 coup and prioritized a discourse of national identity based on unity, and these related ends led to similar recourse to authoritarian thought.[11] While modernism initially promoted a rejection of conservative values, it enjoyed a contradictory relationship with the New State. Vargas's government created a system of cooptation, on the one hand investing in education and the arts more than any previous government in the country's history, yet on the other muting dissenting intellectuals who became functionaries in various state ministries in order to make ends meet (Candido, "A Revolução de 1930" n.p.).

Ramos had a similarly compromised relation to the state, for after his incarceration he was appointed a functionary in the new regime as Federal Inspector of Secondary Education. Struggling to support his family and living in a fellow writer's house in the first months after his release, Ramos entered and won a state-sponsored competition for children's literature, and he also contributed articles on demand for *Cultura Política*, the official publication of the government's Department of Press and Propaganda, even if he was aware of the irony of his position.[12] Yet other intellectual groups participated directly in anticommunist politics that at times allied their actions with Vargas, such as the Brazilian Integralist Action (AIB), a fascist political group founded in early 1932 by author Plínio Salgado. Despite being critical of the 1934 constitution, the Integralists shared Vargas's totalitarian approach to utopian modernization. A decade earlier, Salgado had participated in the Modern Arts Week as a burgeoning modernist. As an Integralist, however, he combatively requested the mobilization of writers and artists for the country's political service via the formation of the National Ministry of Fine Art (Levine, *Vargas* 145, 82), an anti-Vargas stance *In Liberty* illustrates with a newspaper fragment.[13]

Despite the anti-intellectual climate that marked the increasing control over creative expression, several writers and critics did brave public attacks, including Ramos, whose criticism likely played a role in his imprisonment by the Vargas government (Levine, *Vargas* 136–37). Incarcerated for ten months in 1936 as a political prisoner and transported to three separate detention centers—prison, correctional facility, and island penal colony, each a descent into greater spaces of dehumanization—Ramos was never officially charged with a

---

11. Gouveia (55–65) provides an account of the hypocritical relationship between liberal and fascist factions of modernist intellectuals and the New State's manipulative support of the arts.

12. Melo (68–72) and Florent provide more information on Ramos's paradoxical relationships with both the state and the Brazilian Communist Party.

13. Critiquing history's losers' tendency to martyrize leaders, Ramos reproduces a 1937 newspaper excerpt in which Salgado both rebuffs Vargas's attempts to create an alliance against a presidential candidate and claims that Integralists do not fear federal persecution since martyrdom would strengthen the movement (*In Liberty* 182).

crime. Although the implicit offense was his support of communism, he did not officially join the Communist Party until it was legalized in 1945, nearly a decade after his release. Ironically, if Ramos's incarceration was intended to silence him, it had the opposite effect, leading instead to an increased interest in his work on the part of the activist intellectual community. Just as Ramos never learned the official nature of his offense, neither did he discover the reason for his sudden release in January of 1937. Instead, upon his return it became apparent that the reactionary vanguard by the Brazilian Communist Party (PCB), which hoped to publicize its cause via his written account of the ordeal, had claimed him as a symbol.

Although Ramos maintained a diary during his imprisonment, he was subsequently forced to abandon it during transportation to the island colony. The incomplete, multivolume *Memories of Prison* (1953) is thus a fictionalized reconstruction begun nearly a decade after his ordeal and published posthumously, though its mixture of testimonial and fiction did not affect its reception as a document of truth for the general public (Davi 10). Recognizing himself as a member of the bourgeoisie in an alien environment, Ramos resists the temptation to present himself as a militant intellectual or a hero of the masses, and in this sense, he avoids the epic narrative of heroism that testimonial writing during the 1980s would adopt. At the same time, his decision to highlight aesthetic concerns rather than construct a proletariat hero in adherence to socialist realism alienated him from the communist party, which ultimately banned the book within its circles in response to Ramos's damning characterizations of political agents on both sides of the ideological divide (Davi 44).

Ramos makes clear in his introduction that the memoir avails itself of the prison system to create a carceral metaphor for Brazilian society. Thus by claiming to be the missing final chapter of the never-finished memoir, *In Liberty* extends the modernist's prison analogy to historicize the military dictatorship under which Santiago writes. Ramos addresses the decision to wait a decade in his introduction, explaining that "nobody enjoys complete freedom" (11) and admitting that political factors that included increasing censorship and fear of further repercussion prevented him from initiating work on the text. Additionally, he was slowed by literary concerns, not wanting the book to become a list of names like a "civil registry," but also not wishing to use pseudonyms that might turn the book into a type of novel. Santiago's Ramos also ruminates on the need to "liberate" himself from the preconceptions of fiction writing in order to be honest in his diary entries, yet even more ingeniously, Santiago's false document incorporates the postscript to the *Memories of Prison*, in which Ramos's son explains that his father had not written the final chapter but had revealed the missing section would detail both "sensations of liberty" and alienation in Rio de Janeiro upon his release (*Memórias* 2: 229). In dialogue with this description, one of the first sections of *In Liberty* reflects Ramos's estrangement initially walking the streets of Rio a free man. Nonetheless, through multiple levels of interpretation that emerge during the course of the reading, the concept of freedom referenced in the novel's title reveals itself to be more ambiguous than at might first appear, referring to both physical and psychological emancipation, personal and public personas. Santiago appropriates this notion of freedom as an ironic means of discussing censorship without either parodying or repeating Ramos, inhabiting the space between invention and plagiarism.

In addition to Ramos's testimonial style, his complex relationship to authoritarian power would seem to be the ideal subject for Santiago to adapt to the political and aesthetic conditions of his own era's censorship. Yet for Santiago, in a clear dig at Marxist criticism, the "thankless task" of the historian must be augmented by the freedom of the writer, for the relation of traditional history to the circulation of power overlooks the role of cultural responses.[14] Though *In Liberty* primarily details the author's struggles to avoid fictionalizing his own observations, its critique hinges on the final entries in which Ramos abandons a modern individual focus to instead blend history and fiction through a jailed poet. Aside from creating a complex game of mirrors in which this historical narrative doubles the very relationship that exists between Santiago and Ramos, the invented historical narrative builds upon Ramos's own documented preoccupation with national history. In 1940, he wrote "A Short History of the Republic," a children's narrative he planned to enter in another literary contest supported by the Ministry of Education and Culture. A pattern increasingly emerges, for far from heroically depicting national enlightenment, the fragmented text satirizes Vargas's 1930 coup and great men of the historical record, even presenting them *as* children. Realizing the potential risk for returning to prison, Ramos desisted, and the work was only published after his death, yet the example demonstrates two characteristics of the space in-between Santiago mirrors nearly fifty years later: an oppositional role for intellectuals in society, despite state cooptation, and the power of resignifying political events via fiction's freedom from conventions.

---

14. Santiago attacks "traditional history" in *Vale quanto pesa* (51–60), while he discusses the relationship between literature and cultural history in "Para além da história social" (*Nas malhas*).

SANTIAGO, THE FREEDOM OF POSTMODERNISM, AND THE SPACE IN-BETWEEN

The previous section presents Santiago's *In Liberty* as an extension, as opposed to appropriation, of Ramos's identity. If the text foregrounds neither rupture nor parody, the trademarks of Hutcheon's historiographic metafiction, two questions emerge: does this project represent a postmodern aesthetic and how is it related to the oppositional role of the intellectual? To establish this connection, we must examine Santiago's definition of postmodernism within the context of cultural peripheries, which does not correspond to the North American paradigm. The modernist tradition of anthropophagy was founded on parody, most famously outlined in Oswald de Andrade's "Cannibal Manifesto" (1928), in which the oft-cited line "Tupi or Not Tupi" references the supposedly cannibalistic indigenous group in the Amazon (decimated by the European conquest) while simultaneously incorporating canonical European literature to create a uniquely hybrid, Brazilian product. By contrast, rather than frame his reaction to international imperialism, Santiago embraces the arrival of cultural postmodernism as an end of the exhausted practice of modernism. When he imagines that *In Liberty* helps initiate a new phase in Brazilian letters, it is not within the context of relativistic language games, but rather the education of mass society. In peripherally capitalist countries where literacy has a much shorter history, citizenship cannot be measured using modernist methodology. The advent of new technologies and visual media have promised new accessibility, as "the production of meaning ceases to be a monopoly of restricted minorities who are, in conditions of inequality, better trained and thus more sophisticated. With that change, the singular, or authoritarian, interpretation made by a legitimizing group (traditionally, professional critics or experts) also disappears" ("Postmodern Reception" 201). If literature can productively reinvent itself in this new environment alongside visual culture—central to the "spectacle" through which the dictatorship coopted intellectuals' national audience—then it can simultaneously break with the class exclusion inherent to modernism and teach new ways of reading culture.

Jameson famously posited pastiche as a symptom of postmodern superficiality, a form of mimicry that lacks satirical purpose or political motivation, leading instead to "the cannibalization of all the styles of the past" (*Cultural Logic* 18). Santiago instead touts pastiche as the defining *productive* quality of peripheral postmodernism, and history is an important component because it must respond to the previous lack of historicity, whether in dictatorial speeches claiming national unity or the testimonial bestsellers written in opposition (*Nas Malhas* 117). Given his much-criticized claims about third world allegory, it is clear that Jameson is not speaking about critical cannibalization in the Brazilian anthropophagic sense, yet Santiago defines pastiche as a very nuanced and specific form of imitation targeting a cultural dominant—unlike modernist parody, which announces its presence through satire, pastiche consists of repetition with subversive difference—and it cannot be other than political. Precisely because pastiche does not presuppose violent rupture, it is able to "constitute a sympathetic relation with the past which may act as a pointed critique of the present" (Franco, *Critical Passions* 395). Santiago notably engaged in archival research to study Ramos's literary and personal writing style in order to imitate this work. And yet the work is not a hoax; it provides the clues for destabilizing its invented legitimacy. In the author's own formulation, imitation that covertly announces its difference acts as a means of unveiling and recovering concepts that have disappeared from public debate, thus it is inherently oriented toward recovering the past.

As mentioned earlier, the above description of pastiche bears remarkable similarity to the central strategy Santiago laid out in "The Space In-Between." Discussions of Latin American postmodernism were dominated by Hispanic Americanists during the 1990s, yet it is telling that the two Brazilian figures to receive international attention—Santiago and Roberto Schwarz—prefigured regional debates because they were primarily responding to questions of cultural dependency during the 1970s.[15] Both scholars utilize Brazil as a point of entry to frame larger cultural debates between Latin America and Europe, and it is worth noting that both metaphorically evoke the notion of place (*lugar*), specifically that of the intellectual, in the original Portuguese, though this detail is lost when translated into English. The place of Santiago's *entre-lugar* becomes "space in-between," while in the case of Schwarz, *ideias fora do lugar* transforms into "misplaced ideas," signaling a type of order that is transgressed.[16] Thus for Santiago, active defiance is what *places* not only Brazil but also more generally peripheral America "on the map," a cartographical metaphor that he evokes repeatedly in the essay.

Unlike Schwarz, Santiago focuses not on causality but rather the political implications of mimicry itself. Beginning with excerpts from European explorers' and missionaries' comprising descriptions of Indians, the essay evaluates the basic binaries of colonial exploitation that have defined the history of

---

15. While Santiago and Schwarz are the only Brazilians included in Beverley et al., Santiago provides a helpful bibliography of other important Brazilian interventions (241).

16. Reflecting the Marxist underpinnings of social history, Schwarz approaches the question of mimicry in terms of class and material historicism through a reading of Machado de Assis.

Latin American politics—civilization vs. barbarity, center vs. periphery—yet adds a twist by subverting the parameters upon which originality and imitation are based. Because colonial practices historically erased the origins of indigenous culture and then devalued those same peoples for struggling to imitate imposed European values, the phenomenon of duplication became the marker of civilization. Yet its reverberations continue into the twentieth century, which "merely reveals the indigence of an art that is, a priori, poor, due to the economic conditions in which it must survive. It merely sheds light on the lack of imagination of artists forced, due to the lack of an autochthonous tradition, to appropriate models disseminated from within the metropolis" (*Space In-Between* 31). For peripheral American societies, the primary channel for destabilizing this historical practice involves exposing the tautology through which dominant discourse assumes its own unity and purity. If the attribution of originality to a particular model is thus flawed in the first place, then Santiago presents in its place a strategic position from which reactionary intellectuals can reveal contradictions that the dominant center is unable to recognize. This is the space in-between, not in the sense of compromise but rather a "false obedience" that refuses to recognize the autonomy of semantic opposites. Mere imitation equates to silence and therefore complicity. Presence, by contrast, is annunciated through a feigned repetition that later marks its difference with political consequences: "To speak, to write, means to speak against, to write against" (31).

By not stipulating against *whom* or *what* this presence reacts, the essay invites a second level of reading in light of Santiago's later critique of modernism. Its concluding paragraph, the most frequently cited part of the essay, makes no mention of specific geographical positionality as a precondition for deconstructing binary schemes: "Somewhere between sacrifice and playfulness, prison and transgression, submission to the code and aggression, obedience and rebellion, assimilation and expression—there, in this apparently empty space, its temple and its clandestinity, is where the anthropophagous ritual of Latin American discourse is constructed" (38). In effect, Santiago provides a recipe for defying any totalizing model imposed upon Brazilian intellectual production, including that which comes from within. As we have seen, politico-cultural paradigms such as modernism and dictatorial power have equally authoritarian effects upon freedom of thought in Santiago's formation.

Yet what about methodology? American intransigence emerges from a "hidden space" that negates the epistemology of originality, which Santiago illustrates by reading Jorge Luis Borges's "Pierre Menard, Author of El Quijote" (1939). This famous story revolves around the fictitious Menard's attempts to rewrite Cervantes's novel, word for word, in the twentieth century, yet this replica is neither a copy nor a form of plagiarism, according to Menard, who is unconcerned with questions of authenticity. The author instead claims that the identical words shared by the texts do not have the same meaning in their different historical contexts; his achievement is in fact greater than Cervantes's, for recreation of the Spaniard's antiquated language represents anachronism in the contemporary world. Santiago thus concludes that the few fragments that Menard "wrote" are in effect invisible since the model and the copy appear to be indistinguishable, though difference is spatialized by drawing attention to this unseen text: "The invisible work is the paradox of the second text that completely disappears and thereby opens the space of its most evident signification: the cultural, social, and political situation in which the second author is located" (36). Evoking a type of palimpsest, the false imitation—or pastiche, to use Santiago's later terminology—should "affirm itself as a writing upon another writing. . . . Propaganda is effective precisely because it speaks the language of our time" (34).

Both propaganda and the politics of the body emerge as the axes that structure the invisible text in *In Liberty*, which creates a space in-between private and public discourse, intellectual freedom and authoritarian censorship, where the space is temporal rather than geographical or semantic. Similar to Menard's project in Borges's short story, Santiago's false diary anachronistically reproduces Ramos's style and syntax to defamiliarize the contemporary reader. Allegorically, the diary plays the role of invisible text by drawing attention to the intellectual and political policing that continued during the end of the dictatorship, a sense of insecurity about a potential resurgence of oppression not dissimilar to Ramos's own insecurity over the possibility of again facing imprisonment. Intellectual resistance is thus granted a new set of tools through the merging of differing conceptions of the postnational, on the one hand as a hemispheric comparative practice and on the other a localized rejection of authoritarian discourses of progress. Clearly, concurrent testimonial writing was also concerned with speaking against the dictatorship, yet by their referential nature to recent events, such accounts collapsed the past into a focus on the present. As an invisible text, *In Liberty* announces its difference by initiating the return in Brazilian literature to history.

BETWEEN PROPAGANDA AND HISTORY: *IN LIBERTY*, INVISIBLE TEXTS, AND CONTEMPORARY FASCISM

The key both to Brazilian postmodern and in-between spaces is the conscious use of replication to call attention to distinct moments of production. Santiago's Ramos discovers the dangers of repetition when he performs historical research for the unpublished short story he hopes will reignite his motivation to create, though his conclusions are as appropriate for the military's nationalist discourse as they are for modernist scholars. The historian, it turns out, helps exhaust the reader's defenses because she or he is "obligated to answer to the 'truth' of the document . . . [thus] the same facts are repeated to exhaustion. This is how historical truth about events imposes itself among us. Through fatigue rather than attention" (219–20). Ramos thus takes it upon himself to write—and implicitly write against—national mythology by turning his journal entries away from his personal problems to use them as a log of progress. The diary is actually divided into two parts, with the first section featuring Ramos's unease at living in the city. Previous to his incarceration, he had worked in a provincial capital as a public education bureaucrat, marginalized from cultural centers such as Rio. After recording initial preoccupations, the second set of entries deal with the complicated reality of the intellectual seeking to earn a living. Thus Ramos, upon his release, is much more troubled by economic dependence upon his host than he is cultural dependence. Unsure how to support his wife and children given the knowledge of his incarceration by potential employers, Ramos eventually accepts contracted writing for journals legitimizing the New State. In the process of writing on behalf of the very government that imprisoned him, he comes dangerously close to the role of the "impoverished" artist who reproduces the imposed model rather than who actively speaks against power through subversion of codes (*In Liberty* 170). But Ramos becomes aware of this paradox in his diary when he reflects that what he terms "journalistic discourse" has as its ultimate end the establishment of "the power of the master" (180). By writing in programmatic fashion without asserting their individual identities, journalists simply act as vehicles for corporate messages and the medium itself, encouraging a focus on the present that erases historical challenges. The difficult choice facing critics is that the "only option for the intellectual in Brazil is to become a public employee, living reality in two halves, only grasping the truth by closing one eye" (36). Once they are dependent upon the state, important thinkers not only write for a small demographic of educated readers but also have less time to write against the state. Indeed, the mass production of newspapers and propaganda is for Ramos what the mass-production of televised images is for Brazil during the dictatorship's economic miracle.

A month out of prison, when carnival celebrations overtake the city, Ramos now views the events with cynical eyes, particularly its celebration of death as a sacrifice. Ramos anticipates Sussekind's analysis of the dictatorship's use of visual spectacle to distract the population, noting, "Fascist regimes have an obsession with spectacle. Through them, they confuse happiness and sadness, they justify death (the sacrifice for it) with the cheap glitter of carnival fantasies" (146). The search for freedom occurs with acts that exceed the acceptance of everyday existence, whereas the week of apparent freedom from rules that the celebrations offer simply allows citizens to exhaust their resistance and return to complacency for the rest of the year. Facetiously referencing Gilberto Freyre's cultural history of Brazil, he rhetorically asks, "Isn't this the country where differences are erased in favor of a national spirit that mixes blacks and whites, Indians and blacks, rich and poor, masters and slaves? Racial democracy, social democracy—aren't these the words used by our greatest intellectuals and politicians?" (148).

It is therefore appropriate that *In Liberty* is both framed as a form of scholarly work whose authority the reader is invited to call into question and appears initially only to recount Ramos's daily life. As will become clear shortly, Santiago's Ramos is particularly critical of intellectual forms of writing that promulgate institutional values without challenging their audience. The format exemplifies the pattern of creative dissociation central to Doctorow's false documents, as the text explicitly recreates the conventions of academic discourse by starting with two paratextual editorial notes attributed to Santiago. The preface explains the diary as a found document, inventing a history from 1937 to its arrival in Santiago's possession in 1965. In a Kafkaesque gesture, Ramos requests the diary be burned, thus the anonymous friend who failed to destroy the texts hides his identity fearing "judgment by history" (13). In a subtle nod to his own research, Santiago claims he was introduced to the deceased archivist while editing an unpublished draft of Andre Gide's *The Counterfeiters* (1925), which is both a self-reflexive novel that explores the relationship between originals and copies as well as the subject of Santiago's master's thesis. Structurally and thematically, then, this editorial preface provides an important clue to Santiago's relation to the current work, itself a counterfeit of a supposedly unpublished draft.

The second prefatory note provides information on the "edition" of the work, though in admitting editorial intrusion in order to organize and date the various entries, it problematizes any expectations of an authentic document. Santiago describes how he has reproduced Ramos's own handwritten additions from the margins, for the writer revisited and annotated the diary in 1945 shortly before beginning *Memories of Prison*. More challenging is the interpolation of undated sheaves of paper that Ramos must have intended as revisions to the written entries, and the editor has had to interpret where they should best be placed to maintain the consistency of the work. In other words, before the diary even reaches the reader, it has passed through any number of hands that have altered its initial form, from Ramos's own additions to a series of executors entrusted with the dossier of papers. As a palimpsest, *In Liberty* features multiple layers of conflicting historical and political sources, though a great part of the text's ability to convincingly portray Ramos's style comes from incorporating direct references, and at times, nearly verbatim citations from the legitimate *Memories of Prison*.

At first glance, Ramos's personal annotations appear to fall into two categories: political criticism of the growing authoritarianism in the country and banal daily experiences, including the ideological tensions that develop between his wife Heloísa and José Lins do Rego, the writer who shares his home while the couple seeks to get its feet on the ground. A successful historical novelist who romanticizes the past and coolly navigates state bureaucracy, Lins do Rego soon comes to epitomize the complicity that Ramos abhors. Yet while the narration initially seems devoid of purpose or order, Santiago's diarist has in actuality constructed a very tightly woven network of themes that echo and reinforce one another. Ultimately, Ramos returns to three particular motifs throughout the course of the diaries, which cover the period of time from the day after his release in January 1937 through the end of March: the meaning of freedom, the relationship between intellectuals and fascism, and the tension between fiction and history, all of which act as direct extensions of Santiago's earlier hemispheric work.

The "liberty" proclaimed by the title takes on multiple connotations concerning the tenuous state of writing to galvanize individual and collective identity, and again Ramos's annotations are ambiguous enough for Santiago's contemporary readers to recognize their own conditions. "The circumstantial freedom I have experienced since yesterday is much less important than the freedom I have discovered writing these pages" (36), he initially suggests, because the freedom to simply write without creating relieves anxiety, but within the month he reverses course. His minor celebrity status results in new forms of control, as various groups request a testimony of his prison experiences, imagining it on the one hand as the "definitive document against the persecution of communists in Brazil" and on the other as "the definitive work of national literature" (61–62). While Ramos knows that the increase of national security agencies has led to repressive consequences for any socialist sentiment, he ultimately rejects these requests for another reason. Writing designed to substantiate an ideology of heroic resistance is at best propaganda and at worst creates martyrs. Worse still, it enshrines the image of defeat rather than victory. Regarding their utility to posterity, he suggests that "the martyr dies for the historian. He doesn't die for his people" (203). While Ramos is aware that several writers' intercession assisted his release, he complains these same individuals refuse to let him live in freedom, wanting him to revisit the psychological trap he has only just left behind (63).

What then is the proper relation between a writer and his public? Ramos is discouraged to learn how popular he has become as a consequence of his stint in prison rather than the aesthetic merit of his writing (68). Thus when his host Lins do Rego suggests that he enter his recent children's stories in a competition funded by the Ministry of Education and Health, Ramos is conflicted but accepts out of financial need. Additionally, the state-sponsored award might draw national attention to his treatment at the hands of the government, which has largely suppressed media coverage. After winning the award, however, he recognizes how the articles he is commissioned to write coopt his place of opposition. Vargas's system of competition uses prestige to motivate many of his fellow writers, assuring few texts that challenge the public to think outside the valued market.

Ramos's harsh assessment of journalism and "easy" literature is worth quoting at length, for its implication that citizens permit their own subordination is the clearest example of Santiago's own association of modernism and authoritarianism in his scholarly work. At the same time, it conjures up both the destructive effects of leftist ideological patrols and Santiago's hope for what he will later understand as the postmodern challenge to critical lethargy:

> The reader of newspapers (or spontaneous novels) does not want to make any effort when he reads. He contents himself with absorbing another's writing as if he were blotting paper. He allows himself to be guided only by his faculties of memory and not those of reflection. This reader has a fascist perspective of literature. Fascism is not merely strong and authoritarian government, ideally military, which permits the economic forces of the dominant class to reproduce without challenge. Fascism exists every time a human being feels he is the subject of and an accomplice to rules. . . . Fiction only exists when there is conflict, when different forces battle each other inside the book as well as in the process of their circulation throughout society. To find in a book what one already expects to find, what one already knows, is the sad path of fascist art, where even the meanderings and labyrinths of imagination are predetermined so that there isn't any dissenting thought. Fascist art is "realist" in the worst sense of the word. It doesn't realize that its "real" is just the accepted means of representing the complexity of the every day." (116–17)

If Ramos's position as a peripheral intellectual has until now seemed tangential to the space in-between, his equivalence of realism with fascism and censorship now takes on greater implications for intellectual fractures during the military dictatorship and exiles' testimonials. Indeed, the recognition of the ends that nonfiction discourse can serve leads him to rethink his earlier desire to avoid the trap of fiction, since he realizes that "criticism in fiction plays with ambiguity: it reproduces the model (the moment in which the reader, having discovered a likeminded person, begins to sympathize with him), but in the process of reproduction, it begins to instill a hint of discontent that perturbs that same reader" (117).

Ramos's oppositional role stems from neither aligning himself with the political left nor the right, including the groups that advocated on his behalf while imprisoned. He sympathizes with the global and local communist movement as an alternative to Vargas's nationalism, but is perturbed by the party's inability to permit internal dissent or critique the current living conditions in the Soviet Union. He witnessed such "proselytism" in prison, which creates intransigent believers unwilling to consider realities outside the ideological party line, ignoring the role that critical reflection plays in adapting ideas to a local environment. When he does finally acquiesce to writing a document of his times, it is not the one that vying intellectual patrols expect. In order to counteract the nature of the articles he must write in order to support himself, Ramos vows to return to literature to speak against, to write against. Seeking something more substantial than the diary, he wishes to write "anything about opposition between politics and prison, anything about the tragic fate of the intellectual in Brazil, about the desire for death and for life" (170–71). Just as Santiago indirectly denounces his contemporaries by evoking the past, however, Ramos also turns to a foundational episode in Brazil's history to subvert the narrative of progress and to highlight an instance of intellectual deviance. While the historical Ramos composed a satirical children's history of the Brazilian Republic, Santiago's protagonist looks to rewrite the most visible symbol of martyrdom, the 1789 Minas Gerais Conspiracy, a separatist revolt against Portuguese aristocracy that was preemptively quashed when traitors within the group of conspirators informed the government.

During a three-year public trial, the insurrection's leader, Tiradentes, assumed all responsibility, and while his actions saved the lives of other arrested members of the group, he was later hanged and quartered. Poet and coconspirator Cláudio Manuel da Costa, however, died in his cell before the trial started, amid speculation that he may have informed authorities about the movement. Costa's death was officially ruled a suicide after having signed a document unveiling the plotters, although there is some debate among historians as to whether he was murdered. After the establishment of the Republic in 1889, Tiradentes was canonized as a national hero, while Costa was vilified as a traitor. Taking liberties that historians, who must base their revisions on existing accepted facts, cannot, Ramos imagines a narrative in which Costa is murdered precisely because he is capable of implicating the government. The testimony that he supposedly signed is therefore a forgery, a false document that has become truthful by virtue of generations of scholars' acceptance.

Both Ramos's research into the past and his rewriting of the official version of the failed independence movement disturbs the facts that readers take for granted, while again challenging the repetition of fatigue. Just as Santiago uses the lost diary as an invisible text to create a pastiche of Ramos's political identity, Ramos creates a pastiche of the writer Costa. And yet the movement is not only toward the past. Just as Ramos's words ultimately describe contemporary Brazil, so too does the historical fiction with Costa reveal the dangers of repetition as silence and conformity. In the final several entries, Ramos consults numerous historical publications and inserts excerpts from the works into his diary, surprised at how pious faith in the truth of preserved documents makes the task of dissent thankless and largely impossible. Ramos therefore decides the solution is to unveil an alternative to the socioeconomic focus employed by historians; using the language of fiction will allow him to write as if he were Costa and therefore represent the permanence of authoritarian regimes in Brazil in relation to the uncomfortable position that public intellectuals inhabit when they speak out against injustice (208–9). Using Costa's own perspective, Ramos presents a new account of how government actors collaborated to murder the poet, silencing the dangerous intellectual. As Doctorow points out in "False Documents," the goal of creative disavowal is not to completely subvert an existing interpretation but rather to plant the seeds of doubt in the reader's mind. This strategy of displacement is of course a reflexive reference to Santiago's similar historicization of the military dictatorship within *In Liberty*. In fact, the novel is also a testament to the permanence of authoritarian regimes in Brazil, for the reproduced historical accounts of Costa's death are not historical at all.

As it turns out, the specific details of Costa's murder in his cell, the fake autopsy, and a subsequent cover-up are based upon very real events at the time of writing the novel that bear out the parallels between Ramos's incarceration in the past and the corrupt judicial system during the military regime. In 1975, journalist and university professor Vladimir Herzog, a communist sympathizer, voluntarily presented himself and was jailed on suspicion of being a KGB agent. Other journalists later testified to hearing his torture, and the next day he committed suicide in his jail cell, according to a fraudulent medical report (Dassin, *Torture* 201–2). The primary document relating Costa's death as suicide reproduced in Ramos's journal is in fact pulled directly from

Herzog's medical report, in which the military attempts to disclaim responsibility. Included in their ruling were photos that unconvincingly staged his apparent suicide from hanging. Representing yet another invisible text in *In Liberty*, the primary clue to its contemporary origin is that certain vocabulary in the document is anachronistic for the late eighteenth century, when it was supposedly penned (Avelar 160). Fifteen journalists had been prosecuted by the justice system since the promulgation of the Press Law in 1967 (Dassin, *Torture* 121), but the blatant attempt to whitewash Herzog's torture and death galvanized the intellectual and religious communities, and helped usher in controlled liberalization measures that would ultimately quicken the demise of the dictatorship. Within three years, human rights activists successfully had the case recognized by the courts as murder, placing pressure on the government to become accountable for its methods of control. More immediately, mass protests were timed in conjunction with his funeral, while newspapers, radio stations, and television programs operated at a virtual standstill to mark the gravity of the occasion. Echoing the public outcry from 1975, Ramos imagines a similar public mourning after Costa's death by citizens who feel complicit for not having fought against his incarceration. In effect, Santiago tricks the reader to demonstrate how easily authoritative knowledge can be misattributed to supposed representations of the past, both through his own mimicry of Ramos and the government's suppression of information. It is, after all, individuals and institutions in power who are able to attribute new values to history based upon their ideological preferences. In a presentist gesture, Ramos muses that "the past is just a place of reflection that contemporary men can choose (or not) to better direct their position today and tomorrow. Being a place of reflection, the past does not have an inherent value that must be preserved at all costs, but it can and should have value that is conferred by the horizon of expectations of the present" (85). This is certainly the case for Santiago, who utilizes false documents to highlight the contemporary state's own false claims.

CONCLUSION

The diary ends on a note of uncertainty, for it is unclear whether Costa's story has been finished. In the penultimate diary entry, Ramos explicitly identifies with Costa, suggesting the dead poet speaks through him in the very way that Santiago has repurposed Ramos's language. The task of all three men is clear: write against, speak against, from the periphery, though this revelation is by no means climactic. The abrupt final diary entry appears on March 26 and makes no mention of the Costa text. Whether this is because Ramos no longer feels it necessary to reflect on his struggles after having rekindled his passion for writing, or whether the hardships of life simply prevent him from continuing the journal is unclear. In two lines, Ramos recounts going to the docks to pick up his wife, who has returned with their children, and he does not know how they will all fit in his small pension room. Even Santiago-as-editor refrains from contextualizing the absolute lack of closure. Indeed, given that Costa's story is not a part of Ramos's actual oeuvre, the assumption must be that it was lost, much like the diary itself. Ultimately, like the historian, the task of the intellectual is also a thankless one, but this is because it must ethically constitute a permanent commitment to dissent.

In Liberty consists of several false documents, each revealing a historical, allegorical layer, but also inviting the reader to broaden his or her perception of what constitutes modern or postmodern fascism—in other words, monolithic accounts of truth, modernization, and nationhood. In the midst of the wave of testimonial literature, Santiago's novel helped to both initiate postmodern challenges and return to questions of history that would dominate the 1980s in Brazil. Recognizing in Santiago's own evaluation of postmodernism the same patterns that inform peripheral intellectual resistance reveals that the Brazilian scholar anticipated the very questions North American and Hispanic postmodernists were soon asking of their own traditions. In this sense, if the original Inter-American scope of Santiago's postnational historical representation was a consequence of scholarly ignorance of Brazilian letters in the United States during the 1970s, the academic fiction and scholarship provide an underrecognized model for the rest of the hemisphere.

Like Ramos, Santiago refuses to write the document of his times. Instead, the anticonfessional work embodies the work of the oppositional intellectual who calls attention to forms of control across the political spectrum, nation, and hemisphere. Santiago is not critiquing testimonial literature on the grounds that survivors of torture and exile need wait a decade and fictionalize their experiences as Ramos did. Instead, he wishes to temper the trend's paradoxical ahistoricism. *In Liberty* models how history can itself be a form of uncritical repetition ripe for reconception through Brazilian responses to modernist realism. While Santiago's subsequent novels, including *Stella Manhattan* and *Journey to Mexico,* would respectively explore Inter-American relations through metaphorical representations of dictatorial and modernist subjugation of individual expression, it is *In Liberty* that marks a point of transition both in Santiago's oeuvre and in Brazilian letters during the push toward redemocratization. And Santiago's conclusion to "The Space In-Between" makes its dialogue with the false document all the more salient, for

Ramos's assertion of the intellectual's contradictory role is a virtual pastiche of the Inter-American essay's rejection of national commodification: "The Latin American writer demonstrates that we should free ourselves from the image of a smiling carnival and fiesta-filled haven for cultural tourism" (38). This involves an awareness not only of how the government exports the notion of spectacle to the international community but also of how the notion of spectacle was used to divide resistance at home during the 1970s, whether in Brazil or the United States, where Santiago first defined this in-between history.

CHAPTER 7

The Many Deaths of Che Guevara

Jay Cantor's Anxiety of Origins and the Limits of Transnationalism

A 1989 Macarthur Fellow recipient, Jay Cantor has frequently used his fiction to explore the role that media images play in constructions of transnational American history. His experimental blend of genres spanning fiction, screenwriting, graphic novels, and documentary film criticism has led some critics seeking social realism to label his layered texts "postmodern," although Cantor identifies his influences in modernist philosophy and Holocaust studies.[1] Indeed, he wrote several essays during the 1980s attacking postmodernism for transforming politics into entertainment, in one instance implicitly responding to Fukuyama's "end of history." Arguing that the celebrated end of communism was no sign of moral victory, the US author cautions that

> despite the current euphoria that we are history's happy culmination, I think we still need the patriarch's projects and insights. The peoples of Eastern Europe move towards systems, like liberal capitalism, that promise them a greater say in their own making. But that hardly means that in the prosperous West we can't imagine for ourselves a fuller democracy, a greater participation in shaping *our* history. (*On Giving Birth* 4)

---

1. See Berman, Grenier, and Kobak.

Cantor posits instead that the "patriarchs" of modernism—his term for historicist thinkers such as Marx and Nietzsche, against whom Fukuyama writes—provide the most likely model for "remaking" history through the act of defamiliarization, precisely because their flaws and contradictions destabilize the unity of nationalist discourse. The complicated legacy of such thinkers, however, has become essentialized through their more recent association with utopian projects such as the communist "New Man" by postwar political figures including Che Guevara and Chairman Mao. The impending end of the Vietnam War in 1975 signaled the true end of the long 1960s, the author argues, and the failure of the "modern" project for revolutionary transformation was responsible for sparking institutional distrust and bitter irony—the hallmark of emerging postmodernism—as a cover for social ambivalence. Yet rather than producing something new, such attitudes spurn the old without reflecting upon the causes of failure or offering solutions. Influenced by Fredric Jameson's Marxist critique, Cantor claims that "post-modernism sometimes seems a historical term, and sometimes a trademark; what *I* mean by it here is a despairing irony towards the modern projects. . . . [For] some ironies strengthen, and some poison" (*On Giving Birth* 6, emphasis in original).[2] Thus while Cantor admits to being influenced by the self-reflexivity of contemporaries such as Toni Morrison, Thomas Pynchon, and E. L. Doctorow, his early historical focus has more in common with the modernist experimentation of William Faulkner's *Absalom, Absalom!,* and rather than celebrate intertextuality, he focuses on how collective historical events are experienced by the individual (Interview).

While working to reframe the narrative of US exceptionalism, Cantor's scholarly and creative oeuvre has been determined by an obsession with the concept of history and its relation to a different end from the one imagined by Fukuyama: that of individual death (Interview). His primary critical works, *The Space Between: Literature and Politics* (1981) and *On Giving Birth to One's Own Mother* (1992), feature too many references to history—whether defined as a method of reading, a series of symptoms, or a process without end—to list here, and this preoccupation has spilled over into his fiction. Cantor's partially autobiographical portrait of 1960s civil rights and anti–Vietnam War activism, *Great Neck* (2003), explores a multicultural cadre of Jewish-American youth along with their budding activism and solidarity with black Americans, a response to their community's lack of voice during the Holocaust. Alternately, *Krazy Kat* (1987) uses the discovery of the atomic bomb during the

---

2. While Jameson critiques postmodern history's claim to "grind to a halt," Cantor maintain that his work is instead poised *against* history (*On Giving Birth* 95).

1940s to radically reconceive George Herriman's famous cartoon characters as sentient beings suddenly conscious of their precarious mortality, while the graphic novel *Aaron and Ahmed* (2012) explores the complexity of terrorism through a man who becomes an interrogator in Guantanamo Bay after his wife is killed during the 9/11 attacks.

But nowhere has Cantor explored the paradoxical role of death and historical renewal in greater detail than in his debut novel, *The Death of Che Guevara* (1983). Death takes on many connotations in the text, and Guevara is not the only implicit victim. While Cantor uses apocryphal versions of the legend's various diaries to reconstruct Guevara's politicization while crossing the Americas in the 1950s, as well as his subsequent attempt to bring revolution to the hemisphere in the 1960s, the subtext of the late 1970s in North America is never far from the surface. The novel is ultimately a response to the same US imperial culture against which the anti–Vietnam War movement organized— and in which Cantor actively participated—thus providing a vehicle for examining the failure of Guevara and the general modernist project.

In essence, the novel deconstructs the US translation of Guevara's *Bolivian Diaries*, and Cantor's recourse to a false document is particularly appropriate given that Bolivia's president had disingenuously claimed in 1968 that the version smuggled to Cuba was false. All instances of Guevara's (and other insurgents') personal writing are framed by an editorial presence that highlights the oblique politics behind archiving and disseminating a selected ideological image, thus the novel is much more than "diary fiction," the term coined by Gerald Prince in 1975. The false document, however, consciously takes its title from Bjorn Kumm's famous 1967 reportage of the same name, which was one of the first dispatches confirming Guevara's long-rumored demise. In fact, the second half of the novel features a surviving guerilla member piecing together Guevara's downfall through his diaries and newspaper accounts, and the novel ends with the image of Guevara's body attached to a helicopter as a trophy for journalists to view, the very description with which Kumm begins his report. A testament to Cantor's obsessive biographical research that began in 1969, the sprawling novel was written over the course of thirteen years and pared down from nearly five thousand pages of notes (Goldstein 66; Interview). Yet rather than simply serve as sources, the numerous documents he collected are manifested within the novel as journal and diary entries, self-criticism, memoirs, letters, biographies, radio communication transcripts, and even literary fiction. Thus, on the one hand, the false document presents a compendium of the various documents and partial novel found on Guevara's body when he was captured by the Bolivian military, apocryphally extending the *Bolivian Diaries*. Yet on the other, it imagines Guevara's 1950s Latin American travel diaries, anticipating the publication of the "genuine" diaries by over a decade. Perhaps most significantly, the genre-defying work also prophesies the Argentine revolutionary's penchant for fictionalizing and embellishing his experiences in those chronicles.

Despite being coveted by Cuban and European publics upon its publication as a testament to the merits of socialism, the legitimate *Bolivian Diaries* do not present a particularly romantic image of the hardships of jungle warfare, and Cantor reproduces this dynamic in his work by spotlighting Guevara's less heroic features—his asthma, failing health, personal insecurities, and gross miscalculations. The goal, however, is not to discredit the anti-imperial project or the New Man, per se, but rather, through celebrating Guevara's flaws and exposing his purposeful self-fashioning, to recover the humanity lost through his postmodern appropriation and commercial trademarking. In much the same way that he would argue about the "patriarchs" of modernity a few years later, Cantor seeks to defamiliarize the symbol "Che" as a means of remaking history.

Thus, as much as he was drawn to Guevara's anti-imperialist message as a model for criticizing the US involvement in Vietnam, Cantor was also fascinated by the revolutionary's childhood health issues, with which Cantor could identify, along with his obsession with mortality as revealed in the diary. In other words, while admiring the revolutionary's sacrifice, he is critical of the mistakes that brought the Pan-American campaign—and most of the men who fought for it—to an unfortunate end. As the author has explained, "When I began my attempt to make history into fiction, into history *as* fiction, the corpses were mostly coming from Vietnam. History bore down on one like a juggernaut. There was then, too, an active movement against the war, bent on comprehending history, and giving it human dimensions again" (*On Giving Birth* 140–41, emphasis in original).

Because of its refusal to merely celebrate Guevara or adhere to a recognizable genre classification, the false document has aggravated some progressive critics who allege that the failure to rehearse Guevara's triumphs results in a negative portrayal (Grenier 42), though this overlooks the fact that Cantor is attempting to counteract either dogmatic valorization or repudiation. Another critique maintains that Guevara's childhood reminiscences exoticize Argentine sociopolitical history from a US perspective (Foster 85). Argentina features only briefly in the text, but more importantly, Cantor expressly paints Guevara as a product of hemispheric politics, not an icon of any one nation, and it should be expected that portrayals of each country visited ring a little hollow, for Cantor's point is that Guevara's accounts heavily retouch his past. If anything, Cantor agrees that his own positionality should be taken into account, claiming that the novel is "not a story, then, of Che's third world but of the first world, or perhaps a story of the first world as one of its citizens . . . dreamed and feared and longed to join a larger community" (*On Giving Birth* 142). Put another way, in order to explore the revolutionary forces upending Latin American order, Cantor "decides that the way to search out the meanings of these forces is by an imaginative inquiry into a centrally symbolic figure who embodies them" (Flower 314).

While a multitude of biographies has appeared in the fifty years since his death, of which Jon Lee Anderson's 1997 landmark is perhaps the most famous, Guevara has surprisingly received remarkably little fictional treatment. It is a testament to the continued currency of Guevara's documentary project and persona in the hemisphere, then, that *The Death of Che Guevara* was translated into Spanish and Portuguese shortly after its original publication.[3] In the following decades, a few other Inter-American writers would fictionally link apocryphal diaries to Guevara, including Argentine diplomat Abel Posse in *Los cuadernos de Praga* (*The Prague Notebooks*, 1998), which traces Guevara's 1966 stay in the titular city before leaving for the Bolivian mission. Completed shortly after Posse finished his own assignment to Czechoslovakia, the text mixes Guevara's writing with the attempts of a researcher—who may or may not be Posse—to interview a variety of real and fictional individuals, from Jon Lee Anderson to ex-members of the secret police who worked with the incognito revolutionary. Significantly, Posse is best known for his satirical trilogy of Spanish colonialism (1978–1992) closely associated with the rise of the parodic Latin American new historical novel, thus his claim to transcribe images of Guevara's classified diary in the mode of false realism marks a radical shift in style and politics.[4] More recently, Guevara has even been coopted by Brazilian authors. Miguel Sanches Neto's *A Bíblia do Che* (2013) also explores an apocryphal document attributed to Guevara before the Bolivian campaign. Exuding Rubem Fonseca's mixture of hardboiled urban fiction and reflexive literary games, the book details an ex-professor's search for a Bible—now appropriately a coveted collector's item—whose margins supposedly feature Guevara's diary entries during the revolutionary's 1965 trip to Brazil while disguised as a priest.

Yet neither of these texts is able to address Guevara's appropriation by political and media forces to the extent that the first novel featuring Guevara does, quite simply because Cantor's breadth of historical analysis and his appropriation of documents that mediate Che's spectacle are already Inter-

---

3. Translated as *La muerte de Che Guevara* (Madrid: Ediciones Grijalbo, 1985) and *A morte de Che Guevara* (Rio de Janeiro: Editora Record, 1987).

4. The trilogy consists of *Daimón* (*Daimon*, 1978), *Los perros del paraíso* (The Dogs of Paradise, 1983), and *El largo atardecer del caminante* (untranslated, 1992).

American in scope. My intent here is to explore the implications of reframing Guevara's legacy in postnational terms as a North American contribution to what Lois Parkinson Zamora has termed the Inter-American "anxiety of origins" within journalistic fiction, a concept to which I will return near the conclusion. Before beginning an analysis of the novel's reflexive discussion of history within the various American locations it visits, it will be necessary to first contextualize Guevara's cooptation into a postmodern icon, the fetishization of his myth that occurred both through visual means and the Argentine's multiple posthumously published journals. Thereafter, the chapter analyzes the role of utopian postnationalism in Cantor's transnational epic that proved to be Guevara's downfall, which centers on not only Guevara's experiences in Bolivia as a youth and later as revolutionary but also demonstrates Guevara's legacy as part of a continuum of history based on US hegemony in the hemisphere. Indeed, despite ostensibly focusing on events in the late 1960s, Cantor does so as a platform for drawing into the focus the postmodern moment after 1975 and the failed modernist revolutions. This is particularly evident through three sections of "Dates" that correspond to Guevara's birth and death timeline, yet which curiously ignore his own life to instead describe Latin American responses to imperialism and the end of US empire as the country abandons Vietnam to communism.

OF DIARIES, PHOTOGRAPHS, AND DOCUMENTS: GUEVARA'S COMMODIFICATION

In the decades following his 1967 execution, Ernesto "Che" Guevara was transformed into "the quintessential postmodern icon—[signifying] anything to anyone and everything to everyone" (Casey 133). Michael Casey has documented the cultural and tourist spaces that facilitated the Latin American revolutionary's commodification into a global marketing symbol, yet the journalist believes two "texts" have been most important for history's dislocation of man into myth. The first is the mass propagation of a single photograph and the second is Guevara's journals, which have been released by his estate over timed intervals. The famous image is the so-called "Guerillero Heróico," snapped in 1960 by local fashion photographer-turned-state-documentarian Alberto Korda. By some accounts the most reproduced image of the twentieth century, the cropped head shot featuring Guevara staring into the distance was not originally picked up by the state newspaper.[5] In 1967, however, Fidel Castro harnessed the photo's propaganda power during an extended

---

5. Michael Casey and Aleida Guevara reflect in the documentary *Chevolution* (2008) about how Korda's work did not officially go under copyright until the twenty-first century.

PR campaign, unveiling an enormous mural based on the photograph in the Plaza de la Revolución and proclaiming the year after Guevara's death that of the Guerillero Heróico. Fueled by art publishers and the student protests of 1968, the image spread to Europe in the form of a poster before its appropriation by pop art turned the photograph into a red and black graphic, and the graphic quickly morphed into a logo. Each successive shift in medium helped further distance the emblem from the anticapitalist ideals that Guevara supported during his life, and both critics and proponents alike have lamented the absurd commercial products upon which his name has been branded.[6]

Yet if the Guerillero Heróico captured Guevara at the height of his vitality, it was a very different image of Guevara's body that first signaled his potential deification. On October 9, 1967, Bjorn Kumm had the journalistic fortune to travel with a select few Bolivian correspondents from Santa Cruz, Bolivia, where he was covering the government's trial against Marxist professor Régis Debray, to the mountain town of Vallegrande. Upon reaching the village center, the Swede witnessed firsthand the dead body of Guevara as it touched down strapped to a military helicopter's landing gear. The article resulting from this scoop, "The Death of Che Guevara," confirmed the revolutionary's demise for the international community and defined the Swede's career. Kumm does not feign objectivity as he describes the Argentine's half-naked body. His shock at the jocularity of doctors preparing the cadaver for embalming is matched only by his own skepticism regarding the army's conflicting accounts of Guevara's death in combat. Indeed, mysteriously retracted doctor's statements—today the accepted version of his death—suggested the revolutionary might have been executed hours after capture, revealing the Bolivian government's desire to avoid the international attention his trial would bring ("Long Live Guevara" 35–36).

Yet Kumm is neither a Guevara disciple nor simply a detractor of Bolivian military nationalism. The article is blunt in its assessment of the antiimperialist campaign's failure, highlighting the shortsightedness of Guevara's postnational idealism. The US trade block had effectively isolated Cuba from the rest of Latin America, and the insurgents chose to foment revolution in Bolivia because of its central location within the continent, the goal being to unite Latin America by branching into Brazil, Argentina, Peru, and Chile. As Guevara proclaimed in his last major article, an address at the Tricontinental Conference of 1967 in Havana later read publicly by Castro, his goal was to fuel the equivalent of two or even three Vietnams through which the guerilla fronts would eventually exhaust US military resources ("Long Live Guevara" 23). Yet not for the first time in his international guerilla campaigns, the Argen-

---

6. Although diametrically opposed in their ideological valuations of Guevara, Fontava (xxix) and Taibo (11) provide similar laundry lists of his use in corporate product placement.

tine stubbornly insisted upon Cuban leadership, even as the Bolivian communist party argued the movement needed a national base in order to directly engage the population.[7] The resulting ideological split hampered party support from Bolivia's urban centers, and the revolutionary group's outsider status limited its capacity to recruit local conscripts, several of whose desertion aided in the capture of the dwindling numbers of guerillas. In his effort to liberate the continent, Che thus underestimated the importance of local national identity politics. Ironically, then, although villagers did not recognize Guevara when they gathered to view the body, many were quick to associate his recumbent position and long flowing locks with a crucified Jesus Christ. Bolivian photojournalists exaggerated the religious overtones, beginning a long series of visual and textual interventions that would strengthen Guevara's status as an international symbol.[8] Kumm thus notes a bitter irony in how the US-trained Bolivian forces' eradication of Guevara had in fact given birth to his myth and contributed to his immortality as a martyr ("Long Live Guevara" 23).

While a single image may have paved the way for Guevara's evolution into an ad campaign during the 1970s and 1980s, it is the fetishization of his personal writing that has maintained the currency of his political campaigns for sympathetic audiences, their synergy undeniably evident as the "Guerillero Heróico" soon adorned the cover of Cuban editions of the *Bolivian Diaries*. Upon capturing the guerillas in the jungle, the Bolivian military discovered multiple documents in Guevara's backpack, including his diaries, drafts of guerila proclamations, transcriptions of radio messages sent from Cuba, and even the fragments of a novel that the leader had been working on (Ebon 142). The existence of the diary became public knowledge when passages cited from its pages were used as evidence in the trial of Debray back in Santa Cruz, for the French philosopher had been captured while traveling away from Guevara's guerilla base camp. Curiosity over the document's contents prompted a bidding war between European publishing companies, a fever pitch of anticipation encouraged by the Bolivian government through the release of teaser fragments over several months.

Ironically, however, the political left's fear that the CIA would release a doctored version of the diaries in an attempt to discredit Guevara appears to have been mutual. Thus after a high-ranking Bolivian official smuggled out a microfilm copy of the diary to Cuba in early 1968, Castro distributed the jour-

---

7. Numerous African governments counseled against Guevara's 1965 Congo mission, though the "idea that Africa was an African problem did not accord with Guevara's internationalism" (DeGroot 123).

8. See Casey's discussion of photographer Freddy Alborta and the aesthetics of martyrdom (181–86).

nals free of charge throughout the country, effectively undercutting Bolivia's monopoly along with the anticipated profit. Bolivia's furious President Barrientos claimed the Cuban release was a "falsified" and "fictitious diary" before subsequently confirming that his administration had been compromised by a leak (Waters 38). Shortly after this scandal, Stein and Day published the first English translation in the United States as *The Complete Bolivian Diaries of Ché Guevara and Other Captured Documents* (1968), a critical edition in multiple senses of the term that featured an antisocialist introduction as well as three other combatants' recovered memoirs.

In chronological terms, the *Bolivian Diaries* represented Guevara's last testament, yet they were certainly not the last to be published by his estate. The revolutionary had maintained diaries during many of his previous insurgencies dating back two decades, and suddenly an international market appeared for these personal memoirs that promised insight into both the leader and the mentality behind revolution. Concern over the line between fact and falsification would also affect their reception, albeit for distinct reasons from the battle over Castro's supposedly fictitious version of the Bolivian memoirs. Guevara's experiences during the liberation of Cuba (1956–1958), for example, appeared in English translation on the heels of his Bolivian writings as *Reminiscences of the Revolutionary War* (1968). The actual diaries of this period would only be published for the first time in 2011,[9] as it turns out Guevara's reminiscences were actually adaptations of his notes that he had edited in 1963 to promote the model of guerilla insurgency, and his strategic selection and exclusion of details thus produces an "apocryphal Cuban history" (Casey 53).

After a lull in Guevara-mania during the 1980s, the bestselling success of *Diarios de motocicleta* (*The Motorcycle Diaries*, 1992) reintroduced his story to audiences in both Cuba and abroad. Tracing the twenty-three-year-old medical student's adventures as he and a friend crossed Latin America on motorbike in 1952, the narrative provides an account of how Guevara witnessed systemic racism and state oppression across the continent, leading to his eventual radicalization. Yet this publication too represents a reconstruction of his original notes after returning home a changed man, a romanticization of the journey he briefly acknowledges in his introduction (32). Marketed as a sequel to *The Motorcycle Diaries*, *Otra vez* (*Back on the Road*, 2000) follows the budding revolutionary's second trip across Latin America during 1953 and 1954. His increasingly Marxist identification led him to the socialist experiment in Guatemala, and when the US-backed military coup installed a dicta-

---

9. Published in Spanish as *Diario de un combatiente*. The year 2011 also saw the release of a revised edition of his diary from the Congo mission in 1965, *Pasajes de la guerra revolucionaria (Congo)*, first digitized in 2005.

tor months later, Guevara fled to Mexico where he would first meet Castro. This collection is notable because, in addition to its author's annotations, it features extra material such as newspaper clippings as well as numerous letters to Guevara's parents.

Cantor uses the same strategies to document Guevara's continental travels in the first section of the novel, although he remarkably had no knowledge that the "actual" journals would be published in diary form decades later. And Che's writing continues to live on in other genres. In the twenty-first century, a number of Hollywood films have married the textual and visual components of Guevara's myth by basing their scripts on Guevara's diaries, from Walter Salles's *The Motorcycle Diaries* (2004) to the first of Steven Soderbergh's two-part Guevara biopic *The Argentine* (2009), based on *Reminiscences of the Revolutionary War*. Yet the visual adaptation of Guevara's own words onto the screen, as even the most sympathetic reviewers have acknowledged, has served to simplify his politics (Williams 20), much like the two-dimensional photo that has come to universalize his appeal.

VISUAL FALSE DOCUMENTS, CANTOR'S NEWSREELS, AND GUEVARA'S BIOGRAPHY

While adopting a distinct color palette, the original dust jacket design of *The Death of Guevara* is evocative of the "Guerillero Heróico," presenting a stenciled close-up of Guevara's face, thick facial hair under a military beret, and impenetrable eyes gazing into the distance. The image was new to international audiences when Cantor began writing, though as it attained global status, several visual artists began to take aim at the forms of consumption to which Guevara's image has been (re)purposed.[10] Perhaps the most insightful involves the work of D*Face (the alias of Dean Stockton), a London-based graffiti artist who is well known for deconstructing iconic pop figures and styles. His titles frequently engage puns that suggest a critical rereading of social concepts. Thus in the aptly titled piece "Cli-ché," part of his 2007 solo exhibition "Eyecons," the artist displaces the ubiquitous stencil version of Guevara created from Korda's photograph.[11] Preserving both the red background and Guevara's beret, he quite literally defaces the image: in place of a chiseled countenance gazing into the distance, a decomposing face with exposed sec-

---

10. See Franco (*Critical Passions* 110) and Casey (269–71).

11. Access Stockton's full gallery from the "Eyecons" exhibition at: http://www.dface.co.uk/portfolio_page/eyecons/

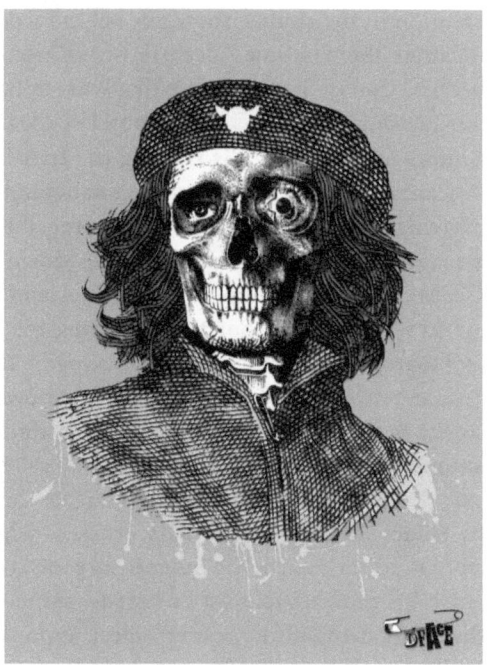

FIGURE 3. "Cli-ché," part of D*Face's 2007 collection "Eyecons"

tions of skull accosts the viewer. The macabre image is chilling, yet its morbidity effectively moves beyond shock-value to highlight two concerns. First, the image makes obvious that to portray Guevara as a static symbol creates an analytical category rather than celebrates an individual, while at the same time, the satire's emphasis upon decay signals the death of any revolutionary value the corporate-endorsed photo might once have possessed. Ultimately, the title "Eyecons" appears to refer to both the mass-produced pop cultural images and D*Face's own remaking of them (see Figure 3).

In essence, Cantor performs the same unmasking of Guevara's death through a textual appropriation of his journals. As Cantor's protagonist says shortly before embarking on his Bolivian campaign, "I'm called Che now. The perfect name: an empty sound that might mean anything" (286). Like D*Face, Cantor defamiliarizes through his reintroduction of Guevara's humanity and death—in figurative and literal terms. Thus, if the urban artist creates visual "eyecons" that challenge his audience to rethink the divorce of individual identity from corporate reproduction, we may in turn think of falsified literary documents as "con-scripts" equally critical of the effects of consumerism and parody. I draw attention to the similar strategies behind works across media not only to demonstrate the continued need to investigate constructions of history but also because Cantor acknowledges that what initially started off as a short story about Guevara in 1969 was first inspired by the Christlike images accompanying Kumm's article before discovering the translated diaries (*On Giving Birth* 127). Cantor pays homage to this visual component at several points, for the surviving guerilla tasked with piecing together Guevara's final days finds it less painful to treat their doomed showdown with the Bolivian military as if it were a fictional film script. At the same time, the artificiality of film also serves as a metaphor for describing the mythical veneer that Guevara's autobiographical poetic license encourages. The revolutionary accentuates "the space between the sentences. Have you ever seen a strip of motion-picture stock? In between the frames there is a thick white line. On the screen the motion looks continuous . . . but there is really that line. A discontinuous dialectic that looks smooth" (93). In fact, from the very beginning, Cantor makes the reader aware that the diary entries—whether under the control of Guevara, his editor Ponco, the other insurgents, or the newspaper accounts upon which his final hours must be based—are neither neutral nor unmediated. Rather, they demand the reader reflect upon the various levels of editing that equally reveal the symbolic capital of Che and obscure the role played by those who worked in his shadow.

The symmetrical structure of the novel is vital for recognizing the ends served by visual and journalistic discourse, but the doubling of places and concepts in the Latin American and the Bolivian diaries also reflects Karl Marx's famous adage that history repeats itself, the first time as tragedy and the second time as farce. The two extended narrative sections containing diary entries are bookended and separated by three brief sections titled "Dates" that initially appear to coincide with Che's life: the first covers the years 1927–1965, and the second 1966, although the third spans 1967–1984. Narrated by an unidentified scholar in what begins as an objective, documentary tone, the "Dates" function as a textual newsreel, jumping between an extensive array of elections, repressions, wars, and coups that narrate a history of resistance from the margins against capitalism, and by extension, the spread of Western democracy through military and economic means. Geographically, these yearly descriptions find their locus in Latin American events before expanding outward to consider the United States and Asia. In this sense, the logic of these "Dates" reflects Guevara's 1964 speech to the United Nations in which he linked the plight of newly independent African nations, Vietnam, and the Caribbean, challenging Washington to look inward at its mistreatment of

African American and Latin American citizens before seeking out injustice internationally.[12] In fact, it is the timeline's treatment of Guevara as a symptom rather than a hero of his times that most clearly establishes him as a conduit to explore collective, hemispheric attitudes.

Opening the novel without context, the first list of dates begins in 1927, corresponding to Guevara's birth, and ends in 1965, the year that he disappeared from Cuban public life. A common device in biographies, this timeline subverts norms, for the dates reveal nothing about Guevara's individual milestones. Instead, they feature hundreds of historical examples of resistance toward growing US hegemony, including the spread of communism, Argentina's refusal to join the Western Allies in breaking with the Axis during World War II, and the CIA's coordinated postwar operations to overthrow socialist-leaning governments in the Western hemisphere. Guevara is barely mentioned, although Fidel Castro features prominently in several different years, including his multiple-hour "History Will Absolve Me" speech before his sentencing to prison on the Isle of Pines in 1953.

Considerably shorter, as it only covers 1966—the year that separates the events of the first and second parts of the novel—the second section of dates reinforces this center-margin dynamic. It starts with Guevara's participation in the Tricontinental Conference in Havana and ends with an account of US military atrocities in northern Vietnam, directly linking the claims from his final public address regarding the creation of multiple Vietnams of guerilla resistance. Significantly, the final set of dates follows the logic of the first, as it is about utilizing Guevara's legacy as glue to tie together global trends. It begins with Che's death in 1967, though the descriptions continue through 1975 and the United States's withdrawal from Vietnam, implying that the insurgency Guevara helped put into motion in the Americas had ramifications far beyond his death. Most surprising, in the third newsreel, the years 1975–1984 (the year after Cantor published the novel) are listed but left blank, inviting the reader to reflect on whose narrative will fill the void left by the death of modernist revolutionary projects. In fact, as the description of facts breaks down into fragmented and jumbled clauses in the final lines, a voice interrupts the objective narration with a pointed barb destined as much for the postmodern reader as Guevara's ghost: "You've misinterpreted the instruction you must take from the history you've been given. Your idealism (which no one asked for) sours into irony. But your irony corrodes only you, and not

---

12. The speech is reproduced as "At the United Nations" (325–39) in Deutschmann's *Che Guevara Reader*.

history" (578). This irony is what Cantor would later describe as the type of postmodern despair that "poisons."

DOUBLING OF HISTORY, TRAGEDY AND FARCE

Set on Cuba's Isle of Pines, *The Death of Che Guevara* features two sections to provide a counternarrative to the developmental democracy later championed by Fukuyama. In the first, after disappearing from public life, Guevara awaits Castro's instructions for Bolivia with a fellow revolutionary in 1965, while in the second, the companion returns in 1968 after Che's biggest disappearing act to piece together an anthologized collection of insurgent diaries. The Isle of Pines served as a penal colony for much of the twentieth century, where both Fulgencio Batista and Castro sent political dissidents under their separate regimes. Yet the island's contested history also calls to mind a different type of colony, one based on US expansionism, for after the Spanish-American War the United States attempted to annex the territory to protect business interests.[13]

While not specifically identifying a source, the first narrative section "Criticism, Self-Criticism" clearly draws on a mysterious German document known as the "R" Memorandum that circulated during the late 1960s and intimated Guevara's disappearance in 1965 was a consequence of a mental and physical breakdown culminating in a period of intense self-evaluation (Ebon 57–60). Instead of a sanatorium, however, Cantor locates Guevara on the Isle of Pines, accompanied by his faithful companion Walter Tulio, affectionately known as Ponco. Having joined the Cuban Revolution under Guevara, Ponco is clearly an incantation of Guevara's actual companion and survivor, Harry Pombo Villegas, whose firsthand account of the Bolivian campaign would appear in 1997, although Cantor was forced to change the name by his publisher to avoid potential litigation (Interview). Encouraged by his companion, whose failing vocal chords partially silence him, Guevara turns from writing self-criticism to creating a true "story" of his life through autobiography to counteract the versions circulated by other groups. Undoubtedly, Cantor's most impressive feat involves the inclusion of invented journal entries that reveal Ernesto's ideological radicalization during the early 1950s when he crossed Latin America on two separate trips. I have noted that the actual diaries would officially appear during the 1990s, though Cantor anticipates both their content and form, including the presence of newspaper clippings and supposed letters to

---

13. Neagle provides an in-depth history of the battle over the island.

Guevara's family. Nonetheless, as Ponco is invited to criticize the revolutionary's writing, he slowly begins to realize that Guevara is reinventing his own formation, and many details presented as fact are strategic fictionalization that downplay his family and the supportive role of women in his life. Ironically, only when Guevara learns of his mother's death in 1965 does the revolutionary end his period of self-criticism and reengage the world. Prophesying his own death, he tasks Ponco with being his future literary executor, and the Cuban accepts without quite understanding the request.

In the second half of the novel, "The Diaries of the Bolivian Campaign," Cantor in effect deconstructs the Stein and Day English translation that appeared in 1968, which included partial fragments of writing recovered from other guerilla members. Having escaped Bolivia on his own, Ponco returns to the Isle of Pines and creates an archive of texts, juxtaposing Che's words with fictionalized versions of the other revolutionaries' recovered accounts. While unexpectedly fulfilling Guevara's request to act as his archivist, Ponco fights the doubt that plagues him regarding Guevara's friendship. Did the Argentine abandon Ponco to die in Bolivia or did he leave his faithful servant precisely so that he could escape? As Ponco chronologically works toward the end of the campaign, the various insurgent diaries create conflicting accounts of Guevara's behavior. At the same time, Ponco's familiarity with Guevara's style from their 1965 interaction allows him to imitate the Argentine's writing, and it becomes increasingly difficult to determine which are Guevara's own words and which Ponco has ventriloquized. The question of whether Guevara is a hero or simply wanted to present himself as such gives way to an even greater assault on reliability: is he even the author of his legend?

If Guevara's diary is tragedy, Cantor cites Marx's view on history to make clear that Ponco's rewriting/repetition should be understood as farce. It becomes evident that Cantor has Ponco return to the Isle of Pines in order to recreate the conditions of the first section, when Guevara sought to rewrite himself during a point of crisis. In this case, Ponco is now in crisis, tasked with both keeping Guevara alive in the minds of future audiences and revising the existing narrative by rewriting Guevara. In effect, Ponco acts as a stand in for Cantor, as both men seek to make sense of an overwhelming array of documents with conflicting accounts. Faced with Guevara's previous notebooks and the insurgents' journals from the campaign, a consequence of Guevara's instructions for everyone to keep a daily record, Ponco decides to put everything first in chronological order, to decide which details matter, and then "decide how to tell the story in its final form. For whom am I telling the story. To make them do what? Or some other question? . . . To make them weep!—that's one answer. Or to make them vomit—that's the answer my own body gives me over and over" (307). Ponco's strong reactions stem from his continued inability to reconcile Guevara's abandonment of the group, whether for his own self-preservation or because he believed the guerillas would have a better chance to escape without him as a burden. While the latter option is supported by Guevara having given Ponco several diaries for safekeeping, the leader's failing health made him increasingly erratic and unwilling to recognize the futility of the project. Ponco's guilt at having survived while so many comrades perished prevents him from eating, such that he is in turn consumed by Guevara's memory while doctors helplessly watch him waste away. But if Ponco feels that he is sacrificing his own life to write Guevara's story, he also seeks a means of including his own voice, wondering in his journal what the limits of his task are: "Can I change things? I review his words, our talks about his own writing. He made his brothers and sisters disappear, his father die of cancer. Because it *felt* that way. Can I change things—depending on how *he* felt to me, how I felt about him? What about *history?*" (362, emphasis in the original). He concludes the following day that he has no right to alter anything, but subsequent clues in the writing cast doubt upon his sincerity. In a few cases his editorial interjections are made visible through italics, but at other times it is impossible to discern what is "authentically" Guevara and what constitutes Ponco's and Cantor's remaking.

At the end of April 1967, for example, the guerillas listen to the radio as Castro reads Guevara's communique from the 1966 Tricontinental Conference in Havana. Ponco reproduces several paragraphs verbatim from the recognized speech, drily remarking that the authorities incorrectly believe that the group is three-hundred-men strong, when in fact only forty-three remain. With Guevara foolishly separating from his second in command and with their equipment broken, the remaining men can no longer contact the outside world. Shortly thereafter, however, the outside world comes to their hideout in the form of *Time-Life* reporter Michael Wolfe, whom the group grants an interview in exchange for transporting information to La Paz. In one of his journal entries, Guevara provides a transcript of the interview, in which Wolfe aggressively questions the leader's tactics of violence as laid out in his "Message to the Tricontinental." To this Guevara responds, "We begin the struggle, and so show the way the fight must be carried out. . . . Right now the people of Bolivia suffer history. We will give them the chance to become agents of history, actors. We perform the actions that history demands of those who would step on to its stage" (378–79). Yet when Wolfe immediately presses Guevara on who decides what history is or does, Guevara has no answer: "How can you say that 'history' demands anything? Don't you interpret 'history' as if it were an oracle, a god? Isn't it *you* that demands?" (379, emphasis in original).

That this barbed question may not be Wolfe's at all, but rather Ponco angrily rewriting the transcript, becomes clear when a subsequent question refers to Guevara abandoning the group before his death, an event that would not take place for another five months. By this time, Wolfe has been found dead in a jail cell, supposedly a suicide, though this is most likely cover for his murder during interrogation by federal troops. At one point in the first section, Guevara expresses delight at having Ponco discover his deception, although Ponco instead seeks to hide his own imposture. How much of this transcript, and with it Guevara's supposed personal annotations, are in fact Ponco's edits designed to claim his own version of Che, much the same way both Cuba and the United States scrambled to do in the aftermath of his death? Adopting Doctorow's terms, Ponco places Guevara's testament on trial, a courtroom interrogation that the revolutionary's execution never permitted. This is accomplished through physical revision, but also through the juxtaposition of the other insurgents' fragmentary journals, which encourage the reader to become an actor, an agent of history.

THE DEATH OF NATIONALISM AND A TALE OF TWO BOLIVIAS

The symmetrical, dual-structure of the narrative sections creates the conditions for understanding the Bolivian campaign as a repetition (with unintended difference) of Che's political awakening in the country over a decade earlier. Above I explored how the setting of the Isle of Pines allows echoes to travel between both timeframes, as both Guevara and Ponco must rewrite Che's myth. Yet the second section, focused on the "Bolivian Diaries," is equally important for providing Guevara the opportunity to revise his previous concepts of nationalism and the Americas by returning to Bolivia, the symbolic center of his 1953 continental motorcycle trek, even as this amounts to misplaced nostalgia. Moving north toward Venezuela in the first section, Guevara and his friend Fernando cross into Bolivia shortly after the 1952 rebellion led by tin miners and indigenous groups who overthrow the government. Inspired by this bottom-up form of resistance against superior federal forces armed by the United States, Ernesto begins to reject his pacifist worldview in order to consider the direct overthrow of power through guerilla warfare. Sensing that Bolivia had discovered its unity through symbols of indigenous nationalism under the Revolutionary Nationalist Movement (MNR), he and Fernando feel the euphoria in the streets. Believing that Bolivia is the first of a series of national revolutions set to reshape the continent, they scour multiple newspapers for news of war. MNR leader Paz Estenssoro had taken over the presidency, challenging foreign influence by undertaking agrarian land reform and nationalizing the mining industry. Yet when Guevara begins to see government officials inhabiting the same cafes as foreign businessmen, he quickly becomes disillusioned with the new order's repetition of the past. Drunk on a sense of moral outrage, he ignores the pleas of his friends on multiple occasions and begins to purposefully antagonize members of the state, with one anti-US rant ending in a fight when he mistakes a low-ranking official for President Estenssoro. Fernando refers to him as Don Quixote (a connection the actual Guevara made in the final letter written to his family), which is appropriate to Ernesto's delusions of heroism and his reckless endangerment of his companions. Instead, the rumors he hears about Castro's failed revolution in Cuba lead him further north to the socialist experiment in Guatemala, from which he flees during a US-backed coup. His claim during the escape to have shot a North American diplomat as his first ever victim marks his full acceptance of violence as the modernist project, setting the stage for his 1956 arrival in Cuba as part of the movement that would initiate the Cuban Revolution.

The book's second section recounts Guevara's return to Bolivia a decade later, yet the mission in Ponco's palimpsest of accounts is a farce. In theory, the site has been chosen based on Debray's intelligence gathering, which suggests the country's politics provide the perfect conditions for revolution, yet Guevara seems to expect the same atmosphere that he had witnessed in 1953 and laments after several months that the Indians have forgotten how to rebel. The leader has formed the Army of National Liberation, whose members Ponco lists in his own journal, yet Che appears to have forgotten that the MNR movement's success came from uniting the peasants, miners, and Indians in a nationalist cause. Mario Monje, the leader of the Communist Party of Bolivia, warns Guevara that his mission will "not be able to unite the masses unless the Bolivian Revolution is also a nationalist revolution, and has a Bolivian head" (327). The Argentine dismisses Monje's position, leading to the latter's withdrawal of support and a lack of necessary supplies from urban centers. Also within the liberation army ranks, the Bolivians who have joined the cause believe that the Cuban leadership treats them unfairly. Guevara's response to the group is emblematic of his misunderstanding of transnational cooperation: "The only nationalism for a country under imperialism is socialist internationalism" (324). Yet perhaps the most jarring example of Guevara's disconnect with the national reality comes from his attempts to convert supporters in the mountains. While Guevara believes the radio's report regarding the planned cooperation of military missions from the United States,

Argentina, Brazil, and Paraguay is a sign that the movement has succeeded in upending continental complacency, his rhetoric means nothing to the villagers, for they have no concept of geography or nation, let alone Cuba and North America (392–94). Guevara attempts to win them over by curing sick children of worms, but his practice of medicine is understood as a form of magic. In Cantor's version, the villagers first begin to associate Guevara with Christ because of his bloody hands, and yet this does not invite their sympathies, for they associate Christianity with the missionaries who have historically attempted to convert them. Shortly thereafter, the radio reports that the Army Rangers have surrounded the guerillas and the end is imminent.

As he balances the perspectives of the various men's journals, Ponco attempts to defer the inevitable ending for as long as possible. He relates how he was entrusted with multiple diaries as the men died or deserted—except for Che's—but at some point, the primary documents can reveal no more, and Ponco confesses that the rest he has learned from newspapers, providing headlines that include Kumm's own article:

"THE DEATH OF CHE GUEVARA"
Guerilla leader killed in Bolivia
Shot in Battle? Or Executed by the Army?
Was he betrayed by peasantry? Or one of his own?
Special from our correspondent (547)

Responding to the contradictory nature of these various media accounts, Ponco imagines different scenarios and dialogues as Guevara waited for his execution by the military. In some he dies with dignity and calm, in others he is mistreated; in some he suffers for days and other accounts are a single sentence. Yet Ponco is unconvinced by the suffering that the Rangers could have actually imposed, for only "someone who Che loved deeply enough to share his thoughts, who loved Che deeply enough to understand him inwardly, only someone like that would be able to torment Che properly, so he might reach his true status" (554). The implication is that Ponco, his most loyal confidant, has been martyrizing Guevara's ghost through his critical dialogue. Ponco understands that Guevara's death is necessary for his myth to accomplish what he could not in the flesh, and given how many times Guevara himself had spoken about his own end, the Cuban imagines his friend's final moments as lifting a burden, as Che was able to imagine himself happy and healthy for one instant in his life, seeing himself "not as the main character, hardly even a hero, in the ambiguous story told by some North American, where he would turn and turn about as the winds of History turned and excited the author's angers and fears" (562). While Ponco has dreaded the final "end" to his account, the experience in fact has the effect of cleansing his conscience. The Cuban realizes that by narrativizing Che's death, he will paradoxically assure his immortality, which permits the longtime companion to begin eating again.

Yet, just like the newsreel sections of dates, Guevara's 1967 demise is in fact not the end. Having adopted Guevara's own interest in writing literature, Ponco appends to the archived reports a short, absurdist play in the style of Samuel Beckett in which characters debate the legacy of Guevara while sitting around his corpse. Unsurprisingly, given the role of doubling in the novel, the play is titled "The Death of Che Guevara," and its epigraph reads: "Because the first time is tragedy and the second time is farce. Because maybe he saved me, and maybe he left me to die" (564). The unexpected inclusion of this play acts analogously to Cantor's novel, a jarring statement about the way that individuals and groups have coopted the Argentine's death in order to support their own ideological programs. As the ensuing final section of "Dates" suggests, his failed project became part of a larger response during the 1970s that challenged North American global dominance at precisely the moment the United States was reflecting upon its bicentennial of independence. The final sentence of these dates pushes beyond the Marxist dynamic between tragedy and farce, and the blank years are clearly an invitation for active participation in that next step: "Let his life interrogate yours, then improvise an answer—the next necessary step. Begin again. It all must be done over!" (579) In other words, the death of the modernist project can serve as a constructive new stage in "Western" democracy, not only an end to history.

CONCLUSION: THE INTER-AMERICAN ANXIETY OF ORIGINS

Cantor's palimpsest of genres, from apocryphal diaries to documented news and radio transmissions, confounds categorization, but more importantly, points to the contradictory currents of historiography. Yet despite the importance of primary sources to Cantor's experiment, the recurring references to Kumm's article establish the important subtexts of journalism and fiction, and this provides a different perspective on Cantor's contribution to hemispheric literature. A trailblazer within Inter-American studies of historical fiction, Lois Parkinson Zamora reads the use of journalistic discourse as a key strategy within post-World War II literature of the Americas. In *The Usable Past* (1997), she outlines how journalistic fictions have historically carried greater importance in Latin America, yet Parkinson stresses their blurring effect stems from exploiting the tension between modernism and postmodern commodification rather than fitting neatly into either category.

While Cantor does not appear in Zamora's analysis, her modernist framework is particularly appropriate for placing his strategies into perspective. Moreover, *The Death of Che Guevara* demonstrates that hemispheric US journalistic fictions can employ similar strategies to Latin American canonical writers. Despite the surge of metafiction in the 1960s in the United States, the gravity of the civil rights movement and the Vietnam War forced US writers to begin responding to concrete historical issues during the 1970s, although Zamora maintains that the dismissive treatment of the past was a consequence of contemporary critical fads rather than authors' texts themselves. Until that decade, the prevailing New Critical and structuralist tendencies encouraged ahistorical readings of American literature that championed myth over social context. Ironically, however, the ensuing postmodern shift did little to remedy this shortcoming because it instead dehistoricized cultural artifacts by highlighting intertextuality over causation (*Usable Past* 19). To combat this divorce from history, she examines works of the Americas that purport to record history through the forms of newspapers and photojournalism, working "in the space between the poles of modernism's subjective representation and postmodernism's presentation of history as a commodity produced by language" (41). Authors incorporate reportorial and interviewing techniques not to claim mimetic authenticity, but rather to challenge the very apparatus of representation. While the incorporation of newspaper conventions has been more broadly applied in Latin America, the rise of New Journalism and the nonfiction novel in the United States has demonstrated a synergistic tendency toward politicizing the act of reporting. Ultimately, she could come no closer to summarizing *The Death of Che Guevara* than her argument that journalistic fictions impose multiple forms and hence perspectives upon the reader to reveal history as an amalgamation of competing genres.

Yet what Cantor understands as the recovery of political imagination, Zamora in turn theorizes as an "anxiety of origins," the basic historical preoccupation that has linked cultural imagination across the Americas during the last century. Cantor openly disagrees with Harold Bloom for claiming that the generation of US antiwar activists lacked the true European nihilism necessary to enact a revolution (*On Giving Birth* 11), but Zamora goes much further to turn Bloom's critical exceptionalism on its head. Drawing upon his famous "anxiety of influence," she posits that the concept is wholly Eurocentric and that the American condition, far from rejecting its precursors, continually demonstrates a desire to connect to a communal identity within the past through a series of strategies that echo the "remaking" Cantor sees as necessary for American history's social impact. She describes American strategies to establish acceptable sources of cultural authority as the five "re's": research, restitution, revaluation, renovation, and resistance (6). This does not mean that American authors have stressed universal tendencies or naively assumed equality between classes and countries, but instead that they seek to identify inclusive processes through which to build on the ideas of regional thinkers. Extending Carlos Fuentes's discussion of historical awareness in a hemisphere where origins are neither universal nor satisfying, it is clear that "creating one's precursors requires that one (re)create the very language of those precursors so they may speak (to us)" (9).

In a manner of speaking, this is exactly the inclusive project that Cantor undertakes, constructing Guevara as his political forbearer on a personal and political level by reproducing his very language. At the same time, he demonstrates how North American authors can productively extend a representational device largely dominated by Latin America, where the harsh legacies of colonialism have meant that the location of cultural origins have been of greater concern. If Guevara as an icon is ahistorical, ambiguous, and largely deprived of political impetus, Cantor creates a usable past through a parable of American imperialism that is both retrospective and prospective. Similar to the patriarchs of modernism, Guevara's memory has become yoked to reductive ideas or deeds. Yet for Cantor, his value as an Inter-American point of origin is as vital to romanticized notions of Latin American revolution during the Cold War as it is to multicultural US identity after Vietnam. Through Cantor's extensive research and the doubling structure of his false document, Ponco recreates the language of his precursor, liberating himself from the anxiety of origins. The goal is to seek the restitution, revaluation, and renovation of a flawed individual whose complexity has been erased by ideological tools. Nonetheless, Cantor neither loves the sinner nor his sins, instead using the patriarch's contradictions to metonymically characterize US–Latin American foreign relations as part of an old political order. As Cantor puts it, we must start all over. Guevara is the device, but the subtext is the modernist project of resistance itself. How the North American reader chooses to remake or resist the purposefully blank dates that appear after the ends of continental revolution and democracy in Vietnam during the 1970s and 1980s constitutes the first step in identifying a new transnational project that does not smugly define Western democracy—or its critique—as a meaningful endpoint.

CHAPTER 8

Renewing History?

John Updike's Critique of Cultural Studies and the Two Americas in Memories of the Ford Administration

THROUGHOUT THIS BOOK, an ongoing task has concerned complicating the ways in which the logic of "two Americas" served to insinuate fundamental political and cultural contrasts between Anglophone, Hispanic, or Lusophone America in support of economic exceptionalism. In the United States during the 1970s, however, the binary also took on distinctly domestic, multicultural implications. Studs Terkel's *American Dreams: Lost and Found* (1980) collected oral histories from citizens across the social spectrum, from politicians to Hollywood actors and recent immigrants to white supremacists, demonstrating the diffuse and contradictory ways in which the dream of prosperity was interpreted in the wake of the 1976 US bicentennial. As a progressive lawmaker responded in his interview, it was increasingly possible to discern "two Americas," one represented by multinationals' influence in the nation's capital and the other by disaffected rural and urban citizens struggling to have their hardships acknowledged (349). Amid disillusionment with Jimmy Carter's first term as well as continued concern with economic problems, the defection of many liberal voters during the 1980 presidential election encapsulated the country's divisions.[1] During his inaugural address, Ronald Reagan promised to initiate "an era of national renewal" (Weisman A1), although ironically

---

1. See Carroll (345–46), whose far-reaching survey of domestic and foreign conflicts during the 1970s has been particularly helpful in weaving together the threads of history, nostalgia, politics, and patriotism in this chapter.

the New Right's conservative platform in fact played on the nostalgic lure of past decades' perceived prosperity. As an endpoint to the series of case studies previously scrutinized, this final chapter considers both the national demise of history—precipitated by progressive divisions during the 1970s—and the postnational reverberations of its renewal, exemplified by the disciplinary return to stability during the 1990s along with the transnational turn.

The 1970s witnessed increasingly divergent agendas between popular and academic conceptions of national history. The surge in historical pulp fiction that accompanied nationwide preparations for the bicentennial, for example, contributed to the trivialization of the country's past as a form of mass entertainment (Carroll 297). Alex Haley's bestselling saga of African American history *Roots* (1976), and its successful television adaptation the following year, stood out from the escapism of many fictional family chronicles, modeling a new path toward belonging for minority groups. Despite acknowledging the necessity of inventing certain details for lack of available records, Haley's Pulitzer-Prize winning novelization of oral histories about his enslaved ancestors was originally marketed as nonfiction. Yet while Haley's appearance on the covers of a variety of magazines, from *Time* and *People* to *Ebony*, demonstrated his appeal across mainstream and African American markets, historians soon began to allege multiple errors. And after an anthropologist accused him of plagiarism, the factuality of his research was cast into doubt. Nonetheless, by tapping into a desire for greater connection to the narrative of American inclusion, Haley's book helped ignite interest in genealogical research to create social community, particularly for ethnic and other minority groups dismissed by consensus narratives (Carroll 298). History in this context represented a form of ideological inheritance as well as the possibility for a common past that united distinct immigrant groups and time periods in an imagined community. Capturing the ethos of social mobility underlying the American Dream, anthropologist Margaret Mead remarked, "George Washington does not represent the past to which one belongs by birth, but the past to which one tries to belong by effort" (qtd. in Harlan 201).

In many ways, Haley's book, and its reception by a public newly encouraged to romanticize its international origins, reflected two ideologically competing forms of nostalgia: the search for social rootedness and a contrasting political escapism, with the latter instead reinforcing the "two Americas" divide. Thus, for example, the 1976 commemoration provided a welcome distraction from Watergate and the fallout from the Vietnam War. And while Nixon's successor, President Gerald Ford (1974–1977), was tasked with healing the country, his attempts to demonstrate governmental accountability to the electorate had backfired. Notably, his disclosure that the CIA had illegally interfered in Latin American democracy during the Cold War only helped further erode public confidence in traditional forms of authority, including the federal government and scientific institutions (Olmsted 117–18). While Ford might publicly boast during the bicentennial that "Americans have united in a new mood of hope and of confidence" ("Toasts"), national polls had seen his initial popularity evaporate after he pardoned Nixon a month into his tenure.

If magazines like *Time* had captured the national mood through Alex Haley's popular impact, they charted a very different sentiment regarding President Ford's approval. Initially featuring a series of positive covers outlining Ford's mission to help heal a divided country that utilized close-up headshots illustrating a battle-tested politician, by October 14, 1974, *Time* had turned Ford into a caricature (see Figure 4). The image featured a cartoon Ford with an outsized head, rolling up his sleeves with a less declarative title than previously supportive issues: "Trying to Fight Back." The phrase referenced not only the increasing critiques by members of his own party, but also a new set of economic issues facing the country. Set against a white background that highlights their starkness, the words "inflation," "recession," and "oil" encapsulated problems at the heart of the US lost decade. On the back of the Arab oil embargo, the country's worst recession since the Great Depression initiated an attendant spiritual crisis as families began to question the security of their financial futures, an instability that would soon be felt across the hemisphere. Taken together, these sentiments prompted a nostalgic turn towards the 1950s, imagined by multiple contemporary television series and films as a peaceful time of economic prosperity free from 1960s social upheaval (Miller 135–36).

In academic spheres, history became polarized as well, as a new wave of American studies scholars rejected nostalgia and instead embraced the social upheaval wrought during the 1960s, highlighting the challenges that peripheral identities posed to the narrative of American unity. Dismayed at the inaccuracy of popular books and film that brought history to a broader North American audience, the scholarly field experienced its own existential crisis. As David Harlan describes in *The Degradation of American History* (1997), US departments fractured during the 1970s under two separate reactionary developments, leading to "two histories" caught as much between past and present as the "two Americas." The New Left condemned how Western history's cast of elite white males came at the expense of addressing the conflicts average citizens experienced in their daily lives. Demythification of past political figures essentially reconceived the practice as a form of "cultural unmasking," contradicting its longstanding didactic role as moral reflection (xix). Shortly thereafter, the arrival of postmodern theory further eroded scholars' status by positing the exponential growth of interpretive paradigms compromised any claim to

FIGURE 4. *Time* Magazine's 1974 cover on President Ford and the economic crisis

comprehensive interpretation. Thus, fallen from its former status as a conversation with great minds, history was no longer an inheritance to be worked for but instead a burden from which to be liberated. Ironically, while social history during the 1960s had helped introduce the study of inequality, historicist insistence upon social context over the content of the canon of scholarship led it to "become an elaborate mechanism for reducing complex texts to the status of documents. It is essentially a restraining device" (Harlan 192).

Harlan is an advocate of history's ability to unite different groups, though he is not touting a return to conservative methods that erased marginal perspectives; rather, he is concerned that young scholars are trained only to seek a never-ending chain of social disparity without stressing the importance of proffering answers to the irregularities. Yet Harlan's purpose is not to announce the end of history, for he stresses the cyclicality of ideological trends, believing both postmodernism and the New Left to have run their courses during the 1980s. By 1992, a newly self-aware tendency was gaining momentum that no longer reduced the discipline to a mere product of its sociopolitical context, and Harlan thus asserts historical writing's renewal has nothing to do with Reagan's "national renewal," but instead suggests that reconsidering the affective roles of historical texts has more comprehensive implications. In other words, through what methods can a historian inspire empathy for people and ideas seemingly of little contemporary relevance? As evidence of how this trend affected both young and established practitioners, he examines the trajectory of Hayden White, one of the central figures originally involved in the poststructuralist assault. In "The Historical Text as Literary Artifact" (1974), White broaches many of the concerns later voiced by Harlan, writing that "history as a discipline is in bad shape today because it has lost sight of its origins in the literary imagination. In the interest of *appearing* scientific and objective, it has repressed and denied to itself its own greatest source of strength and *renewal*" (*Tropics* 99, my emphasis). Harlan claims that during the 1980s White's rhetorical analyses devolved into academic relativism, but with "Historical Emplotment and the Problem of Truth" (1992), he "contributed more than anyone else to the return of moral imagination in American historical writing" (106). The article's objective analysis of revisionist history and the Holocaust touched a nerve with many in cultural studies, though Harlan maintains White completes the promise of his earliest explorations regarding the historian's burden. Significantly, this involves "coming to terms with our chosen predecessors" within changing contemporary conditions, rethinking why they were previously canonized as heroes or villains (126).

Nonetheless, reconciling US popular and academic endeavors in this era of introspection remains a complex task. If the New Left's support of minority representation dovetailed with the aims of social history, the extent to which postmodern and cultural history could be seen to overlap was not as clear. Timothy Parrish notes the incongruity between scholarly and mainstream concerns, as "for most Americans, history is not what academics write for other academics. If history is to be found in books, it will be sought in books that are far removed from the kinds of intellectual debates [scholars] have been rehearsing" (14). Parrish's point is that fiction—for better or worse—reaches a broader audience and therefore exercises a greater effect upon the general imagination of the past, yet his underlying disappointment concerns the insular, disconnected nature of critical debates. In a diagnosis of turn-of-the-century issues, which eerily reprises the country's bicentennial history craze, he worries the market for popular biographies bolsters uncritical forms of nostalgia and national belonging. Texts that conscientiously borrow techniques from popular fiction in order to stimulate monetary gain "are read by hundreds of thousands of Americans, and their message is reinforced on television networks such as C-Span and the History Channel. Such works appear blissfully unaware that the authenticity of narrative history has been challenged from any postmodern theoretical perspective" (15). While Parrish does not condone this type of popular scholarship, he also takes to task novelists who, like their counterparts, prioritize easy consumption over uncomfortable challenges to the national myths of progress. Thus, he wonders at the ubiquity of Philip Roth and John Updike on a contemporary *New York Times Book Review*'s list of best novels, despite the fact that both authors conjure up abstract notions of the historical without seeking to challenge the canon (35).

Departing from the above evaluation, in this chapter I am concerned with how Updike's *Memories of the Ford Administration* (1992) not only demonstrates complex historical engagement (while offering a means of bridging the popular-academic disconnect) but also attacks the "restraining device" approach to historiography in which all texts are reduced to their function as documents. Indeed, while the dates concerning White's shift toward renewal (1974–1992) are of importance to the scope of this book, it is particularly telling how Updike's approach to US history, nationalism, and ethical renewal also evolved over exactly the same timeframe. Revisiting the failed biography of the nation's fifteenth president, James Buchanan (1857–1861), which he abandoned twenty years earlier and published as the play *Buchanan Dying* (1974), Updike lampoons the effects of cynical poststructural theory in American studies departments and explores the conservative nostalgia that gripped the nation during the bicentennial period. While Parrish's portrait of wider society's preference for popular fiction over dry academic fare is valid, Updike's text is paradoxically successful precisely because it presents itself as an academic dialogue between scholars. Notably, he frames the novel as a historian's commissioned submission to a disciplinary journal detailing President Gerald Ford's incumbency (1974–1976). Yet the historian also includes multiple sections of a revisionist monograph on Buchanan upon which he staked his career, though, like Updike, he abandoned it because of misgivings about postmodern relativism and the ambiguous role of fiction in his work. While Updike originally struggled with how to tie together the overwhelming, contradictory research he performed, his reproduction of the conventions of academic writing provides a clever way to interweave authoritative footnotes, presidential dispatches, correspondence, newspaper articles, and interviews. In many ways a response to the fallout of 1970s texts like Haley's *Roots*, Updike's false document claims to be nonfiction, though its numerous inconsistencies purposefully invite the reader to question its status. Similarly taken to task for several errors in his description of Fordian US popular culture, Updike confesses, "I could not have written the episodes of the Ford era without the frame of . . . [the journal] *Retrospect*, of my impudent assumption of the historian's robes" ("Reply" 60).

It should be noted that this type of experimentation did not appear only in works by fiction writers. As publications like Lawrence Levin's *The Unpredictable Past* (1993) illustrate, cultural historians documented the hostility they faced from the establishment by writing about the process of revising the biographies of canonical figures during the 1970s. Also at the same moment, several "traditional" historians had begun to incorporate the role of literary fiction into historical writing, rather than portraying historical scholarship and creative fiction as adversarial discourses. Simon Schama's *Dead Certainties* (1991), notably caused waves for its overt incorporation of fictional invention, though Schama claimed, in terms similar to White's, that he wished to call attention to the unrecognized processes of selection and narration behind even the most scholarly of work, as opposed to revel in relativism (322). It is not surprising then, that historians believe Updike's hybrid approach repays attention in their own field: "Viewed as a book about history, the novel is concerned less with Ford, or even with Buchanan, than with the nature of memory; the process of writing history; and indeed whether 'the past' can be recovered at all in any authentic sense, by professional historians or anyone else" (Boyer 72).

Written on the heels of the Pulitzer-winning final instalment of the Rabbit Angstrom series, *Rabbit at Rest* (1990), Updike's fifteenth novel has received considerably less attention than many of his other works. Given the association of the Rabbit series with US Cold War history, Updike may seem an unlikely postnational candidate, and yet the writer's trajectory in some ways echoes the multicultural and hemispheric turns during the 1980s. As the author proclaimed in a 1987 interview, "The Great American Novel hardly takes place in America at all" (Mcnally and Stover 197). Citing the international impact of Gabriel García Márquez, Mario Vargas Llosa, and Machado de Assis, Updike continues, "Latin Americans are in some way where Americans were in the nineteenth century. They really have a whole continent to say; suddenly they've found their voice; they're excited about being themselves and their continent and their history" (201). It was under such influence that Updike wrote one of his least successful experiments, *Brazil* (1994), a magical realist retelling of Tristan and Isolde across racial and class lines in Rio de Janeiro that was generally panned. *Memories of the Ford Administration* emerges from this same experimental period, though instead of geographically spanning the Americas, it adopts the internal postnational critique that Brazilian and Hispanic American authors frequently employed during redemocratization. Literally reviving the biographical research he performed on Buchanan during the 1970s, Updike removes the veneer of the bicentennial celebrations by unraveling their typical associations with independence and the Founding Fathers. In fact, it becomes clear that Updike's alter-ego historian is subconsciously drawn to Buchanan because the disintegration of the union in 1860 serves as a counterpoint to the bicentennial celebrations a century later. Thus, according to the author, the text explores "the impossibility of recovering the past, whether as nostalgia or as history" ("A 'Special Message'" 827), which his narrator illustrates in both his account of the War Between the States and his partisan recollection of Ford's similarly tumultuous presidency.

The false document's overt self-awareness has resulted in associations with historiographic metafiction (Vargo 109), yet in contrast to the latter's insistence upon the fictionality of nonfiction, Updike conceives of this exchange as mutual, examining the indebtedness of historical practices and literary representations to one another. Furthermore, despite multiple moments of irony, he establishes intertextuality with academic discourse and historical documentation rather than parodying the agreed-upon record. In this sense, the divergence is perhaps best illuminated as an update to White's older formalist concerns in "The Historical Text as Literary Artifact"—with a caveat. The novel's frame as an academic journal submission actually reverses White's conceptual terms, presenting instead a literary text as historical artifact. Updike is well aware the book's title evokes nonfiction and therefore works against its designation as a novel (Cavett 229), yet the coexistence of autobiography, biography, and political history frustrates readers' abilities to determine whether the novel falls neatly into any singular narrative genre, whether comedy, tragedy, romance, or satire, to use White's categories of tropes.

Perhaps in part due to its supposedly postmodern revision of a realist project, *Memories of the Ford Administration* garnered a mixed critical response, although this does not do justice to the academic nature of the poststructural debates Updike refutes.[2] Unfairly dismissed as a "series of complaints Updike has with the nature of history" (Schiff 138), the novel is less interested in exposing the shortcomings of historiography than in highlighting both academic and creative writers' complex, interdependent relationship in determining revisionist "truth." Although Updike's historian ultimately rejects the

---

2. Reviewers accustomed to the *Rabbit* tetralogy's realism profess confusion as to why Updike would recycle sections directly from *Buchanan Dying* (Gates 59). Advocates in turn celebrate the novel's ability to reconsider the limits of biography as postmodern appropriation (Schiff 135; Vargo 108).

antihumanism of deconstruction, it is, paradoxically, by laying bare the historian's multiple failures that Updike provides an illustration of Harlan's model for the renewal of the historical discipline. By demonstrating that the critique of American identity is embroiled in the same identity politics that the New Left and poststructuralists decry, the novel avoids conservative nostalgia—in fact, Ford's administration is judged to be largely forgettable—and imagines a postnational response in which identifying common ground can have a role to play in projects of social inclusion. In order to establish this imperative renewal of ethical imagination, I will need to first rehearse Updike's own attitude toward history and his subsequent decision to repurpose Nixon-era research to comment on the challenges of representing history as a conversation across time periods, for the book's setting around the bicentennial is no accident. The chapter will lastly survey White's own shift from "The Historical Text as Literary Artifact" to the thorny issue of moral truth at the same moment that Updike's novel appeared, setting the stage for the novel's critique of theoretical excess and the resulting potential for reactivating what Harlan terms the moral historical imagination.

THE RENEWAL OF UPDIKE'S AND WHITE'S APPROACHES TO HISTORY

As a warning to readers who assume published interviews represent spontaneous interaction, Charles Thomas Samuels characterizes his 1968 discussion with John Updike as both a "fabricated interview" and a "work of art," a reference to Updike's insistence upon rewriting his oral responses before publication ("The Art of Fiction" 22). Given this obsessive precision with language, Updike's defiant declaration after Samuels alleges an absence of American history in his oeuvre calls attention to itself: "My fiction about the daily doings of ordinary people has more history in it than history books, just as there is more breathing history in archeology than in a list of declared wars and changes in government" (37). Revealing his intention to write a biographical work about President Buchanan in the next breath, Updike asserts that fiction's affective power allows readers to emotionally experience the past in ways that scholarly works cannot. Although he eventually abandoned this plan, Updike salvaged his extensive research six years later as a play, *Buchanan Dying*. An extensive "Afterword" to the play serves multiple functions, including acting as an annotated bibliography and detailing his archival research and communication with academics. While initially intrigued by scholars' descriptions of Buchanan as the worst of all presidents, his "only quality the absence of all qualities" (202, 240–41), Updike's analysis does not bear out such harsh evaluation, though he recognizes the limits of his role: "Needless to say, I am no historian" (210). Indeed, while he admits to mistakenly changing the date of an encounter in his play, Updike is adamant that the historical record was at no point "knowingly distorted" (192).

Twenty years later, when the writer revisited the failed novel and the play as the basis for *Memories of the Ford Administration*, his attitude toward Buchanan and the past had radically shifted. Not only did he take on the persona of a historian in novelizing his own previous failure but also he openly courted the effects of factual distortion in the name of postmodern skepticism. Updike's shifting sense of historical authenticity was in part a consequence of his reflection on researching archival documents and existing manuscripts, for he claims that his original intention to create a factual novel was complicated by the obvious "novelistic touches" in his primary biographical source, despite its claims to objective fact (*Buchanan Dying* 183). This discovery marked Updike, for in the new novel he exaggerates these novelistic touches in an experiment designed to test how viable postmodern claims to erode the line separating the two genres were. In addition to inverting the roles of fiction and history, however, Updike is clearly concerned with cultural trends in literary American studies, and his protagonist Alfred Clayton provides a cautionary tale.

Based upon his previous failure to "reanimate" Buchanan in a realist vein, Updike knows how difficult it is to do "justice" to a historical figure ("A 'Special Message'" 826). Particularly aware of the "fakery" involved in the construction of literary history, he decided to make its aesthetic and ethical tensions his central issues, as he revealed in a fictional interview in *Vogue* Magazine. Adding to the game of mirrors between Updike and his protagonist Clayton, the interview questions are posed by Henry Bech, one of Updike's recurring fictional characters,[3] whose contrapuntal status as a frustrated author provides a vehicle for satirizing critical tendencies. Clayton's profession is vital, for "with a historian within the living plot engaged in trying to write about Buchanan, I might thereby bestow upon myself a writing license, the necessary freedom of the imagination which had been hitherto constrained by my constitutional unwillingness to do all the faking—what Henry James called the *escamotage*— that goes into a historical novel" ("Henry Bech Interviews" 823). Initially identifying himself as a traditional or positivist historian, Clayton is reluctant to engage in fakery, for he has been trained to worship the empirical record, not

---

3. Updike returned to the satirical academic figure on several occasions, including *Bech: A Book* (1970), *Bech Is Back* (1982), and *Bech at Bay: A Quasi-Novel* (1998).

imagine the blanks outside existing documents. Updike channels White as he concludes of his experiment that "insofar as history lives in the telling, and persuades us we are there, it is a species of fiction" ("Reply" 60). The difference: *Memories of the Ford Administration* purposefully calls attention to its fakery through Clayton's invasive commentary in the margins of his memoir, directed at the journal's editors.

Shortly after Updike's 1968 declaration about the province of living history in his work, White would arrive at similar conclusions. In "The Historical Text as Literary Artifact," which interrogates narrative historians' presumed objectivity in representing the past, he contends that in order to attribute meaning to what would otherwise be merely a chronicle of unrelated occurrences, historiography creates causation through literary conventions. (Tellingly, he draws his concepts from Northrup Frye's 1957 literary study *Anatomy of Criticism*.) Thus, via processes such as emplotment, White's term for the creation of different types of plot structures, historians shape a series of events into recognizable narrative genres (i.e., comedy, tragedy, romance, and satire), which are as important in determining how the reader interprets the text as is the actual content (*Tropics* 83). For White, "*How* a given historical situation is to be configured depends on the historian's subtlety in matching up a specific plot structure with the set of historical events that he wishes to endow with a meaning of a particular kind. This is essentially a literary, that is to say, fiction-making, operation" (85, emphasis in original). The agenda behind asserting the fundamental literariness of historical discourse, White claims, has little to do with undermining the authority of history, but rather forcing its practitioners to acknowledge that they predetermine their subject by packaging it for interpretation. In other words, historians do not simply discover facts, but instead construct them by suggesting causation and consequence, and drawing attention to the processes of rhetoric guards against "ideological distortions."

The same year that Updike repackaged his earlier conception of the past, White also revisited his earliest and most influential work in relation to trauma studies in "Historical Emplotment and the Problem of Truth," particularly the ethics of representing Nazism within the Holocaust. "Can these events be responsibly emplotted in any of the modes, symbols, plot types, and genres our culture provides for 'making sense' of such extreme events in our past?" (37) he wonders. Or is it possible that they belong to a certain special class of events like the American Civil War that have been permitted only one single kind of meaning—as tragedy? The answer is no, for our moral imagination is not static and is constantly revised by shifting ideological frames. Thus, if presenting anything other than a denunciatory, realist account of the

Third Reich was once unthinkable, the difference between content and form has become more fluid in recent years, as portrayals of the perpetrators that move beyond their status as villains increasingly appear in humorous or fantastical forms. White singles out Art Spiegelman's graphic novel *Maus* (1986), for example, in part because "it makes the difficulty of discovering and telling the whole truth about even a small part of [the Holocaust] as much a part of the story as the events whose meaning it is seeking to discover" (41). The correspondence of this description to Updike's plotting is clear, for while Buchanan's failure to prevent the Civil War is typically attributed to his untenable position between opposing political forces, the skepticism toward patriotism that defines Clayton's era leads him to mold Buchanan after Ford as an inept statesman, a forgettable president.

FORD, AMERICAN STUDIES, AND A FORGETTABLE DECADE

Despite minority groups' emerging desire to establish stronger bonds of identity, many individuals turned away from the social issues they had championed in the 1960s and embraced an individualistic model of self-improvement, prompting New Journalist Tom Wolfe's famous characterization of the 1970s as the "Me Decade."[4] Indeed, Updike's historian-narrator is a prime example of the "Me Decade" phenomenon. Completely insulated in his academic bubble from issues relating to foreign diplomacy or economic stagnation, he narcissistically focuses upon the era's supposed sexual liberation and the academic politics at a fictional women's liberal arts college in New England. Having recently left his family, Clayton more readily identifies with Nixon, for the historian sees a kindred spirit in that Nixon too "abandoned" his post.

Perhaps the most salient detail of Clayton's memoir, given its title, is how perfunctory Ford's presence is. After alienating both sides of the political aisle, Ford would lose his bid for reelection to Jimmy Carter in an election where apathy manifested through low voter turnout. Updike discovered historians were unkind to Buchanan, yet contemporary journalists were equally critical of Ford, claiming that "there is no whiff of charisma."[5] Even more colorful accounts surmised that the new market for disaster books and film adaptations such as *Jaws* (1974/1975) served as a metaphor for the nation under Ford (Carroll 183). Yet in contrast to many members in the acting president's own

---

4. See Miller for more on the shift toward individualism during the 1970s.
5. See *New York Times* reporter Israel Shenker's 1974 publication *The End of a Presidency* (Carroll 161).

party, who viewed him as unprepared for the office, Clayton's glowing evaluation goes beyond conservative support:

> As far as I could tell, Ford was doing everything right—he got the Mayaguez [cargo ship] back from the Cambodians, evacuated from Vietnam our embassy staff and hangers-on . . . went to Helsinki to meet Brezhnev and sign some peaceable accords, slowly won out over inflation and recession, restored confidence in the Presidency, and pardoned Nixon, which saved the nation a mess of recrimination and legal expense. As far as I know, he was perfect. (354)

Although it is his job to remember the past, Clayton concludes his submission by admitting to the journal's editors that the "more I think about the Ford Administration, the more it seems I remember nothing" (369). This reads less as a confession of failure to address the journal's call for papers than an indictment of a forgettable era. Yet the tongue-in-cheek title of historian Peter Carroll's account of the decade, *It Seemed Like Nothing Happened* (1982), reveals that Clayton's seeming dismissal of the period's importance—which became lost between the end of the Vietnam War and Reagan's shift toward the New Right—was not uncommon (ix).

Although Updike draws attention to the decade's absence through his protagonist's escape to the pre-Civil War era, this is certainly not for lack of interest in Cold War national politics. Each of the novels in his bestselling *Rabbit* tetralogy takes stock of a decade preceding its publication, providing a "living history" of the United States (Vargo 108) in which the historical and literary cannot be divorced from the social and political commentary.[6] *Memories of the Ford Administration* also reflects upon a preceding decade, though in contrast to the mimetic construction of the Rabbit Angstrom tales, the historian-narrator admits to having consulted the types of reference books that produce "instant history" of popular culture in order to provide greater authority to his spotty recollections of the period (9). There are several reasons for this shift in strategy. By inserting segments of his failed popular-revisionist history of Buchanan into Clayton's journal submission, Updike establishes a link between these two less-celebrated presidents. Immediately after taking office in 1974, Ford informed Congress of his intentions to heal a divided nation: "I do not want a honeymoon with you. I want a good marriage" (*Public Papers of the Presidents* 6).

---

6. Ristoff explores the Rabbit series as "contemporary history" (*Updike's America* xviii–xix), while later he rebranded Updike's approach as a more radical form of historical appropriation in *John Updike's Rabbit at Rest* (1998)

Ironically, Clayton subconsciously interprets the metaphorical divorce of the Union under Buchanan through the lens of his own rocky marriage, though the novel opens on a much more formal note, imitating a memo sent to the editors of an academic journal:

From: Alfred L. Clayton, A. B. '58, Ph.D. '62
To: Northern New England Association of American Historians, Putney, Vermont

Re: Requested Memories and Impressions of the Presidential Administration of Gerald R.Ford (1974–77), for Written Symposium on Same to Be Published in NNEAAH's Triquarterly Journal, *Retrospect.* (*Memories* 1)

Thus prefaced, Clayton's submission frames the entirety of the book, though the academic rigor of the biography and editorial marginalia contrasts with the central memoir. Writing fifteen years after the events he narrates, the academic remains unfazed by his sexist past, and while he discusses university politics, he also pays tribute to the era's sexual liberation by including details about his separation from his wife and subsequent philandering.

It is within the surfeit of private information that Clayton embeds alternating sections of excerpts culled from Buchanan's revisionist biography. The never-finished book initially appears in full chapter-length segments, though by the end of Buchanan's crumbling presidency its form is reduced to a mere list of "hard facts" from existing historical sources. While the purpose of the biography's inclusion is initially unclear, it emerges that the two alternating narratives inform one another as its formal degeneration begins to mirror Clayton's personal life. Moreover, the juxtaposition of the two texts reveals Buchanan's biography to in fact be an autobiographical transposition of the researcher's personal life.

Given that Updike noted upon the novel's publication that "'postmodern' never was much of a label anyway" ("Henry Bech Interviews" 824), it stands to reason that his purpose lies in exposing the general excesses of academic theory that swept across the humanities, and he reserves particular derision for literary and American studies scholars. While White reveals how history must incorporate literary elements in the process of narrativizing, there is no small irony in the reciprocal influence of literary criticism upon Clayton, who decides to reframe his initial project after a deconstructionist arrives in his college's English Department. The literary critic's anachronistic book touches upon virtually every token minority group in American cultural studies, claiming that Whitman and Emerson suppressed their awareness that "American expansionism was fueled by black slavery, child labor, domestic oppression of women, and government-sponsored swindling and slaughter of Native Americans" (359). Updike is clearly not impressed with this appropriation, but Clayton explains his recourse to new theory as opportunism. "So why not *my* text, also deconstructed?" he wonders. "I began to overcome my mistaken reverence for the knowable actual versus supposition or fiction, my illusory distinction between fact and fancy. Here, dear NNEAAH and editors of *Retrospect* . . . is a section of my text, composed under the benign overarch of the Ford Administration, and no doubt partaking of some of that Administration's intellectual currents" (35).

Instead of imagining history as a conversation with great minds of the past, Clayton promotes his research for a contemporary audience of peers. He must carve out his own niche to garner professional accolades, a fact he cynically evokes for his editorial audience as if to make them accomplices: "You know how it is, fellow historians—you look for a little patch not trod too hard by other footsteps, where maybe you can grow a few sweetpeas. My efforts, neverending as research led to more research, and even more research led back to forgetfulness and definitive awareness that historical truth is forever elusive" (*Memories* 13–14). It is apparent that Clayton hides behind academic and quantitative jargon to avoid admitting his own ethical responsibility, deadpanning that his wife and children, whom he decides to leave, "had been deconstructed, but didn't know it yet. I would have to tell them," completely negating the negative human emotional impact: "It was a not uncommon crisis in this historical era, yet there is a difference between an event viewed statistically, as it transpired among people who are absorbed into a historical continuum, and the same event taken personally, as a unique and irreversible transformation in one's singular life" (52). This pattern of ethical nihilism eventually leads to Clayton's personal and professional collapse as well as a moment of reckoning that has symbolic repercussions for the academic field's renewal.

EXHAUSTING DECONSTRUCTION, RENEWING THE ETHICAL IMAGINATION

Updike attributes his frustrated attempt at "exhuming" Buchanan to excessive research that left him "frozen by the theoretical discoverability of everything" (*Buchanan Dying* 259). This same overdetermination plagues Clayton to the point of destroying his project, particularly as his dereferential, postmodern stance unravels. As he puts it to the editors, he was "merely writing more history, and without the pre-postmodernist confidence" of narrative historians, thus his "opus ground to a halt of its own growing weight, all that comparing of subtly disparate secondary versions of the facts, and seeking out of old newspapers and primary documents, and sinking deeper and deeper into an exfoliating quiddity that offers no deliverance from itself, only a final vibrant indeterminacy" (*Memories* 360). Second, the logic of the linguistic turn challenges his previous understanding of the discipline as an objective transcription of facts. As a poststructural convert, he wonders if his contemporary recollections are not "modern fiction—for surely this reconstruction, fifteen years later, is fiction—[which] thrives only in showing what is not there" (296). He thus compensates for intrusive literary elements by directing editorial notes at the journal's editors, although their hyperexplanatory nature paradoxically lessens rather than strengthens his authoritative status.

Clayton soon begins an affair with the deconstructionist's wife, an act that subconsciously determines his research on Buchanan. Indeed, it is the "conflict between union and separation" that propels events in both Buchanan's and Clayton's narratives (Schiff 137). While Buchanan, figuratively wed to the North, battles against the secession of the South prior to the Civil War, Clayton struggles to mediate between his estranged wife and his new mistress. By narcissistically imagining his own personal travails paralleling the larger process of the country's political history, Clayton trivializes the mass death that resulted from the Civil War, though he remains largely ignorant of the allegorical significance with which he imbues Buchanan's presidency. In White's and Harlan's terms, Clayton may choose his predecessor, though his reckoning comes when he is forced to confront the moral bankruptcy of his professional and personal motivations.

The subjective intrusion of the personal into his biography provides irony because of the great lengths to which Clayton goes to observe the conventions of traditional professional writing. Thus, he highlights in italics direct citations from documented sources and frequently identifies biographical sources in-text. The project comes to an uncomfortable impasse, however, when certain gaps cannot be filled by archival documents. One of his greatest preoccupations becomes whether Ann Coleman, who died of fever after mysteriously breaking off her engagement to Buchanan, may have actually committed suicide, despite the lack of any documentation to that effect. When all sources, personal correspondence, and newspaper accounts are inconclusive, Clayton begins to openly consider the merits of subjective emplotment. As he admits, he takes pleasure in discovering where earlier historians "fudged" the gaps in the record, for the archival "texts are like pieces of a puzzle that only roughly fit. There are little irregular spaces between them, and through these cracks, one feels, truth slips. History, unlike fiction and physics, never quite jells" (165–66). Faced with a paucity of documentation, Clayton fancifully imagines Ann Coleman's final night, and, like Schama in *Dead Certainties* or Haley in *Roots,* invents dialogue and characters' thoughts to which he could have had no access.[7] This is Clayton at his most literary, and although he professes embarrassment at the invented dialogue's departure from verifiable events, he nonetheless justifies his counterfactual version in which the two reconcile and marry, perhaps willing his own reconciliation, through the "indeterminacy" of reconstruction.

Clayton's admission regarding the liberties his narrative takes has an unintended consequence, as it triggers his suspicion that the content of documents he has hitherto assumed truthful may also have similarly fictionalized aspects. Although he intends to write a deconstructionist history, Clayton's reconsideration of the infallibility of documentation actually represents the moment when he instead deconstructs his own approach to the narrative past. Rather than simply cite sources in italics, he now openly questions the sources' veracity and logic (166), modeling the same doubt readers are invited to cast upon his own personal writing.

While the overlapping metaphors of dis/union linking the novel's two narrative threads have received critical attention, it is a third parallel that is most telling with regard to textual relations: Clayton's response to the American profession itself, which is challenged in conjunction with his professional and private life. Despite his initial disavowal of fiction, Clayton cannot help but acknowledge that his own project is dependent upon the conventions of literature, though this is ultimately less a liability than it is a quality, a point brought home after he abandons the manuscript. He apologizes to the editors of *Retrospect,* citing personal distractions and the fact that Buchanan's later life is already better documented than his youth. True enough, the remaining sections of the manuscript are little more than brief summaries and citations, with little attempt to link them up into a coherent narrative. If for White narrativization and emplotment are what transform a list of events into history, then Clayton's example illustrates an opposing "unemplotment."

All of these various challenges come to a head as Clayton's research collapses, the indeterminacy of textual traces taking its toll on his sense of personal and public impunity. When his estranged wife asks at a community event how his project is proceeding, he disingenuously hides behind the profession to avoid admitting his failure: "Doesn't history demonstrate over and

---

7. Updike also confronted this aporia when writing about Coleman for *Buchanan Dying* (184–90).

over how hard it is to say what actually *did* happen, so that even the Nazis' fanatically documented extermination of six million Jews . . . [is] still seriously debated?" (*Memories* 254, emphasis in original). Literature as revisionist history is typically celebrated as a corrective to a record that reflects the interests of dominant groups, though Clayton's allusion to the denial of the Holocaust draws attention to one of the most cynical abuses of historical revisionism. By demonstrating the double-edged hypocrisy that relativism serves—by removing the scholar from having to commit to any position that could be exposed to ethical criticism—Updike uses Clayton's case to address the relationship of postmodernism to the humanities.

White's own reconsideration of the ethics of representation in "Historical Emplotment and the Problem of Truth" speaks to this cowardice. Moving beyond the question of postmodern or conservative denialism, White suggests that modernist modes of representation may be uniquely able to communicate both the reality of the World War II and its experience. When he councils that the concept of realism "must be revised to take account of experiences that are unique to our century and for which older modes of representation have proven inadequate" (52), he gestures toward the representation of all events perceived to be traumatic to any national or ethnic identity. In Harlan's terms, if history is merely a form of textual reconstruction, then its power to instill ethical judgment is lost upon both historian and the public.

Before acquiescing to the postmodern fad, Clayton had characterized his original motivation for teaching in ethical terms: "As I understand it, if you deconstruct history, you take away its reality, its guilt, and for me its guilt is the most important thing about it—guilt and shame, I mean, as a final substratum of human reality" (103). Unsurprisingly, these are the two emotions he stifles until the authority he craves is doomed by the end of history. Yet while the historian's actions may preclude the *practice* of history, his spectacular failure serves as a moral lesson on the field's *purpose*. The most important part of White's analysis is not that tragedy is narrativized in predetermined ways, but instead that postmodern theory can, paradoxically, also reinforce traditional humanism, using "ethically empty insight to support a set of deeply ethical beliefs" (129).

FAILURE AS RENEWAL

While *Memories of the Ford Administration* has not received attention on par with Updike's more traditional novels—much less been explored as a timely critique of postmodern historiography—the experimental book generates a positive alternative to the failure it thematizes. According to Harlan's prescription, if representation of the past is to be elevated from a vehicle for professional promotion to its former status encouraging the public's identification with unexperienced locations and times, the reasons behind its desire to be treated as a scientific form of social inquiry must be addressed (209–13). Moreover, it must be conceived as a conversation with the dead, rather than a laboratory for truth claims, but this does not mean that it should uncritically accept the findings of past generations of overwhelmingly white male voices. Yet if the New Left asserted that American culture was too heterogeneous to engage in a grand conversation, Harlan effectively demonstrates the much more constructive effect that nostalgia generated by works such as Haley's *Roots*—despite its inaccuracies, ethical concerns, and popular status—has for activating citizens' participation in their social and national histories. Far from advocating for a return to consensus or traditional figures as the masters of the record, this freedom to select any voice is what he means by choosing one's predecessors. For in contrast to the nostalgia of escapism, the search for greater rootedness is an ethical decision designed to open up the past to a larger array of groups for interpretation.

Additionally, historiography must abandon the pretense of objectivity—not as a consequence of postmodern skepticism, but because it is through openly subjective judgment that practitioners can most powerfully address the contemporary needs of their readers. Third, the value of ethical decision-making must take precedence over the context in which the documents are produced. "If historians were no longer obligated to analyze historical documents in their proper historical context, would they not start reading their own biases into them?" (187) Harlan asks. Like White or Berkhofer, his answer is no, for the antidote to ideology is not objective data but rather the rhetorical ability to inspire empathy for human beings who faced the types of challenges that are, if not universal, certainly not bound by national experience.

Similar to Harlan, Updike believes that history is not inherited, but rather chosen as a means of informing the present. Clayton mistakes imposing his own preoccupations onto Buchanan for choosing a predecessor whose challenges can be extended into the present as knowledge. It is in this aspect that Clayton's downfall, despite his apparent self-consciousness and skepticism, serves as a model for taking "empty" insight into tragedy and turning it into productive ethical insight. In the final instance, it is not relativism that catches up with Clayton but rather his moral vacancy when taking advantage of women, his colleagues, and even his own children. Once his mistress learns of his infidelities and reconciles with her husband, Clayton becomes doubly divorced from his project, and his frustration continues to haunt him at the end of George H. Bush's term. He explodes, "I *hate* history! Nothing is simple, nothing is consecutive, the record is corrupt. Further, the *me* inside these brackets appears no wiser that [sic] the one outside them, though he (the former) is fifteen years older" (*Memories* 307, emphasis in original). This climax of frustration illustrates the dangers of churning out history through predetermined theoretical lenses, for while Clayton ultimately fails to deconstruct Buchanan, he now accepts that his project was doomed from the beginning because it was based not on dialogue but on personal ambition. Tellingly, at the time of submission to the journal he has returned to his traditional role in both society and his host department.

In fact, Ford's defeat by Carter coincides with the end of Clayton's radicalism, as he goes back to his family. This return to the status quo mirrors both the trajectory of historiography, which weathered the postmodern storm and returned to a general period of traditional practice the following decade, and the conservative politics of the 1980s under Reagan. Just as the memoir opens with Clayton watching Ford's inauguration on television with his estranged children, it closes with the family following Carter's inauguration ceremony from the sofa. Still viewing his own life through the lens of national politics, Clayton interprets his lukewarm reception by his family as emblematic of Carter's indifferent national welcome, for he was never totally accepted by either the North or the South. Yet his earlier assessment of Ford's tenure has become more measured with age, as he ambiguously concludes to the *Retrospect* editors, "The Ford years. What else can you say about them/him? Or, really, any of them? These men, our Presidents, do their confused best, toward the end of their lives usually, and there's no proving that different decisions would have produced better results" (366). The historian no doubt confuses Ford's unpreparedness for the national stage with the desire for history to absolve his own faults.

Despite its examination of the university, Updike's novel is not a veiled disciplinary attack on studies of the past. Clayton's aborted venture into postmodern theory does not privilege literature as a means of deconstructing historiography, but instead avows literature's complementary relation. Updike's novel renews the historical imagination, embracing subjectivity, demonstrating through his conversation between Clayton, Buchanan's "ghost," and the reader that the act of seeking out the human experience of the past creates inheritance, not an ideological lens that focuses on power inequalities. Despite the fragmented nature of Buchanan's biography, Updike manages to bring his legacy to bear on the present, even as it becomes clear that Clayton misses the opportunity to meaningfully choose his predecessor because of his focus upon both skepticism and rupture. Ultimately, the national markers upon which

Clayton sets his sights mean nothing if he cannot emplot a story that speaks to multiple audiences, irrespective of the social and ethnic exceptionalism consensus history has been guilty of in the past.

As both "fabrication" and "work of art," a gesture to bestselling biographies and professional scholarship, *Memories of the Ford Administration* novelizes history in order to educate. Its creative approach to the literal "two Americas" on the eve of the Civil War finds a corollary in the divisions of the lost decade, and this division in turn echoes the "two histories" that evolved as a consequence of New Left and postmodern attacks. Establishing the literary text as a subjective historical artifact signals a productive postnational approach to American cultural studies, but more importantly, it generates new vocabulary for critically exploring contemporary forms of popular literature and biography. Acknowledgment of the reciprocal relationship between the two disciplines does not compromise historical fiction's political dimensions, but rather takes into account the shifting conventions of political and cultural nationalism, in the process exploiting the nostalgia used to construct these opposing discourses, whether the inclusive push for collective belonging or the conservative motives behind economic escapism.

POSTSCRIPT

Fake News and the New Lost Decade

REPORTS OF the end of history were greatly exaggerated. As the year 2020 approaches, if the postmodern period seems—certainly in academic terms—further behind us than ever before, cultural approaches continue to represent a central tenet of contemporary historiography. On the one hand, critical realism has assumed a central role in both the social sciences and the humanities, yet on the other, scholarship has become so acculturated to the principal poststructural claims that their iconoclasm no longer merits consideration as foreign. Thus, postmodernism has become institutionalized by the entertainment industry through music sampling, reality television, and cinematic self-reflexivity, its oppositional identity undermined in the process. Yet many of the lessons from the era of the lost decade remain unresolved and as relevant for contemporary area studies as they are for hemispheric cultural diplomacy. As responses to Argentina's continued debt restructuring with the International Monetary Fund have demonstrated, Inter-American organizations are still dominated by structural economic analyses equating development with democracy, suggesting that we are more than ever in need of alternative methodologies to US national models that can account for localized ethnographic and historical realities. The international debate over the future of the North American Free Trade Agreement provides just one of many examples, as the United States recently played Canada and Mexico against each other to renegotiate the accord, while Venezuela's increasing political and economic instability has led to its suspension from the South American trade bloc MERCOSUR without addressing its humanitarian crisis.

In the ten years leading up to this book, the term "lost decade" has again appeared in relation to economic downturn, although this time around its origins had little to do with Latin American debt. The United States's protracted recovery after the global 2008 financial crisis it precipitated is projected to have long-term effects not yet fully understood for the country or the region.[1] In fact, Brazil's initial resilience to the global recession, coupled with overtaking the position of sixth largest economy in the world in 2012, led to an attendant rise in the study of Portuguese language and Brazilian culture at universities across the hemisphere. Despite these subtle reversals, however, many other political trends may look surprisingly similar to the conditions underlying the Inter-American lost decade. In the first decade of the twenty-first century, numerous left-leaning governments began to distance themselves from neoliberal policies and US influence as part of the so-called regional "pink tide." Yet despite Mexico's 2018 election of President Andrés Manuel López Obrador, the most visible responses to recession and disillusionment with the government have helped the pendulum swing back in favor of neoliberal populism as evidenced by Donald Trump and the so-called "Trump of the Tropics" in Brazil, Jair Bolsonaro. Successfully touting themselves as outsiders to the political establishment, Trump and Bolsonaro are not only products of deep domestic, social, and ethnic divisions but also messengers of conservative nostalgia, their fusion of protectionism and multinational expansion rooted in the desire to return each country to its political and social status prior to the Inter-American lost decade. And in an even more alarming gesture of ahistoricism, Bolsonaro campaigned on reinstating military dictatorship-era policies regarding gender inequality and the control of information (Gielow and Fernandes n.p.).

Yet what does this mean for literary and cultural studies, especially with the precariousness of federal funding for humanities under these current administrations? Postmodernism has been supplanted by a general return to critical realism since the late 1990s, one that incorporates some of the concepts behind earlier false documentation. Yet, changing technology has played an even more important role in expanding the form and format of such historical engagement. While new Inter-American writers have emerged to explore similar methodologies, with Pulitzer Prize-winner Junot Diaz's *The Brief Wondrous Life of Oscar Wao* (2007) having received particular attention for its transnational gamut, much like the sources that increasingly inform historians' work, false documents may no longer be primarily written texts.

---

1. See Chinn and Frieden.

The growing popularity of mockumentaries and historically self-aware films during the 1990s has led to greater appropriations within digital media and the field of adaptation studies,[2] while the ease with which digital technologies can manipulate and circulate images on social media means that truth is increasingly tied to the echo chambers within which internet influencers, and in turn their followers, surround themselves.

While these competing forms of media offer new opportunities to teach different demographics about historical questions of democracy and self-determination, recent debates about so-called "fake news" and its influence on national elections reveal that the greater awareness about sources, content, and analytical reading skills that false documentation encourages is particularly crucial for the functioning of democratic norms. Deprived of the grounds on which to distinguish facts from "alternative facts," it becomes increasingly difficult to place national judgments on trial, to return to Doctorow's pedagogical defense of false documents. Campaigns of misinformation have most notably been discussed in relation to the 2016 presidential election in the United States, but the 2018 elections for similar offices in Brazil, Colombia, Costa Rica, Mexico, and Venezuela prompted both civil leaders and journalists to question how this will affect future free speech and fair voting protection. The phenomenon has been noted on a variety of fronts, from experts at the World Economic Forum to journalists at civil liberty nonprofits.[3] And yet, recalling a long history of sensitivity toward cultural imperialism, a variety of organizations spanning the Southern Cone to the Caribbean have also come together to express concern that the terminology borrowed from North America has obscured Latin America's own extensive record of media censorship ("Open Letter"). Ironically, the debate over fake news simultaneously reveals a loss of public historicity and amnesia toward the recent authoritarian pasts that the writers explored in this book work to deconstruct.

In this sense, fiction in any of its multiple forms or connotations still plays an important creative role in opposition to the language of the regime that Doctorow identified more than four decades ago. As Doctorow reminds us, the art of fiction is not without its pitfalls, but it is perhaps the only profession that is forced to admit its own lies. The future of Inter-American studies similarly rests on confronting its own shortcomings—particularly its lack of institutional status within the US—but even more important are the collaborations it offers between fields spanning the humanities and sciences. Despite the increasing rhetoric of interdisciplinarity in job searches and administrative

---

2. Much has been written on self-aware cinema by film scholars since 2000, but historian Rosenstone's seminal *Visions of the Past* (1995) signaled the shift toward new media and technologies.

3. See Rodríguez ("'Fake Guns'") and Tedenek.

initiatives, the neoliberal push toward specialization makes the reality of such cross-field initiatives a practical challenge. Comparative work is particularly important in such a context to help bridge the many fields encompassed by area studies, as well as to alter the prism through which historical frames operate by finding balance between local and global flows of culture.

For these reasons, triangular approaches to political and hemispheric relations offer an important channel for reformulating the oppositional methodologies used to analyze nationalism. While I have attempted to emphasize the importance of Brazil to hemispheric work, the power of Inter-American gestures lies in recognizing that they are always partial and fragmentary—the opposite, then, of total history. This book has focused on the largest linguistic traditions in the hemisphere, though there is much to be gained by expanding the future scope of analysis to target other regional legacies of colonialism, including the French and British Caribbean and Canada as well as Andean and indigenous traditions. History can either be used to establish regional convergence or create national and class divisions, yet the usable past explored here corroborates Doctorow's olive branch between what Alun Munslow has titled "interpretive" and "adaptive" history.[4] While the interpretive approach corresponds to historians who infer their conclusions from documented evidence, adaptive historians practice primarily outside the academy, and, in their roles as journalists, fiction writers, filmmakers, street artists, or blog writers, they highlight speculative constructions of the past to invoke ethical considerations about the choices made and thus inform future repetitions of the past. While interpretive historians have feared—and rightly so—that this popular use by untrained figures can lead to simplifications, misconceptions, and market-determined decisions, most adaptive proponents operate in good faith. The goal is not to diminish the roles of accuracy and ethics needed to create educational representations that can transfer across social boundaries but rather to recognize that the proliferation of media available can both expand dissemination of important topics but conversely also dilute the power of these messages through sheer diversity of options. Ultimately, given the impossible plurality of geographies, ethnicities, cultures, languages, and political trajectories coexisting within the hemisphere, Doctorow's conclusions are consonant with Inter-American cultural synthesis, for as messy or incomplete as it may be, history "is one of the few things we have in common here" (Levine, "Independent Witness" 42).

---

4. Munslow ultimately distinguishes between three conflicting epistemological "choices" of history: what he terms reconstructionist, constructionist, and deconstructionist.

WORKS CITED

Aínsa, Fernando. "La nueva novela histórica latinoamericana." *Plural*, vol. 240, no. 20–21, Sept. 1991, pp. 82–85.

———. *Reescribir el pasado: historia y ficción en América Latina*. CELARG, 2003.

Aldridge, Alfred Owen. *Early American Literature: A Comparatist Approach*. Princeton UP, 1982.

Almandoz Marte, Arturo. *Modernization, Urbanization and Development in Latin America, 1900s-2000s*. Routledge, 2015.

Anderson, Benedict R. *Imagined Communities: Reflections on the Origin and Spread of Nationalism*. Verso, 1983.

Anderson, Perry. *A Zone of Engagement*. Verso, 1992.

Antillano, Laura. *Perfume de Gardenia*. Seleven, 1982.

———. Personal Interview. 5 April 2018.

———. *Solitaria solidaria*. Editorial Planeta Venezolana, 1990.

Archila, Mauricio. "Ser historiador social hoy en América Latina." *Historia Social*, vol. 83, 2015, pp. 157–169.

Avelar, Idelber. *The Untimely Present: Postdictatorial Latin American Fiction and the Task of Mourning*. Duke UP, 1999.

Bach, Caleb. "Tomás Eloy Martínez: Imagining the Truth." *Americas*, vol. 50, no. 3, 1998, pp. 14–21.

Barrientos, Juan José. "Reynaldo Arenas, Alejo Carpentier y la nueva novela histórica hispanoamericana." *Historia, ficción y metaficción en la novela latinoamericana contemporánea*. Ed. Mignon Domínguez. Corregidor, 1996, pp. 49–67.

Baudrillard, Jean. *The Illusion of the End*. Stanford UP, 1994.

Bauer, Ralph. "The Changing Profession: Hemispheric Studies." *PMLA*, vol. 124, no. 1, 2009, pp. 234.

———. "Early American Literature and American Literary History at the 'Hemispheric Turn.'" *American Literary History*, vol. 22, no. 2, 2010, pp. 250–265.

Baumgarten, Carlos Alexandre. "O novo romance histórico brasileiro." *Via Atlântica*, vol. 4, 2000, pp. 168–175. Web. Accessed 7 March 2010.

Belnap, Jeffrey Grant, and Raúl A. Fernández, eds. *José Martí's "Our America": From National to Hemispheric Cultural Studies*. Duke UP, 1998.

Berg, Edgardo H. "Fronteras móviles: consideraciones acerca de la producción narrativa de 'no ficción' en la Argentina." *Celehis*, vol. 4, no. 4–5, 1993, pp. 93–105.

Berkhofer, Robert. *Beyond the Great Story: History as Text and Discourse.* Belknap P, 1995.

———. *Fashioning History: Current Practices and Principles.* Palgrave Macmillan, 2008.

———. "A New Context for a New American Studies?" *Locating American Studies: The Evolution of a Discipline.* Ed. Lucy Maddox. John Hopkins UP, 1999, pp. 279–304.

Berman, Paul. "Diary of a Revolutionary." *New Republic,* vol. 189, no. 24, 12 December 1983, pp. 37–38.

"Betancourt Party Seems Winner in Orderly Venezuelan Election" *New York Times,* 28 October 1946, p. 6.

Beverley, John, et al., eds. *The Postmodernism Debate in Latin America.* Duke UP, 1995.

Bevilacqua, Winifred Farrant. "An Interview with E. L. Doctorow." *Conversations with E.L Doctorow.* Ed. Christopher D. Morris. UP of Mississippi, 1999, pp. 129–143.

Bolton, Herbert Eugene. "The Epic of Greater America." *Do the Americas Have a Common History?: A Critique of the Bolton Theory.* Ed. Lewis Hanke. Knopf, 1964, pp. 67–100.

Boyer, Paul. "Notes of a Disillusioned Lover: John Updike's Memories of the Ford Administration." *American Literary History,* vol. 13, no. 1, 2001, pp. 67-78.

Brands, Hal. *Latin America's Cold War.* Harvard UP, 2010.

Brannigan, John. *New Historicism and Cultural Materialism.* St. Martin's P, 1998.

Britto-García, Luis. "Critiques of Modernity: Avant-Garde, Counterculture, Revolution." *South Atlantic Quarterly,* vol. 92, no. 3, 1993, pp. 515–527.

Buchenau, Barbara, et al. "Normative Programs and Artistic Liberties: Inter-American Case Studies in Historical Fiction and the Campaigns for Cultural Dissociation." *Do the Americas Have a Common Literary History?* Barbara Buchenau and Annette Paatz, eds. Peter Lang, 2005, pp. 195–200.

Burke, Peter. "Gilberto Freyre e a história cultural." *Gilberto Freyre e os estudos latino-americanos.* Eds. Joshua Lund and Malcolm Mcnee. Instituto Internacional de Literatura Iberoamericana, 2006, pp. 335–350.

———. *New Perspectives on Historical Writing.* Pennsylvania State UP, 1992.

Byerman, Keith Eldon. *Remembering the Past in Contemporary African American Fiction.* U of North Carolina P, 2005.

Candido, Antonio. "O papel do Brasil na nova narrativa." *Revista de crítica literaria latinoamericana,* vol. 7, no. 14, 1981, pp. 103–19.

———. "A Revolução de 1930 e a Cultura." *A Revolução de 1930 e a Cultura.* ERUS, 1983. Web. Accessed 16 December 2016.

Cantor, Jay. *The Death of Che Guevara.* Knopf, 1983.

———. *Great Neck: A Novel.* Knopf, 2003.

———. *On Giving Birth to One's Own Mother: Essays on Art and Society.* Knopf, 1991.

———. Personal Interview. 14 December 2017.

———. *The Space Between: Literature and Politics.* Johns Hopkins UP, 1981.

Capobianco, Ken. "An Interview with Jay Cantor." *Journal of Modern Literature,* vol.17, no. 1, 1990, pp. 3–11.

Carroll, Peter N. *It Seemed Like Nothing Happened: The Tragedy and Promise of America in the 1970s.* Holt, Rinehart and Winston, 1982.

Casey, Michael. *Che's Afterlife: The Legacy of an Image.* Vintage, 2009.

Cavett, Dick. "A Conversation with John Updike." *Conversations with John Updike.* Ed. James Plath. UP of Mississippi, 1994, pp. 229–236.

Chartier, Roger. *Cultural History: Between Practices and Representations.* Cornell UP, 1988.

Che Guevara, and Daniel James. *The Complete Bolivian Diaries of Ché Guevara, and Other Captured Documents.* Stein and Day, 1968.

Chevigny, Bell Gale, and Gari Laguardia, eds. *Reinventing the Americas: Comparative Studies of the Literature of the United States and Spanish America.* Cambridge UP, 1986.

Chinn, Menzie D., and Jeffry A. Frieden. *Lost Decades: The Making of America's Debt Crisis and the Long Recovery.* W. W. Norton, 2012.

Chomsky, Noam. "A View from Below." *The End of the Cold War: Its Meaning and Implications.* Ed. Michael Hogan. Cambridge UP, 1992, pp. 137–50.

Colás, Santiago. *Postmodernity in Latin America: The Argentine Paradigm.* Duke UP, 1994.

Cohen, Samuel S. *After the End of History: American Fiction in the 1990s.* U of Iowa P, 2009.

Cohn, Deborah N. *The Latin American Literary Boom and US Nationalism during the Cold War.* Vanderbilt UP, 2012.

Cohn, Dorrit. "Signposts of Fictionality: A Narratological Perspective." *Poetics Today,* vol. 11, no. 4, 1990, pp. 775–804.

Cosson, Rildo. *Fronteiras contaminadas: Literatura como jornalismo e jornalismo como literatura no Brasil dos anos 1970.* Editora UnB, 2007.

Coutinho, Eduardo F. "Postmodernism in Brazil." *International Postmodernism: Theory and Literary Practice.* Eds. Johannes Willem Bertens and Douwe Fokkema. John Benjamins, 1997, pp. 327–334.

Cowart, David. *History and the Contemporary Novel.* Southern Illinois UP, 1989.

Cramer, Gisela, and Ursula Prutsch. "Nelson A. Rockefeller's Office of Inter-American Affairs (1940–1946) and Record Group 229." *Hispanic American Historical Review,* vol. 86, no. 4, 2006, pp. 785–806.

Crassweller, Robert D. *Perón and the Enigmas of Argentina.* Norton, 1987.

Cunha-Giabbai, Gloria de, ed. *La narrativa histórica de escritoras latinoamericanas.* Corregidor, 2004, pp. 11–26.

Dalcastagnè, Regina. *O espaço da dor: O regime de 64 no romance brasileiro.* Editora da Universidade de Brasília, 1996.

Dassin, Joan. "Testimonial Literature and the Armed Struggle in Brazil." *Fear at the Edge: State Terror and Resistance in Latin America.* Eds. Juan E. Corradi et al. U of California P, 1992, pp. 161–83.

———. *Torture in Brazil: A Shocking Report on the Pervasive Use of Torture by Brazilian Military Governments, 1964–1979.* U of Texas P, 1998.

Davi, Tania Nunes. *Subterrâneos do autoritarismo em* Memórias do cárcere *(de Graciliano Ramos e de Nelson Pereira dos Santos).* EDUFU, 2007.

Davies, Lloyd Hughes. "Portraits of a Lady: Postmodern Readings of Tomás Eloy Martínez's *Santa Evita.*" *Modern Language Review,* vol. 95, no. 2, 2000, pp. 415–423.

———. *Projections of Peronism in Argentine Autobiography, Biography and Fiction.* U of Wales P, 2007.

Davis, Natalie Zemon. *The Return of Martin Guerre.* Harvard UP, 1983.

De la Campa, Román. *Latin Americanism.* U of Minnesota P, 1999.

De la Cruz, Rafael. "Decentralization: Key to Understanding a Changing Nation." *The Unraveling of Representative Democracy in Venezuela.* Eds. Jennifer L. McCoy and David J. Myers. John Hopkins UP, 2004, pp. 181–201.

DeGroot, Gerard. *The Sixties Unplugged: A Kaleidascopic History of a Disorderly Decade.* Harvard UP, 2008.

Dickstein, Morris. "Black Humor and History: Fiction in the Sixties." *Partisan Review,* vol. 43, no. 2, 1976, pp. 185–211.

Doctorow, E. L. "False Documents." *E. L. Doctorow: Essays and Conversations.* Ed. Richard Trenner. Ontario Review P, 1983, pp. 16–27.

———. *Ragtime*. Random House, 1975.

Domínguez, Mignon, ed. *Historia, ficción y metaficción en la novela latinoamericana contemporánea*. Corregidor, 1996.

Ebon, Martin. *Che: The Making of a Legend*. New American Library, 1969.

Edwards, Todd L. *Brazil: A Global Studies Handbook*. ABC-CLIO, 2008.

Ellison, Ralph, William Styron, Robert Penn Warren, and C. Vann Woodward. "The Uses of History in Fiction." *Southern Literary Journal*, vol. 1, no. 2, 1969, pp. 57–90.

Ernst, Kirsten. "Brazilian Pastoral?: Nature, Nation, and Exile in Ana Maria Machado's *Tropical sol da liberdade*." *ISLE*, vol. 22, no. 2, 2015, pp. 349–367.

Esteves, Antônio R. *O romance histórico brasileiro contemporâneo (1975–2000)*. UNESP, 2010.

Evans, Richard J. *In Defense of History*. W. W. Norton, 1999.

Fernández, Edmée. "El Guzmancismo en la novela venezolana." *Revista de Literatura y Artes Venezolanos*, vol. 2, no. 1, 1996, pp. 71–84.

Fernández Retamar, Roberto. *Caliban and Other Essays*. U of Minnesota P, 1989.

Firmat, Gustavo Peréz, ed. *Do the Americas Have a Common Literature?* Duke UP, 1990.

Fitz, Earl. *Inter-American Literary History: Six Critical Periods*. Peter Lang, 2017.

———. "Old World Roots/New World Realities: A Comparatist Looks at the Growth of Literature in North and South America." *Council on National Literatures/Quarterly World Report*, vol. 3, no. 3, 1980, pp. 8–11.

———. *Rediscovering the New World: Inter-American Literature in a Comparative Context*. U of Iowa P, 1991.

———. "Spanish American and Brazilian Literature in an Inter-American Perspective: A Comparative Approach." *Comparative Cultural Studies and Latin America*. Eds. Sophia McClennen and Earl Fitz. Purdue UP, 2004, pp. 69–88.

Fleishman, Avrom. *The English Historical Novel: Walter Scott to Virginia Woolf*. John Hopkins UP, 1971.

Florent, Adriana Coelho. "Roupa suja se lava em casa: Graciliano Ramos, escritor e comunista na era de Vargas." *Intelectuais e estado*. Eds. Marcelo Ridenti et al. Editora UFMG, 2006, pp. 143–62.

Flower, Dean. "Fiction Chronicle." *Hudson Review*, vol. 37, no. 2, 1984, pp. 301–16.

Fluck, Winfried. "A New Beginning?: Transnationalisms." *New Literary History*, vol, 42, no. 3, 2011, pp. 365–84.

Flynn, Thomas. "Foucault's Mapping of History." *The Cambridge Companion to Foucault*. Ed. Gary Gutting. Cambridge UP, 2005, pp. 29–48.

Foley, Barbara "From *USA* to *Ragtime*: Notes on the Forms of Historical Consciousness in Modern Fiction." *American Literature*, vol. 50, no. 1, 1978, pp. 85–104.

———. *Telling the Truth: The Theory and Practice of Documentary Fiction*. Cornell UP, 1986.

Fontava, Humberto. *Exposing the Real Che Guevara and the Useful Idiots Who Idolize Him*. Sentinel, 2007.

Ford, Gerald R. *Public Papers of the Presidents of the United States: Gerald R. Ford, 1974*. US G. P. O., 1975–1979.

———. "Toasts of the President and Queen Elizabeth II of the United Kingdom (July 7, 1976)." *The American Presidency Project*. Eds. Gerhard Peters and John T. Woolley. Web. Accessed 2 May 2017.

Forster, Gabrielle da Silva. "Os meandros da memória em *Tropical sol da liberdade*: descortinando 1968 pelo olhar da mulher brasileira." *Revista Cerrados*, vol. 21, no. 34, 2012, pp. 52–68. Web. Accessed 3 March 2018.

Foster, David William. "Imagining Argentine Socio-Political History in Some Recent American Novels." *Yearbook of Comparative and General Literature*, vol. 39, 1990–1991, pp. 75–86.
Foucault, Michel. *Power/Knowledge: Selected Interviews and Other Writings 1972–1977*. Ed. Colin Gordon. Pantheon Books, 1980.
Fox, Claire F. *Making Art Panamerican: Cultural Policy and the Cold War*. U of Minnesota Press, 2013.
Franco, Jean. *Critical Passions: Selected Essays*. Duke UP, 1999.
———. *The Decline and Fall of the Lettered City: Latin America in the Cold War*. Harvard UP, 2002.
———. "The Nation as Imagined Community." *The New Historicism*. Ed. H. Aram Veeser. Routledge, 1989, pp. 203–12.
Fuentes, Carlos. *La nueva novela hispanoamericana*. Editorial Joaquín Mortiz, 1969.
Fukuyama, Francis. "The End of History?" *National Interest*, vol. 16, 1989, pp. 3–18.
———. *The End of History and the Last Man*. Free Press, 1992.
Ganduglia, Silvia. "La representación de la historia en *La novela de Perón*." *Ideologies and Literature*, vol. 4, no. 1, 1989, pp. 271–297.
García Canclini, Néstor. *Hybrid Cultures: Strategies for Entering and Leaving Modernity*. Routledge, 1995.
Gates, David. "Now Old, Buck Redux." *Newsweek*, vol. 120, no. 19, 9 November 1992, p. 68.
Gauthier, Marni J. *Amnesia and Redress in Contemporary American Fiction: Counterhistory*. Palgrave Macmillan, 2011.
Geertz, Clifford. *The Interpretation of Cultures: Selected Essays*. Basic Books, 1973.
Gielow, Igor, and Talita Fernandes. "Objetivo é fazer Brasil semelhante ao que 'era há 40, 50 anos,' diz Bolsonaro." *Folha de São Paulo*, 15 October 2018. Web. Accessed 12 December 2018.
Giles, Paul. "Commentary: Hemispheric Partiality." *American Literary History*, vol. 18, no. 3, 2006, pp. 648–55.
Goldstein, William. "Jay Cantor." *Publishers Weekly*, 8 January 1988, pp. 65–66.
Gonçalves Vieira, Ilma Socorro. "O diálogo entre literatura e história na obra de Ana Maria Machado." *Trança de histórias: a criação literária de Ana Maria Machado*. Eds. Maria Teresa Goncalves Pereira and Benedito Antunes. Editora UNESP, 2004, pp. 35–52.
González Echevarría, Roberto. "Archival Fictions: García Márquez's Bolívar File." *Critical Theory, Cultural Politics, and Latin American Narrative*. Ed. Steven Bell. U of Notre Dame P, 1993, pp. 183–207.
———. *Myth and Archive: A Theory of Latin American Narrative*. Cambridge UP, 1990.
González Stephan, Beatriz. "Escritura de memorias subalternas." *Texto Crítico*, vol. 5, no. 10, 2002, pp. 21–34.
Gouveia, Saulo. *The Triumph of Brazilian Modernism: The Metanarrative of Emancipation and Counter-Narratives*. North Carolina Studies in the Romance Languages and Literatures, 2013.
Grandin, Greg. *Empire's Workshop: Latin America, The United States, and the Rise of New Imperialism*. Metropolitan Books, 2006.
Green, Anna, and Kathleen Troup. *The Houses of History: A Critical Reader in Twentieth-Century History and Theory*. New York UP, 1999.
Green, Duncan. *Silent Revolution: The Rise and Crisis of Market Economics in Latin America*. 2nd ed. Monthly Review P; Latin American Bureau, 2003.
Greenblatt, Stephen. "Towards a Poetics of Culture." *The New Historicism*. Ed. H. Aram Veeser. Routledge, 1989, pp. 1–14.

Grenier, Cynthia. "The Death of Che Guevara and Family Portrait with Fidel." *American Spectator*, July 1984, pp. 42–43.
Grover, Mark L. "Latin American History: Concerns and Conflicts." *History Teacher*, vol. 21, no. 3, 1988, pp. 349–366.
Guevara, Che. *The Motorcycle Diaries Notes on a Latin American Journey*. Ocean Press, 2003.
Guevara, Che, and David Deutschmann. *Che Guevara Reader*. Ocean Press, 2003.
Guevara, Che, and Daniel James. *The Complete Bolivian Diaries of Ché Guevara, and Other Captured Documents*. Stein and Day, 1968.
Guevara, Che, and Mary-Alice Waters. *The Bolivian Diary of Ernesto Che Guevara*. Pathfinder, 1994.
Guevara, Ernesto. *Back on the Road: A Journey to Latin America*. Grove, 2001.
Gullar, Ferrera. *Na vertigem do dia*. Civilização Brasileira, 1980.
Gussow, Mel. "Novelist Syncopates History in Ragtime." *Conversations with E. L. Doctorow*. Ed. Christopher D. Morris. U of Mississippi P, 1999, pp. 4–6.
Hanke, Lewis, ed. *Do the Americas Have a Common History?: A Critique of the Bolton Theory*. Knopf, 1964.
Harlan, David. *The Degradation of American History*. U of Chicago P, 1997.
Harrison, Robert. "The 'New Social History' in America." *Making History: An Introduction to the History and Practices of a Discipline*. Eds. Peter Lambert and Phillipp Schofield. Routledge, 2004, pp. 109–20.
Hellinger, Daniel. *Venezuela: Tarnished Democracy*. Westview Press, 1991.
Henderson, Harry B. *Versions of the Past: The Historical Imagination in American Fiction*. Oxford UP, 1974.
Hernández, Mark A. *Figural Conquistadors: Rewriting the New World's Discovery and Conquest in Mexican and River Plate Novels of the 1980s and 1990s*. Bucknell UP, 2006.
Hodges, Donald C. *Argentina's "Dirty War": An Intellectual Biography*. U of Texas P, 1991.
Holden, Robert H., and Eric Zolov. *Latin America and the United States: A Documentary History*. Oxford UP, 2000.
Hoyos Ayala, Héctor. *Beyond Bolaño: The Global Latin American Novel*. Columbia UP, 2015.
Hunt, Lynn, ed. *The New Cultural History*. U of California P, 1989.
Hurup, Elsebeth, ed. *The Lost Decade: America in the Seventies*. Aarhus UP, 1996.
Hutcheon, Linda. *A Poetics of Postmodernism: History, Theory, Fiction*. Routledge, 1988.
———. *The Politics of Postmodernism*. Routledge, 1989.
Jackson, David K. "The Prison-House of Memoirs: Silviano Santiago's *Em Liberdade*." *Tropical Paths: Essays on Modern Brazilian Literature*. Ed. Randal Johnson. Garland Publishing, 1993, pp. 199–222.
Jameson, Fredric. *Postmodernism, or, The Cultural Logic of Late Capitalism*. Duke UP, 1991.
Jenkins, Keith, and Alun Munslow, eds. *The Nature of History Reader*. Routledge, 2004.
Joseph, Gilbert M. "Close Encounters: Towards a New Cultural History of US-Latin American Relations." *Close Encounters of Empire: Writing the Cultural History of US-Latin American Relations*. Eds. Gilbert M. Joseph et al. Duke UP, 1998, pp. 3–46.
Joyce, Patrick. "The Return of History: Postmodernism and the Politics of Academic History in Britain." *Past & Present*, vol. 158, February 1998, pp. 207–35.
King, Stewart, and Jeff Browitt. *The Space of Culture: Critical Readings in Hispanic Studies*. U of Delaware P, 2004.
Kobak, Jim. "Review of *On Giving Birth to One's Own Mother*." *Kirkus Reviews*, 15 January 1991, p. 85.

Kumm, Bjorn. "The Death of Che Guevara." *New Republic*, 11 October 1967, pp. 13–15.

———. "Guevara Is Dead, Long Live Guevara." *Transition*, vol. 35, 1968, pp. 18–23.

La reforma del estado: proyecto de reforma integral del estado. Comisión Presidencial para la Reforma del Estado, 1988.

LaCapra, Dominick. *History and Criticism*. Cornell UP, 1985.

Leal Cunha, Eneida. "Os entre-lugares de Silviano Santiago." *Leituras críticas sobre Silviano Santiago*. Ed. Eneida Leal Cunha. Editora UFMG, 2008, pp. 7–21.

Leal Cunha, Eneida, and Wander Melo Miranda. "O Intelectual Silviano Santiago: Entevista." *Leituras Críticas Sobre Silviano Santiago*. Ed. Eneida Leal Cunha. Editora UFMG, 2008, pp. 171–210.

Leisy, Ernest Erwin. *The American Historical Novel*. U of Oklahoma P, 1950.

Levander, Caroline F., and Robert S. Levine, eds. *Hemispheric American Studies*. Rutgers UP, 2008.

Levin, David. *In Defense of Historical Literature: Essays on American History, Autobiography, Drama, and Fiction*. Hill and Wang, 1967.

Levine, Lawrence W. *The Unpredictable Past: Explorations in American Cultural History*. Oxford UP, 1993.

Levine, Paul. "The Writer as Independent Witness." *Conversations with E. L. Doctorow*. Ed. Christopher D. Morris. UP of Mississippi, 1999, pp. 41–52.

Levine, Robert M. *The Vargas Regime: The Critical Years, 1934–1938*. Columbia UP, 1970.

Lewis, Bart L. *The Miraculous Lie: Lope De Aguirre and the Search for El Dorado in the Latin American Historical Novel*. Lexington Books, 2003.

Lomas, Laura. *Translating Empire: José Martí, Migrant Latino Subjects, and American Modernities*. Duke UP, 2008.

Lombardi, John V. *Venezuela: The Search for Order, the Dream of Progress*. Oxford UP, 1982.

López, Kimberle S. *Latin American Novels of the Conquest: Reinventing the New World*. U of Missouri P, 2002.

Luengo Comerón, Isabel. "Un viaje al pasado de Venezuela en la novela *Solitaria solidaria* de la escritora venezolana Laura Antillano." *El viaje en la literatura hispanoamericana: el espíritu colombino*. Eds. Sonia Mattalia et al. Iberoamericana; Vervuert; 2008, pp. 889–900.

Lukács, Georg. *The Historical Novel*. Tr. Hannah and Stanley Mitchell. Beacon P, 1963.

Lyotard, Jean-François. *The Postmodern Condition: A Report on Knowledge*. U of Minnesota P, 1984.

Machado, Ana Maria. *Contracorrente: Conversas sobre leitura e política*. Ática, 1999.

———. "Diversidade." *Democracia: cinco princípios e um fim*. Ed. Carla Rodrigues. Editora Moderna, 1996, pp. 51–64.

———. *Tropical sol da liberdade*. Editora Nova Fronteira, 1988.

Malard, Letícia. "Romance e história." *Revista Brasileira de Literatura Comparada*, vol. 3, 1996, pp. 143–49.

Mallmann, Maria Izabel. *Os ganhos da década perdida: Democracia e diplomacia na América Latina*. EDIPUCRS, 2008.

Márquez Rodríguez, Alexis. *Historia y ficción en la novela venezolana*. Monte Ávila Editores, 1991.

Martí, José, and Philip Sheldon Foner. *Our America: Writings on Latin America and the Struggle for Cuban Independence*. Monthly Review Press, 1977.

Martin, Gerald. "Tomás Eloy Martínez, Biography and the Boom: *La novela de Perón* (1985) and *Santa Evita* (1995)." *Bulletin of Latin American Research*, vol. 31, no. 4, 2012, pp. 460–72.

Martínez, Tomás Eloy. "Ficción e historia en *La novela de Perón.*" *Hispamérica,* vol. 17, no. 49, 1988, pp. 41–49.
———. "La batalla de las versiones narrativas." *Boletín Cultural y Bibliográfico,* vol. 23, no. 8, 1986, pp. 21–31. Web. Accessed 5 March 2017.
———. *Las memorias del general.* Planeta, 1996.
———. *Las vidas del general.* Aguilar, 2004.
———. "Mito, historia y ficción: idas y vueltas." *Visiones cortazarianas: historia, política, y literatura hacia el fin del mundo.* Ed. Alejandra Mora. Aguilar, 1996, pp. 109–31.
———. *Réquiem por un país perdido.* Aguilar, 2003.
———. *The Perón Novel.* Tr. Asa Satz. Pantheon Books, 1988.
———. "The Truth in Fiction." *New Perspectives Quarterly,* vol. 22, no. 3, 2005. Web. Accessed 2 Feb. 2018.
McClennen, Sophia. "Area Studies Beyond Ontology: Notes on Latin American Studies, American Studies, and Inter-American Studies." *A Contracorriente,* vol. 5, no. 1, 2007, pp. 173–84.
———. "Inter-American Studies or Imperial American Studies?" *Comparative American Studies,* vol. 3, no. 4, 2005, pp. 393–413.
McDonald, Terrence J, ed. *The Historic Turn in the Human Sciences.* U of Michigan P, 1996.
McHale, Brian. *Postmodernist Fiction.* Methuen, 1987.
Mcnally, T. M., and Dean Stover. "An Interview with John Updike." *Conversations with John Updike.* Ed. James Plath. UP of Mississippi, 1994, pp. 192–206.
Melo, Ana Amelia M. C. "Pensando o Brasil: os escritos de Gracilian Ramos durante o Estado Novo." *De sertões, desertos e espaços incivilizados.* Eds. Angela Mendes de Almeida et al. FAPERJ; MUAUD Editora, 2001, pp. 65–74.
Menton, Seymour. *Latin America's New Historical Novel.* U of Texas P, 1993.
Mignolo, Walter. "Human Understanding and (Latin) American Interests: The Politics and Sensibilities of Geohistorical Locations." *A Companion to Postcolonial Studies.* Eds. Henry Schwarz and Sangeeta Ray. Blackwell, 2005, pp. 180–202.
Miller, Douglas T. "Sixties Activism in the 'Me Decade.'" *The Lost Decade: America in the Seventies.* Ed. Elsebeth Hurup. Aarhus UP, 1996, pp. 133–43.
Miranda, Wander Melo. *Corpos escritos: Graciliano Ramos e Silviano Santiago.* Editora UFMG, 1992.
Munslow, Alun. *Deconstructing History.* London: Routledge, 1997.
Neagle, Michael. *America's Forgotten Colony: Cuba's Isle of Pines.* Cambridge UP, 2016.
Neyret, Juan Pablo. "Una escritura imposible. La construcción de la historia en *La novela de Perón,* de Tomás Eloy Martínez." *Puntos de partida, puntos de llegada.* Ed. Adriana Bocchino. Estanislao Balder, 2003, pp. 202–9.
Nist, John. *The Modernist Movement in Brazil: A Literary Study.* U of Texas P, 1967.
Novick, Peter. *That Noble Dream: The "Objectivity Question" and the American Historical Profession.* Cambridge UP, 1988.
Nunes, Ana. *African American Women Writers' Historical Fiction.* Palgrave Macmillan, 2011.
Nye, Russel. "History and Literature: Branches of the Same Tree." *Essays on History and Literature.* Eds. Robert Bremner et al. The Ohio State UP, 1966, pp. 123–59.
Olderman, Raymond. *Beyond the Waste Land: The American Novel in the Nineteen-Sixties.* Yale UP, 1972.
Olmsted, Kathryn S. "US Intelligence Agencies during the Ford Years." *A Companion to Gerald R. Ford and Jimmy Carter.* Ed. Scott Kaufman. Wiley Blackwell, 2016, pp. 114–29.

Olster, Stacey Michele. *Reminiscence and Re-creation in Contemporary American Fiction.* Cambridge UP, 1989.

"Open Letter on Fake News and Elections in Latin America." *Democracia Abierta,* 12 January 2018. Web. Accessed 5 April 2018.

Pacheco, Carlos. "Reinventar el pasado: la ficción como historia alternativa de la América Latina." *Kipus, Revista Andina de Letras,* vol. 6, 1997, pp. 33–42.

Park, Stephen M. *The Pan American Imagination: Contested Visions of the Hemisphere in Twentieth-Century Literature.* U of Virginia P, 2014.

Parrish, Timothy. *From the Civil War to the Apocalypse: Postmodern History and American Fiction.* U of Massachusetts P, 2008.

Passmore, Kevin. "Poststructuralism and History." *Writing History: Theory & Practice.* Eds. Stefan Berger et al. Arnold, 2003, pp. 118–40.

Pease, Donald. "New Perspectives on US Culture and Imperialism." *Cultures of United States Imperialism.* Eds. Amy Kaplan and Donald Pease. Duke UP, 1993, pp. 22–37.

Pease, Donald, and Robyn Wiegman, eds. *The Futures of American Studies.* Duke UP, 2002.

Pellegrini, Tânia. "Brazil in the 1970s: Literature and Politics." *Latin American Perspectives,* vol. 21, no. 1, 1994, pp. 56–71.

———. "A ficção brasileira hoje: os caminhos da cidade." *Revista de Filología Románica,* vol. 19, 2002, pp. 355–70. Web. Accessed 12 June 2015.

———. *Gavetas vazias: Ficção e política nos anos 70.* Mercado das Letras, 1996.

Pérez-Brignoli, Hector, and Ernesto Ruiz. "History and Quantification in Latin America: An Assessment of Theories and Methods." *Social Science History,* vol. 8, no. 2, 1984, pp. 201–15.

Perkowska, Magdalena. *Historias híbridas: La nueva novela histórica latinoamericana (1985-2000) ante las teorías posmodernas de la historia.* Iberoamericana, 2008.

Perón, Juan Domingo. *Los libros del exilio, 1955-1973.* 2 vols. Ediciones Corregidor, 1996.

Pinto-Bailey, Cristina Ferreira. "Memory, History, Illness: The Female Body and the Body Politic in Ana Maria Machado's *Tropical sol da liberdade.*" *Romance Quarterly,* vol. 63, no. 4, 2016, pp. 183–89.

———. "Sincronicidades: História, memória e ficção em Ana Maria Machado e Griselda Gambaro." *Estudos de Literatura Brasileira Contemporânea,* vol. 45, 2015, pp. 121–37.

Poblete, Juan, ed. *Critical Latin American and Latino Studies.* U of Minnesota P, 2003.

Pons, María Cristina. *Memorias del olvido: Del Paso, García Márquez, Saer y la novela histórica de fines del siglo XX.* Siglo XXI, 1996.

Posada Mejía, Germán. *Nuestra América: notas de historia cultural.* Instituto Caro y Cuervo, 1959.

Posse, Abel. *Los cuadernos de Praga.* Atlantida, 1998.

Poster, Mark. *Cultural History and Postmodernity: Disciplinary Readings and Challenges.* Columbia UP, 1997.

Pratt, Mary Louise. "Arts of the Contact Zone." *Profession,* 1991, pp. 33–40.

Prince, Gerald. "The Diary Novel: Notes for the Definition of a Sub-Genre." *Neophilologus,* vol. 59, 1975, pp. 475–81.

Pulgarín, Amalia. *Metaficción historiográfica: la novela histórica en la narrativa hispánica posmodernista.* Editorial Fundamentos, 1995.

Punte, María José. "Perón: personaje de novela." *RILCE,* vol. 20, no. 2, 2004, pp. 223–39.

Radway, Janice. "What's in a Name?" *American Quarterly,* vol. 51, no. 1, 1999, pp. 1–32.

Rama, Ángel. "Los contestatórios del poder." *Novísimos narradores hispanoamericanos en marcha, 1964-1980.* Marcha Editores, 1981, pp. 9–48.

Ramos, Graciliano. *Memórias do Cárcere.* 2 vols. Publicações Europa-América, 1980.

———. "Pequena História da República." *Alexandre e Outros Heróis*. 9th ed. Liv. Martins, 1972.

Reising, Russell J. *The Unusable Past: Theory and the Study of American Literature*. Methuen, 1986.

Ribeiro, José Antônio Pereira. *O romance histórico na literatura brasileira*. Secretaria da Cultura, Ciência e Tecnologia, 1976.

Richard, Nelly. "The Latin American Problematic of Theoretical-Cultural Transference: Postmodern Appropriations and Counterappropriations." *South Atlantic Quarterly*, vol. 92, no. 3, pp. 453–549.

Ristoff, Dilvo. *John Updike's Rabbit at Rest: Appropriating History*. Peter Lang, 1998.

———. *Updike's America: The Presence of Contemporary American History in John Updike's Rabbit Trilogy*. Peter Lang, 1988.

Rivas, Luz Marina. *La novela intrahistórica: tres miradas femeninas de la historia venezolana*. Dirección Cultura de la Universidad de Carabobo, 2004.

———. "La novela intra-histórica y el caribe hispánico en la ficción femenina." *Estudios*, vol. 9, no. 18, 2001, pp. 103–24.

———. "La perspectiva marginal de la historia en la obra de Laura Antillano." *Revista de Literatura y Artes Venezolanas*, vol. 2, no. 1, 1996, pp. 15–31.

Robinson, Alan. *Narrating the Past: Historiography, Memory and the Contemporary Novel*. Palgrave MacMillan, 2011.

Rockefeller, Nelson. "Discurso del Excmo. Sr. Nelson A. Rockefeller, Secretario de Estado Auxiliar de los Estados Unidos, en la reunión del Comité Consultivo Económico Financiero Interamericano celebrada en la Unión Panamericana, en Washington, el 16 de enero de 1945." Organization of American States, 1945.

———. *The Rockefeller Report on the Americas: The Official Report of a United States Presidential Mission for the Western Hemisphere*. Quadrangle Books, 1969.

Rodríguez, Ileana. "Postmodern Theory and Cultural Criticism in Spanish America and Brazil." *A Companion to Latin American Literature and Culture*. Ed. Sara Castro-Klarén. Blackwell, 2008, pp. 602–19.

Rodríguez, Katitza. "'Fake News' Offers Latin American Consolidated Powers An Opportunity to Censor Opponents." *Electronic Frontier Foundation*, 2 April 2018. Web. Accessed 5 May 2018.

Rojas, Carlos A. Aguirre. "Braudel in Latin America and the US: A Different Reception." *Review (Fernand Braudel Center)*, vol. 24, no. 1, 2001, pp. 25–46.

Rowe, John Carlos. "Culture, US Imperialism, and Globalization." *A Concise Companion to American Studies*. Ed. John Carlos Rowe. Wiley-Blackwell, 2010, pp. 284–302.

———. *The New American Studies*. U of Minnesota P, 2002.

———, ed. *Post-Nationalist American Studies*. U of California P, 2000.

Sadowski-Smith, Claudia, and Claire Fox. "Theorizing the Hemisphere: Inter-Americas Work at the Intersection of American, Canadian, and Latin American Studies." *Comparative American Studies*, vol. 2, no. 1, 2004, pp. 5–38.

Saldívar, José David. *The Dialectics of Our America: Genealogy, Cultural Critique, and Literary History*. Duke UP, 1991.

———. *Trans-Americanity: Subaltern Modernities, Global Coloniality, and the Cultures of Greater Mexico*. Duke UP, 2012.

Samuels, Charles Thomas. "The Art of Fiction XLIII: John Updike." *Conversations with John Updike*. Ed. James Plath. UP of Mississippi, 1994, pp. 22–45.

Samuels, Shirley. *Reading the American Novel, 1780–1865*. Wiley-Blackwell, 2012.

Santí, Enrico. "Latinamericanism and Restitution." *Latin American Literary Review*, vol 20, no. 40, 1992, pp. 88–96.

Santiago, Silviano. *As raízes e o labirinto da América Latina*. Rocco, 2006.
———. *Em Liberdade*. Paz e Terra, 1981.
———. *Nas malhas da letra: ensaios*. Companhia das Letras, 1989.
———. *O cosmopolitismo do pobre: crítica literária e crítica cultural*. Editora UFMG, 2004.
———. "Reading and Discursive Intensities: On the Situation of Postmodern Reception in Brazil." *boundary 2*, vol. 20, no. 3, 1993, pp. 194–202.
———. *The Space In-Between: Essays on Latin American Literature*. Ed. Ana Lúcia Gazzola. Duke UP, 2001.
———. *Uma literatura nos trópicos: ensaios sobre dependência cultural*. Ciência e Tecnologia do Estado de São Paulo, 1978.
———. *Vale quanto pesa: Ensaios sobre questões político-culturais*. Paz e Terra, 1982.
Schama, Simon. *Dead Certainties (Unwarranted Speculations)*. Knopf, 1991.
Schiff, James A. *John Updike Revisited*. Twayne, 1998.
Scott, Sir Walter. *Peveril of the Peak*. A. Constable and Co., 1822.
Serrafero, Mario D. "Menem and Kirchner: Two Faces of Peronism?" *Presidents and Democracy in Latin America*. Eds. Manuel Alcántara, Jean Blondel, and Jean-Louis Thiébault. Routledge, 2018, pp. 205–30.
Shukla, Sandhya, and Helen Tinsman. "Introduction: Across the Americas." *Imagining Our Americas*. Eds. Sandhya Shukla and Helen Tinsman. Duke UP, 2007, pp. 1–33.
Skłodowska, Elzbieta. *La parodia en la nueva novela hispanoamericana (1960–1985)*. J. Benjamins Publishing, 1991.
Sinder, Valter. "A reinvenção do passado e a articulação de sentidos: O novo romance histórico brasileiro." *Estudos Históricos*, vol. 14, no. 26, 2000, pp. 253–64.
Smith, Henry Nash. "Can 'American Studies' Develop a Method?" *Locating American Studies: The Evolution of a Discipline*. Ed. Lucy Maddox. Johns Hopkins UP, 1999, pp. 1–16.
Socorro, Milagros. "Convertir la intimidad en hecho colectivo: Entrevista con Laura Antillano." *Imagen*, vol. 100, no. 68, 1990, pp. 8–9.
Spaulding, A. Timothy. *Re-forming the Past: History, the Fantastic, and the Postmodern Slave Narrative*. The Ohio State UP, 2005.
Styron, William. *The Confessions of Nat Turner*. Random House, 1967.
Sussekind, Flora. *Literatura e vida literária: Polêmicos, diários e retratos*. 2nd ed. Editora UFMG, 2004.
Taibo II, Paco Ignacio. *Ernesto Guevara, también conocido como el Che*. Planeta, 1997.
Tarver Denova, Hollis Micheal, and Julia C. Frederick. *The History of Venezuela*. Greenwood, 2005.
Tedeneke, Alem. "Fake News Poses a Threat to Democracies across Latin America and Worldwide." *World Economic Forum*, 14 March 2018. Web. Accessed 5 April 2018.
Tedesco, Laura, and Jonathan Barton. *The State of Democracy in Latin America: Post-Transitional Conflicts in Argentina and Chile*. Routledge, 2004.
Terkel, Studs. *American Dreams: Lost and Found*. Pantheon Books, 1980.
Thompson, E. P. "History from Below." *Times Literary Supplement*, 7 April 1966, pp. 279–80.
———. *The Making of the English Working Class*. Pantheon Books, 1964.
Thompson, Willie. *Postmodernism and History*. Palgrave Macmillan, 2004.
Tosta, Antonio Luciano de Andrade. *Confluence Narratives: Ethnicity, History, and Nation-Making in the Americas*. Bucknell UP, 2016.
Tuchman, Barbara W. *Practicing History: Selected Essays*. Knopf, 1981.

Turner, Joseph W. "The Kinds of Historical Fiction: An Essay in Definition and Methodology." *Genre*, vol. 12, no. 3, 1979, pp. 333–55.

Umbach, Rosani Úrsula Ketzer, and Andrea Quilian de Vargas. "*Tropical sol da liberdade*: Narrativa e resistência em tempos de barbárie." *Literatura em Debate*, vol. 7, no. 12, 2013, pp. 263–80. Web. Accessed 11 March 2017.

Unzueta, Fernando. *La imaginación histórica y el romance nacional en Hispanoamérica*. Latinoamericana Editores, 1996.

Updike, John. *Buchanan Dying*. Knopf, 1974.

———. "Henry Bech Interviews Updike Apropos of His Fifteenth Novel." *More Matter: Essays and Criticism*. Knopf, 1999, pp. 821–25.

———. *Memories of the Ford Administration*. Knopf, 1992.

———. "Reply." *Novel History: Historians and Novelists Confront America's Past (And Each Other)*. Ed. Mark C. Carnes. Simon and Schuster, 2001, pp. 57–60.

———. "A 'Special Message' for the Franklin Library's Signed First Edition Society's Printing of *Memories of the Ford Administration*." *More Matter: Essays and Criticism*. Knopf, 1999, pp. 825–27.

Valdés. Mario J. *Inter-American Relations*. Garland, 1985.

Valente, Luiz Fernando. "Fiction as History: The Case of João Ubaldo Ribeiro." *Latin American Research Review*, vol. 28, no. 1, 1993, pp. 41–60.

———. *História e ficção: convergências e contrastes*. Registros do SEPLIC 12, Universidade Federal do Rio de Janeiro, 2002.

———. "*Viva o povo brasileiro*: Ficção e anti-historia." *Letras de hoje*, vol. 25, no. 3, 1990, pp. 61–74.

Vann, Richard. "The Reception of Hayden White." *History and Theory*, vol. 37, no. 2, 1998, pp. 143–61.

Vargo, Edward. "Updike, American History, and Historical Methodology." *The Cambridge Companion to John Updike*. Ed. Stacey Olster. Cambridge UP, 2006, pp. 107–21.

Vartuck, Pola. "Por um Cinema Popular, Sem Ideologias: Entrevista de Cacá Diegues a Pola Vartuck." *O Estado de São Paulo*, 31 August 1978.

Vecchi, Roberto. "Memória no feminino: *Tropical sol da liberdade* de Ana Maria Machado." *Revista Brasileira*, vol. 65, 2010, pp. 252–63.

Veeser, H. Aram, ed. *The New Historicism*. Routledge, 1989.

Ventura, Susana Ramos. "Identidade, identidades: percursos de uma pesquisa." *Nau Literária*, vol. 2, 2006, pp. 113–32. Web. Accessed 6 December 2016.

Waters, Mary-Alice. Introduction to *The Bolivian Diary of Ernesto Che Guevara*. Ed. Mary-Alice Waters. Pathfinder, 1994, pp. 11–47.

Weinhardt, Marilene. "O romance histórico na ficção brasileira recente." *Nem fruta, nem flor*. Ed. Regina Helena Machado Aquino Corrêa. Edições Humanidades, 2008, pp. 131–72.

———. "Outros palimpsestos: ficção e história, 2001–2010." *Literatura crítica comparada*. Ed. João Luis Pereira Ourique et al. Universitária PRECJ/UFPEL, 2011, pp. 31–55.

Weinstein, Mark. "The Creative Imagination in Fiction and History." *Genre*, vol. 9, no. 3, 1976, pp. 263–77.

Weisman, Steven. "Reagan Takes Oath as 40th President; Promises an 'Era of National Renewal.'" *New York Times*, 21 January 1981, p. A1.

Weldt-Basson, Helene Carol, ed. *Redefining Latin American Historical Fiction: The Impact of Feminism and Postcolonialism*. Palgrave Macmillan, 2013.

Welskopp, Thomas. "Social History." *Writing History: Theory & Practice*. Eds. Stefan Berger, Heiko Feldner, and Kevin Passmore. Arnold, 2003, pp. 203–22.

Wesseling, Elisabeth. *Writing History as a Prophet: Postmodern Innovations of the Historical Novel*. J. Benjamin Publishing, 1991.

White, Hayden. "Historical Emplotment and the Problem of Truth." *Probing the Limits of Representation: Nazism and the "Final Solution."* Ed. Saul Friedlander. Harvard UP, pp. 37–52.

———. *Metahistory: The Historical Imagination in Nineteenth-Century Europe*. Johns Hopkins UP, 1973.

———. *Tropics of Discourse: Essays in Cultural Criticism*. John Hopkins UP, 1978.

Williams, Claire. "*Los diarios de motocicleta* as Pan-American Travelogue." *Contemporary Latin American Cinema: Breaking into the Global Market*. Ed. Deborah Shaw. Rowman and Littlefield, 2007, pp. 11–27.

Windschuttle, Keith. *The Killing of History: How Literary Critics and Social Theorists Are Murdering Our Past*. Free Press, 1997.

Wise, Gene. "'Paradigm Dramas' in American Studies: A Cultural and Institutional History of the Movement." *American Quarterly*, vol. 31, no. 3, 1979, pp. 293–337.

Yúdice, George. "¿Puede hablarse de posmodernidad en América Latina?" *Revista de Crítica Literaria Latinoamericana*, vol. 15, no. 29, 1989, pp. 105–28.

———. "Testimonio and Postmodernism." *Latin American Perspectives*, vol. 18, no. 3, 1991, pp. 15–31.

Zambrano, Gregory. "Narrar desde la memoria: La historia posible (Laura Antillano, Ana Teresa Torres, y Milagros Mata Gil)." *Texto Crítico*, vol. 5, no. 10, 2002, pp. 243–53.

Zamora, Lois Parkinson. *The Usable Past: The Imagination of History in Recent Fiction of the Americas*. Cambridge UP, 1997.

———. *Writing the Apocalypse: Historical Vision in Contemporary US and Latin American Fiction*. Cambridge UP, 1989.

Zamora, Lois Parkinson, and Wendy B. Faris, eds. *Magical Realism: Theory, History, Community*. Duke UP, 1995.

INDEX

A Bíblia do Che (Neto), 177
Aaron and Ahmed (Cantor), 175
Absalom, Absalom! (Faulkner), 49, 174
Admiral's Vigil, The (Roa Bastos), 59
agency, 12–18, 20, 34, 36, 88, 100, 138
AI-5, 125–26, 129, 133, 137, 139–40, 151–52
AIB. *See* Brazilian Integralist Action (AIB)
Aínsa, Fernando, 41–42, 60, 60n14, 61–62
Alliance for Progress, 1–2
Almanac of the Dead (Silko), 25–26
Álvares Cabral, Pedro, 66
Alvarez, Julia, 25
American Dreams: Lost and Found (Terkel), 195
American Tabloid (Ellroy), 25
anachronism, 30, 60–62, 64, 70, 82n10, 163
Anatomy of Criticism (Frye), 205
Anderson, Benedict, 27
Anderson, Jon Lee, 177
Andrade, Oswald de, 160
Angústia (Ramos), 155
anthropological turn, 40
Antillano, Laura, 99–103, 100n4, 106–15, 111n8, 115–23
Anzaldúa, Gloria, 14
apocryphal history, 12, 20, 54
archival fiction, 5, 20, 63–64
archives, 20–21, 35, 43, 64–65, 79, 107–11, 113, 120, 133, 138, 144–45

Arenas, Reynaldo, 59–60
Argentina, 18, 21, 23, 35, 48, 61, 73–95, 75, 135–36, 176–79, 187, 217
Argentine, The (film), 182
Artaud, Antonin, 150
Artificial Respiration (Piglia), 59
As raízes e o labirinto da América Latina (The Roots and the Labyrinth of Latin America) (Santiago), 150
August (Fonseca), 68
authority: of historians, 31; of history, 30, 62, 205; humor and, 52; of nonfiction, 5–6; unmasking of, 55
Avelar, Idelber, 126, 134–36, 147, 153n7

"Back in Bahia" (Gil), 140
Bakhtin, Mikhail, 61–62, 68
Balderston, Daniel, 56n9
Barrenechea, Antonio, 19
Barrientos, Juan José, 59–60
Barth, John, 25, 48, 50, 52
Baudrillard, Jean, 9
Bauer, Ralph, 19
Beasley-Murray, Jon, 78
Bech: A Book (Updike), 204n3
Bech at Bay: A Quasi-Novel (Updike), 204n3
Bech Is Back (Updike), 204n3
Belnap, Jeffrey, 103
Beloved (Morrison), 25

236 • INDEX

Berger, Thomas, 50
Berkhofer, Robert, 17–19, 70–71
Between God and the Devil (Lobo), 24
Blanco, Eduardo, 114n13
Bloom, Harold, 193
Bolivia, 175, 179–80, 181, 189–92
Bolivian Diaries (Guevara), 175–76, 180–81
Bolsonaro, Jair, 218
Book of Daniel, The (Doctorow), 4
Borderlands/La Frontera (Anzaldúa), 14
Borges, Jorge Luis, 48, 77, 162–63
Braudel, Fernand, 35
Brazil, 8, 35, 39, 47–48, 59n12, 64–69, 125–41, 149–72, 177, 218
Brazil (Updike), 201
Brazilian Integralist Action (AIB), 157
Brickhouse, Anna, 16
Brief Wondrous Life of Oscar Wao, The (Diaz), 218
Buarque de Holanda, Sérgio, 150
Buchanan, James, 200, 202, 203–4, 206, 208. See also *Memories of the Ford Administration* (Updike)
Buchanan Dying (Updike), 202n2, 203, 211n7
Burke, Peter, 39, 42

Calibán: Notes toward a Discussion of Culture in Our America (Fernández), 40, 104–5
Callado, Antônio, 68
Campa, Román de la, 14
Canada, 15–16, 105, 150, 217, 220
Candido, Antonio, 5, 65, 155
Cannibal Democracy (Nunes), 16
"Cannibal Manifesto" (Andrade), 160
Cantor, Jay, 173–94, 174n2
capitalism: in Brazil, 127; and concept of individual, 41; freedom and, 135; historical novels and, 32–33; history and, 32; intellectual imperialism and, 35; Perón and, 85; postmodernism and, 129
Carpentier, Alejo, 56, 59–60, 63n17
Carroll, Peter, 207
Carter, Jimmy, 195
Casey, Michael, 178, 178n5
Castro, Fidel, 178–81, 185

Castro, Manuel Antônio de, 128
Catch-22 (Heller), 52n6
censorship, 3, 8, 127–28, 127n3, 140, 144–45, 151–52, 154–56, 158–59, 219
Center for Inter-American Relations (CIAR), 2
Central Intelligence Agency (CIA), 2, 180, 196
Cervantes, Miguel de, 5, 29, 162–63
Chartier, Roger, 39
Chávez, Hugo, 98
Chevolution (film), 178n5
Chile, 110, 135–36, 138, 179
Chomsky, Noam, 10
CIA. See Central Intelligence Agency (CIA)
CIAR. See Center for Inter-American Relations (CIAR)
Citizenship and Crisis in Contemporary Brazilian Literature (Lehnen), 25
"Cli-ché," 183 fig. 3, 182–83
Cohn, Deborah, 2, 19, 50n4
Colás, Santiago, 31, 57, 77
Cold War, 2n2, 35, 52n6, 53n7, 100n5, 194, 197, 201, 207
Collor, Fernando, 66
colonialism, 14, 40, 161–62, 177, 194, 220. See also neocolonialism
Color Defect, A (Gonçalves), 69
comic historical novel, 51
Committee for State Reform (COPRE), 98, 98n3, 99, 100, 111, 121
commodification, of Guevara, 178–82
communism, 85, 97n1, 156, 158, 166, 168–69, 173–74, 185
Communist Party (Bolivia), 190
Communist Party (Brazil), 152, 158
Confessions of Nat Turner, The (Styron), 50
Confluence Narratives (Tosta), 47
Congo, 180n7
consumerism, 9, 22, 128, 142–47, 183
contact zone, 47, 71, 86
Contras, 2
Coover, Robert, 50, 52
COPRE. See Committee for State Reform (COPRE)

Costa, Cláudio Manuel da, 168–71
counterhistory, 27, 30, 136
Cowart, David, 53
critical realism, 218
Cuadernos Americanos (journal), 60, 60n14, 63
Cuadernos de Praga, Los (The Prague Notebooks) (Posse), 177
Cuba, 55–56, 59–60, 94, 178–81
Cuban Revolution, 35, 97, 103, 125, 190
Cultura Política (Brazilian propaganda), 157
cultural history, 8, 10–11, 38–41, 113, 139–41, 199, 201
Cultural History (Chartier), 39
"Cultural Logic of Late Capitalism, The" (Jameson), 29
cultural turn, 36–38
Culturas híbridas (Hybrid Cultures) (García Canclini), 78, 86
Cultures of United States Imperialism (Pease and Kaplan, eds.), 17

D*Face, 183 fig. 3, 182–83
Dalcastagnè, Regina, 126
Dark Night of Niño Avilés, The (Rodríguez Juliá), 59
Dash, Michael, 122
Dassin, Joan, 133n12
Davis, Natalie Zemon, 38–39
Dead Certainties (Schama), 201, 211
Death of Artemio Cruz, The (Fuentes), 50, 186–87
Death of Che Guevara, The (Cantor), 175–77, 182–93
"Death of Che Guevara, The" (Kumm), 179–80
decollection, 78, 87, 89–93, 95
Defoe, Daniel, 5, 55
Degradation of American History, The (Harlan), 197–99
DeLillo, Don, 25
democracy, 3, 7–11, 35, 76–77, 79, 94–95, 121, 131, 140–41, 147–48, 165, 194, 217, 219
Democracy: Five Principles and a Purpose (Souza), 148
Democratic Action Party (Venezuela), 97

dependency theory, 20, 35–36, 40, 151
deterritorialization, 77–78, 87–93, 123
Dialectics of Our America, The (Saldívar), 105
diary, false, 69, 152–53, 163
Diaz, Junot, 218
Didion, Joan, 54–55
Diegues, Carlos, 127n3, 152
"Dirty War," 74–75, 79–80, 94
Dividing the Isthmus (Rodríguez), 24
Do the Americas Have a Common Literature? (Firmat), 15–16
Doctorow, E. L., 4–6, 25, 29–30, 44–45, 50, 52, 55, 174, 189, 219–20
documentary model, 6, 20, 28, 32–34, 41–45
documentary novel, 49, 55
Dogs of Paradise, The (Posse), 59
Don Quixote (Cervantes), 5, 29, 162–63
dos Passos, John, 49, 55

Elbrick, Charles, 130
Ellison, Ralph, 50, 52n6
Ellroy, James, 25
Em Liberdade (In Liberty) (Santiago), 149, 149n1, 151–57, 159–60, 163–72
Emperor of the Amazon, The (Souza), 68–69
empiricism, 44, 55
"End of History, The?" (Fukuyama), 9–10; rejection of, 11–12, 77, 173
End of History and the Last Man, The (Fukuyama), 9–10
essentialism, 18, 36–37, 43, 51, 154
Estado & Reforma (magazine), 98–99
Estenssoro, Paz, 190
Esteves, Antônio R., 59n12, 60n15, 67n22, 68n24
Everlasting (Callado), 68
exceptionalism, 9, 11–13, 28, 71, 105, 136, 174, 193, 195, 215
Explosion in a Cathedral (Carpentier), 59–60

"fake news," 219
Falklands War, 75
False Chronicles from the South (Vega), 24
"false diary," 69, 152–53, 163

false documents: in Brazil, 65–66; in Cantor, 175, 194; defined, 5–6; Doctorow and, 105, 169; dos Passos and, 55; in Franco, 58; in González Echevarria, 63; historical revisionism and, 50; historiographic metafiction and, 202; in Martinez, 85; new history and, 41–45; origin of term, 4–5; parody vs., 60, 64; in Santiago, 154, 158–59, 165, 170–71; in Updike, 202

"False Documents" (Doctorow), 5, 44

Famous All over Town (Santiago), 26

fascism, 32, 154, 157, 157n11, 163–71

Faulkner, William, 49, 174

feminism, 21–22, 30–31, 36, 38, 40–42, 102–3, 106–7, 111–15, 134n13

Feracho, Lesley, 19

Fernández, Raúl, 103

Fernández Retamar, Roberto, 40

Ferré, Rosario, 59

Ficçao e confissão (Candido), 155

fiction: archival, 5, 20, 63–64; authority of, 5; borders of, 79–84; Clayton and, 211; diary, 175; Doctorow and, 219; documentary, 5, 21, 49, 55; and ethical imagination, 50n3; experimental, 21; memorialist, 132n10; new historical, 7, 12, 42, 48, 56, 59, 61–62, 63n17, 68n24, 69, 100n6, 131; politicization and, 30; in Santiago, 167; satirical, 52; testimonial, 155–59

Firmat, Gustavo, 15–16, 19

Fitz, Earl, 6, 15

Fleishman, Avrom, 51

Fondle Fever (Gomes), 68

Fonseca, Rubem, 68, 177

Ford, Gerald, 2, 196–97, 198 fig. 4, 200–210

Foucault, Michel, 37–38, 64, 150

"foundational fictions," 27

Fox, Claire, 17, 19

Franco, Jean, 2, 57–58, 153n7

Freyre, Gilberto, 39, 165

Frye, Northrup, 205

Fuentes, Carlos, 50, 56, 59, 63n17, 194

Fukuyama, Francis, 9–10, 173–74

functionalism, 36–37

Futures of American Studies, The (Pease), 14

Gabeira, Fernando, 129–30, 130n7, 155

Gallegos, Rómulo, 97n1, 99

García Canclini, Néstor, 4, 19, 78–79, 86–89, 93, 95, 154n9

García Márquez, Gabriel, 50, 59, 63n17

Gazzola, Ana Lúcia, 149n1

Geertz, Clifford, 36

Geisel, Ernesto, 128

General in His Labyrinth, The (García Márquez), 59

Gil, Gilberto, 140

Giles, Paul, 18

globalization, 9, 14, 16, 57

Gomes, Eustáquio, 68

Gonçalves, Ana Maria, 69

González Echevarría, Roberto, 5, 56n9, 60, 63

González y González, Luis, 113n12

Goulart, João, 125

Gravity's Rainbow (Pynchon), 50

Great Neck (Cantor), 174

Greenblatt, Stephen, 40

"Guerillero Heróico" (photograph), 178–80

Guevara, Aleida, 178n5

Guevara, Che, 174–92

Gullar, Ferreira, 142

Guzmán Blanco, Antonio, 101, 106–9, 114, 121

Haley, Alex, 196, 211

Hallucinations. Or, the Ill-Fated Peregrinations of Fray Servando (Arenas), 59–60

Hanke, Lewis, 16

Harlan, David, 19, 197–99, 203, 213

Harp and the Shadow, The (Carpentier), 59

Hegel, Georg Wilhelm Friedrich, 10, 33

Heller, Joseph, 52n6

Hemispheric American Studies (Levander and Levine, eds.), 16

Hemispheric Imaginings (Murphy), 16

hemispheric turn, 2, 13, 17, 201

"Hemispheric Vertigo" (Ortíz), 105

Henderson, Harry, 51

Herriman, George, 175

Herzog, Vladimir, 128, 151, 169–70
"Historical Emplotment and the Problem of Truth" (White), 199, 205–6, 212
Historical Novel, The (Lukács), 32
historical revisionism, 7, 48–56, 116, 122, 212
"Historical Text as Literary Artifact, The" (White), 199, 202, 205
historical turn, 3, 11, 20, 32, 49, 56
historicity, 29, 52–53, 55, 62, 160, 219
historiographic metafiction, 12, 19, 34–35, 61, 70–71; false documents and, 202; Hutcheon and, 54, 61, 66, 160; Machado and, 131; Menton and, 61; new historicism and, 41; and postmodern paradigm, 28–32, 44; revisionism and, 54; self-awareness and, 44; self-awareness of, 45; use of term, 25, 70; Valente and, 68
History and Memory in the Two Souths (Cohn), 19
Horizonte (magazine), 76, 91
Hour of the People, The (Martínez), 85
humor, 51–53, 61–62
Hunt, Lynn, 39
Hutcheon, Linda, 28–31, 53–54, 57, 61, 160
hybrid culture, 84–89, 93
Hybrid Cultures (García Canclini), 21, 86

I, the Supreme (Roa Bastos), 7, 56, 59
"ideological patrols," 127n3, 152, 154, 167
imperialism, 12–18, 35–36, 57, 85, 103–5, 150, 160, 178–79, 190, 194
In Defense of Historical Literature (Levin), 50
In Liberty (Santiago), 68–69
In the Time of the Butterflies (Alvarez), 25
Integralists, 157
International Monetary Fund, 217
Interpretation of Cultures, The (Geertz), 36
intrahistory, 64, 64n18, 110–16, 122–23
Invincible Memory, An (Ribeiro), 68
It Seemed Like Nothing Happened (Carroll), 207

Jameson, Frederic, 9, 29, 154n9, 160–61, 174, 174n2
JFK (film), 25

José Martí's "Our America": From National to Hemispheric Cultural Studies (Belnap and Fernández), 103
Joseph, Gilbert, 17
journalism. *See* New Journalism

Kaplan, Amy, 17
Kirchner, Néstor, 77n4
Kogawa, Joy, 25
Korda, Alberto, 178
Krazy Kat (Cantor), 174–75
Kumm, Bjorn, 175, 179–80

LaCapra, Dominick, 5n6, 43–44
Laclau, Ernesto, 78
Latinamericanism, 14–15
Lehnen, Leila, 25
Leisy, Ernest, 49
Levander, Caroline, 4, 16
Lévi-Strauss, Claude, 35
Levin, David, 50
Levin, Lawrence, 201
Levine, Robert, 16
Libra (DeLillo), 25
Lima Souto, Edson Luís, 126
linguistic turn, 32, 36–38, 40, 210
"literariness" of history, 49–50
Little Big Man (Berger), 50
Lobo, Tatiana, 24
Lomas, Laura, 105
"London, London" (Veloso), 140
Long Dusk of the Traveler, The (Posse), 59
López Obrador, Andrés Manuel, 218
López Rega, Jose, 74, 74n2, 81, 89–91
lost decade: in Argentina, 94; in Brazil, 66; cultural application of term, 8–9; economic origins of term, 7–8; neoliberalism and, 57, 58; reappearance of term, 218; in United States, 8–9, 197; in Venezuela, 98, 100, 104, 111
Lukács, Georg, 32, 34–35, 61

Machado (Santiago), 149–50
Machado, Ana Maria, 126–27, 130–48

Machado de Assis, 48
magical realism, 25, 31, 52, 65, 201
Making Art Panamerican (Fox), 17
Making of the English Working Class, The (Thompson), 34–35
Malard, Leticia, 67n22
Mao Zedong, 174
"March of One Hundred Thousand," 125
Márquez Rodríguez, Alexis, 114n13–114n14
Martí, José, 102–12, 123
Martin, Gerald, 84–85
Martínez, Tomás Eloy, 59, 73–76, 78–82, 81n9, 82n11, 83–95, 94n18
Marx, Karl, 174, 184, 187
Marxism, 147
Masters and the Slaves, The (Freyre), 39
Mata Gil, Milagros, 112
McHale, Brian, 53–54
Mead, Margaret, 196
Mejía, Posada, 39
Memorias del general, Las (The General's Memoirs) (Martínez), 73–75, 79, 83, 94–95
Memories of Prison (Ramos), 158–59, 165–68, 170–71
Memories of the Ford Administration (Updike), 200–215
Menem, Carlos, 77n4, 94n18
Menton, Seymour, 58, 59n12, 60–62, 66, 100n6
MERCOSUR, 218
metafiction, historiographic. *See* historiographic metafiction
metahistory, 56, 68, 105, 153, 160–61, 161n16
Metahistory (White), 37
Miami (Didion), 54–55
mimicry, 161–62, 161n16
Minas Gerais Conspiracy, 151, 168
Miranda, Ana, 69
misinformation, 81, 219
MNR. *See* Revolutionary Nationalist Movement (MNR)
mockumentaries, 219
modernism, 49, 54, 86–87, 91, 147, 152–53, 155–59, 162, 174, 193–94

Monroe Doctrine, 15, 17
Moraes, Vinicius de, 140
Morrison, Toni, 25, 174
Motorcycle Diaries, The (film), 182
Motorcycle Diaries, The (Guevara), 181–82
movies, 25, 178n5, 182, 219, 219n2
Mumbo Jumbo (Reed), 50
Munslow, Alun, 9n12, 220, 220n4
Murphy, Gretchen, 16

National Reorganization Process, 74–75
nationalism, 2n2, 3, 22–26, 32, 36, 43, 77–78, 89, 107–11, 140, 147–48, 152, 168, 179, 189–92, 220
neocolonialism, 108–9. *See also* colonialism
Neto, Miguel Sanches, 177
New Criticism, 34
New Cultural History, The (Hunt), 39
new historical novel, 28, 41, 56–69, 77, 114n14, 130, 177
new historicism, 17, 38–41, 113
New Historicism, The (Veeser, ed.), 41, 57–58
New Historicism Reader, The (Veeser, ed.), 41
New Journalism, 20, 31, 54–55, 83, 193, 206
New State (Brazil), 151–52, 157, 157n11, 164
Newcomb, Robert, 19
News from the Empire (Paso), 59
newsreels, 182–86
Nietzsche, Friedrich, 174
"Nightmare" (Pinheiro), 140
1968, Year That Never Ended (Ventura), 125n1, 133
Nixon, Richard, 1–2, 52, 196–7
nonfiction novel, 54–56, 69, 83n12, 128, 193
North American Free Trade Agreement, 217
novel: comic historical, 51; counterhistory and, 27; documentary, 32–34, 49, 55; new historical, 28, 41, 56–69, 77, 114n14, 130, 177; nonfiction, 54–56, 69, 83n12, 128, 193; political function of, 27; -factual, 65–69; redemocratization, 127–30; traditional historical, 19, 28, 32–34
Novela de Perón, La (The Perón Novel) (Martínez), 76–78, 80–82, 81n9, 83–84, 86–95
Novick, Peter, 31

"Nuestra América" (Martí), 39, 103–4, 109
Nunes, Zita, 16, 19
Nye, Russel, 50n3

O cosmopolitismo do pobre (The Cosmopolitanism of the Poor) (Santiago), 150
"O entre-lugar do discurso latinoamericano" ("Latin American Discourse: The Space In-Between") (Santiago), 150, 153–55, 161, 171–72
O que é isso, companheiro? (What's This, Comrade?) (Gabeira), 129–30
Obasan (Kogawa), 25
Office of Inter-American Affairs, 1–2, 2n1
On Giving Birth to One's Own Mother (Cantor), 173–74, 176, 184, 193
One Hundred Years of Solitude (García Márquez), 50, 63n17
ontology, 37, 54
Order and Progress (Freyre), 39
Organization of American States, 3
Orientalism (Said), 14
Ortíz, Ricardo, 105
Other America, The (Dash), 122
Otra vez (Back on the Road) (Guevara), 181–82

Pan-Caribbean intrahistory, 111–15
Panama, 10
Panorama (magazine), 74, 75
Parra, Teresa de la, 114n15
Parrish, Timothy, 199
Paso, Fernando del, 59, 63n17
pastiche, 29, 62, 152–53, 153n6, 160–61, 169, 172
"Pátria Minha" (Moraes), 140
Paz, Octavio, 150
Pease, Donald, 14, 17
Pérez, Andrés, 98, 101
Pérez Jiménez, Marcos, 97n1
Perfume de Gardenia (Scent of Gardenias) (Antillano), 100, 100n4–100n5
Perón, Isabel, 74–75
Perón, Juan, 73–74, 74n2, 75, 80, 82, 85. See also *Perón Novel, The* (Martínez)

Perón Novel, The (Martínez), 59, 76–80, 82–84, 89–94
Peronism, 76–81, 85, 94
"Pierre Menard, Author of the Quixote" (Borges), 48, 162–63
Piglia, Ricardo, 59
Pinheiro, Paulo Cesar, 140
"pink tide," 218
Piñon, Nélida, 68–69
Pinto-Bailey, Cristina Ferreira, 132n10, 134n13
Poblete, Juan, 4
Poetics of Postmodernism, A (Hutcheon), 28–29
Politics of Postmodernism, The (Hutcheon), 28–29
Ponco, 184, 186–90, 192
populism, 21, 74, 78–79, 84–89, 94, 125, 218
positivism, 34, 52, 106, 204
Posse, Abel, 59, 177
postdictatorial literature, 22, 126, 134–39, 147
Posthegemony (Beasley-Murray), 78
Posthumous Memoirs of Bras Cubas, The (Machado de Assis), 48
postmodernism: in Brazil, 128, 153–54, 160–61; capitalism and, 129; cultural and social debates about, 28–30, 57; democracy and, 147–48; freedom of, 160–63; historicity and, 29; historiographic metafiction and, 28–32, 44; hybridity and, 86; Martínez and, 73, 77, 84; new historical novel and, 56–65; ontology and, 54; Perón and, 73–74; reception within Latin American criticism, 11–12, 14, 17–18, 30–31, 57–59, 61, 63, 86–89; relation to historiography, 9–10, 36–40, 197–200; skepticism of, 4–5, 21, 113n11, 173–74, 204, 213; video and, 29
Postmodernity in Latin America (Colás), 77
postnationalism, 9, 18, 21, 78, 151, 178
poststructural theory, 28, 31, 36, 41, 45, 48–49, 61, 94, 136, 153, 199–200, 202–3, 210, 217
Pratt, Mary Louise, 47
propaganda, 21, 75, 85, 91, 108, 157, 163–70, 178
pseudo-factual novel, 65–69
pseudo-factuality, 44, 55, 60
Public Burning, The (Coover), 50, 52
Purgatory (Martínez), 78

Pynchon, Thomas, 50, 52, 174

Rabbit at Rest (Updike), 201
Radway, Janice, 13–14
Ragtime (Doctorow), 4, 50, 52
Rama, Ángel, 56, 59, 65
Ramírez, Sergio, 24
Ramos, Graciliano, 152–53, 153n5, 154–59, 157n13, 164–68, 170–71
Ranke, Leopold van, 33–34, 50
Reagan, Ronald, 195
realism, 23, 33, 48, 50, 55, 68, 126, 156, 171, 177, 212; critical, 218; magical, 25, 31, 52, 65, 201; social, 32, 43–44, 49, 56, 156, 173
redemocratization, 2, 22, 57, 126–31, 134–37, 144, 147, 171, 202
reductionism, 36–37
Reed, Ishmael, 50, 52n6
reflexivity, 29, 55, 174, 217
relativism, 24, 29–30, 42, 51, 199–201, 212–13
Reminiscences of the Revolutionary War (Guevara), 181–82
Renaissance Self-Fashioning (Greenblatt), 40
Republic of Dreams, The (Piñon), 68
Retamar, Roberto Fernández, 104–5, 109
Return of Martin Guerre, The (Davis), 38–39
revisionism, historical, 7, 48–56, 116, 122, 212
Revolutionary Nationalist Movement (MNR), 189–90
Ribeiro, João Ubaldo, 68
Richard, Nelly, 154n9
Rivas, Luz Marina, 102, 112, 113n12, 114–15, 115n16
Roa Bastos, Augusto, 7, 56, 59, 63n17
Robinson Crusoe (Defoe), 5, 55
Rockefeller, Nelson, 1–2
Rockefeller Report on the Americas, The, 1
Rodríguez, Ana Patricia, 24
Rodríguez Juliá, Edgardo, 59, 63n17
romance-reportagem, 128–30, 133–34, 143
Roosevelt, Theodore, 15
Roots (Haley), 196, 211
Roth, Philip, 200
Rowe, John Carlos, 4

Said, Edward, 14
Saldívar, José David, 102, 105, 123
Salgado, Plínio, 157, 157n13
Salles, Walter, 182
Salvador (Didion), 54–55
Samuels, Charles Thomas, 203
Santa Evita (Martínez), 59, 73, 76–78, 83n13, 93n17
Santí, Enrico, 14
Santiago, Danny, 26
Santiago, Silviano, 4, 25, 65, 68–69, 130, 130n7, 149–59, 159n14, 160–63, 171–72
São Bernardo (Ramos), 155
Schama, Simon, 201, 211
Schwarz, Roberto, 87, 147, 161, 161n16
scientific colonialism, 14
scientifism, 36, 50
Scliar, Moacyr, 68
Scott, Sir Walter, 32
self-aware documentary fiction, 5, 49
self-aware films, 219, 219n2
self-awareness, 44, 70, 130, 143, 202
Shakespeare, William, 104
"Short History of the Republic, A" (Ramos), 159
Shukla, Sandhya, 16
Silko, Leslie Marmon, 25–26
Silva, Dionísio da, 68
Silva, Francisco Manuel da, 140n14
Silva Gruesz, Kirsten, 19
Sin, The (Silva), 68
skepticism: epistemological, 31, 73; experimental, 50; objectivity and, 41; postmodern, 4–5, 113n11, 204, 213
Skłodowska, Elzbieta, 63n16
Slaughterhouse V (Vonnegut), 50
social realism, 32, 43–44, 49, 56, 156, 173
social turn, 34–36
Society and Culture in Early Modern France (Davis), 38
Soderbergh, Steven, 182
Solitaria solidaria (Alone but Committed) (Antillano), 100–101, 100n6, 101–3, 106–11, 115–23

Sommer, Doris, 19, 27
Sotweed Factor (Barth), 50
Souza, Herbert, 148
Souza, Márcio, 68–69
Space Between, The: Literature and Politics (Cantor), 174
Space In-Between, The (Gazzola), 149n1
"Space In-Between, The" (Santiago). *See* "O entre-lugar do discurso latinoamericano" ("Latin American Discourse: The Space In-Between") (Santiago)
Spanish-American War, 105, 112, 186
Stella Manhattan (Santiago), 25, 171
Stockton, Dean. *See* D*Face
Stone, Oliver, 25
"Strange Force" (Veloso), 141
Strange Nation of Rafael Mendes, The (Scliar), 68
Styron, William, 50
Sussekind, Flora, 151–52, 164
Sweet Diamond Dust and Other Stories (Ferré), 59

Tapajós, Maurício, 140
Tempest, The (Shakespeare), 104
Teresa de Mier, Fray Servando, 60
Terkel, Studs, 195
Terra Nostra (Fuentes), 50, 56, 59
terrorism, 136–37, 175
testimonial fiction, 155–59
testimonio, 84, 112–13, 113n11
That Noble Dream (Novick), 31
"thick description," 16, 39–40
Thompson, E. P., 34–35, 37
Time (magazine), 197, 198 fig. 4
Tinsman, Helen, 16
Tiradentes, 168–69
"To Translate Oneself" (Gullar), 142
Torres, Ana, 112
Tosta, Luciano, 47
Transamerican Literary Relations and the Nineteenth-Century Public Sphere (Brickhouse), 16–17
Translating Modernity (Lomas), 105

Tropical Dreams (Scliar), 68
Tropical sol da liberdade (Tropical Sun of Liberty) (Machado), 126–27, 131–34, 136–37, 142–48
Tropics of Discourse (White), 37
Trump, Donald, 218
Tulio, Walter. *See* Ponco
Turner, Joseph, 51

Uma literatura nos trópicos (A Literature in the Tropics) (Santiago), 150–51
Unamuno, Miguel, 112
universalism, 36–37
Untimely Present, The: Postdictatorial Latin American Fiction and the Task of Mourning (Avelar), 135–36
Updike, John, 200–203, 202n2, 203–4, 206–15
USA Trilogy (dos Passos), 49, 55
Usable Past, The (Zamora), 192–93

V (Pynchon), 50
Valente, Luiz, 67, 67n23, 68
Van Woodward, C., 50
Vargas, Getúlio, 151, 156–57, 157n13, 159
Vargas Llosa, Mario, 59
Vartuck, Pola, 127n3, 152
Vecchi, Roberto, 132n10
Veeser, H. Aram, 41, 57
Vega, Ana Lydia, 24
Velásquez, Rámon, 100–101, 115
Veloso, Caetano, 140–41
Venezuela, 74, 77–78, 81, 97, 97n1, 98–109, 113–14, 114n13, 119, 121–22, 189, 217–19
Venezuelan Review, 102
Ventura, Zuenir, 125n1, 133
Viagem ao México (Journey to Mexico) (Santiago), 150, 171–72
Vidas Secas (Ramos), 155
video, 29, 87
Vietnam War, 3, 9, 23–24, 59, 174–76, 185, 193–94, 196, 207
Visions of the Past (Rosenstone), 219n2
Vonnegut, Kurt, 50

War of the End of the World, The (Vargas Llosa), 59
Warren, Robert Penn, 50
Waverley (Scott), 32
Webber, Andrew Lloyd, 77
Weinhardt, Marlene, 69
"What's In a Name?" (Radway), 13–14
White, Hayden, 37, 37n7, 49–50, 84, 149, 199, 202, 205–6, 212

Wolfe, Michael, 188–89
Wolfe, Tom, 206

Yúdice, George, 11, 154n9

Zambrano, Gregory, 114n15
Zamora, Lois Parkinson, 15–16, 19, 178, 192–94
Zárate (Blanco), 114n13

GLOBAL LATIN/O AMERICAS
FREDERICK LUIS ALDAMA AND LOURDES TORRES, SERIES EDITORS

This series focuses on the Latino experience in its totality as set within a global dimension. The series showcases the variety and vitality of the presence and significant influence of Latinos in the shaping of the culture, history, politics and policies, and language of the Americas—and beyond. It welcomes scholarship regarding the arts, literature, philosophy, popular culture, history, politics, law, history, and language studies, among others.

False Documents: Inter-American Cultural History, Literature, and the Lost Decade (1975–1992)
    FRANS WEISER

Public Negotiations: Gender and Journalism in Contemporary US Latina/o Literature
    ARIANA E. VIGIL

Democracy on the Wall: Street Art of the Post-Dictatorship Era in Chile
    GUISELA LATORRE

Gothic Geoculture: Nineteenth-Century Representations of Cuba in the Transamerican Imaginary
    IVONNE M. GARCÍA

Affective Intellectuals and the Space of Catastrophe in the Americas
    JUDITH SIERRA-RIVERA

Spanish Perspectives on Chicano Literature: Literary and Cultural Essays
    EDITED BY JESÚS ROSALES AND VANESSA FONSECA

Sponsored Migration: The State and Puerto Rican Postwar Migration to the United States
    EDGARDO MELÉNDEZ

La Verdad: An International Dialogue on Hip Hop Latinidades
    EDITED BY MELISSA CASTILLO-GARSOW AND JASON NICHOLS

www.ingramcontent.com/pod-product-compliance
Lightning Source LLC
Chambersburg PA
CBHW020647230426
43665CB00008B/342